FORM IN MODERN ENGLISH

Form

in Modern English

Dona Worrall Brown

Wallace C. Brown
UNIVERSITY OF KANSAS CITY

Dudley Bailey
UNIVERSITY OF NEBRASKA

NEW YORK / OXFORD UNIVERSITY PRESS

Printed in the United States of America

PREFACE

This is a grammar of modern English, designed primarily for college Freshman courses, but it could also be used in courses in descriptive grammar and in the teaching of English. Grammar is presented in this book not as a set of 'definitions' of grammatical meanings, but as a system of symbolic devices by which these meanings are expressed in the written language. Therefore, the student learns to think of grammar as patterns of word order, inflections, function words, permanent forms, marks of punctuation, and other 'structural' devices. In addition to squaring more accurately with the facts of the language, this approach has the advantage of facilitating the 'transfer' from descriptive grammar to the problems of composition, thus narrowing the gap that is often said to exist between these subjects. Clearly an emphasis on the ways by which grammatical meanings are expressed will be more helpful to the young writer struggling to express his own ideas than any so-called 'definitions' could be.

This transfer, however, does not take place automatically: it calls for a different formulation of the old familiar precepts. For this reason, in addition to the descriptive materials, we have included a section in which the most common problems in grammatical usage and mis-usage are re-examined. Our treatment of these problems, however, goes beyond the mere re-stating of rules: the primary emphasis is placed upon exploring the reasons *why* certain kinds of mistakes occur—reasons which have their origin not so much in ignorance of the 'rules' of grammar as in a misunder-standing of the nature of the language itself.

Many modern grammarians prefer to make a complete break with the traditional vocabulary of grammar by devising a wholly new terminology. Although this is advantageous in some ways, it has severe practical limitations imposed by the very fact that it is unfamiliar. The traditional terms, on the other hand, have been standardized: they are a permanent part of the language; and they are entrenched in dictionaries, handbooks, and other reference works used in all college English courses. In this book, therefore, we have retained most of the conventional terminology—although of necessity a few new terms have been introduced. Thus students will find that they are still dealing with the familiar names for the parts of speech and that a phrase is still a phrase and a clause a clause, in spite of the fact that these grammatical categories are described in a way somewhat different from the usual one.

The organization of the book follows the logic of the materials. It starts with the simplest problems and proceeds by easy stages to the more complex and difficult. This plan has been adopted, in spite of its limitations, because we believe it is a mistake to assume that 'everyone knows the fundamentals of grammar'; and it is all too clear that unless college students are firmly anchored in these simple matters at the beginning, they will be at sea throughout the remainder of the course. Another reason for not slighting the basic materials arises from the fact that the structural approach to grammar requires a complete reorientation toward the subject—a reorientation that cannot be effected by plunging the student *in medias res*. According to our plan, the book falls into four distinct divisions. The first three chapters discuss the general principles of the subject. The next seven describe the individual parts of speech as form categories. The next two are devoted to the more com-plex sentence structures with emphasis on the device of nesting and the phenomenon of structural layers. The last section (Chapters XIII, XIV, and XV) deals with the principles of modern usage and the application of the earlier materials to the many problems of grammatical usage and mis-usage in the forms of words and in the construction of the modern English sentence.

We have usually employed an essay-like method of presentation instead of the traditional textbook format. This has been done in order to improve the appearance of the page and to encourage the student to read more carefully and thoughtfully. But running heads have been provided as a guide to the subject-matter on each page, and the full index is a source of quick and easy reference. Finally, there is an abundance of exercises at the end of the book, some of which may be used as subjects for themes as well as materials for class discussion and for examinations.

In general terms, we are indebted to those great grammarians whose work anticipates the modern structural approach to grammar, especially the work of Otto Jespersen, Henry Sweet, Joseph Vendryes, Edward Sapir, and Leonard Bloomfield. But our most direct obligation is to the work of Charles Carpenter Fries, particularly to his *American English Grammar*. Our book, however, is not the kind that Dr. Johnson deplored—the digest of two others in order to make a third; for we have not hesitated to give our own interpretations wherever a fresh explanation or insight seemed to accord better with the facts of the language or to provide greater clarification of the subject.

Finally, we wish to acknowledge the comments and suggestions of the following readers who examined all or portions of the manuscript on behalf of the publishers: Professors Leonard F. Dean, University of Connecticut; Albert Elsasser, Princeton University; Albert R. Kitzhaber, University of Kansas; W. Edson Richmond, Indiana University; and W. Freeman Twaddell, Brown University. These readers are, of course, in no way responsible for the opinions expressed in this book.

D. W. B.
W. C. B.
D. B.

Kansas City, Missouri
Lincoln, Nebraska
April 23, 1958

CONTENTS

FORM IN MODERN ENGLISH

'There's a glory for you!'

'I don't know what you mean by "glory," ' Alice said.

Humpty Dumpty smiled contemptuously. 'Of course you don't—till I tell you. I meant "there's a nice knock-down argument for you!" '

'But "glory" doesn't mean "a nice knock-down argument," ' Alice objected.

'When *I* use a word,' Humpty Dumpty said, in rather a scornful tone, 'it means just what *I* choose it to mean—neither more or less.'

'The question is,' said Alice, 'whether you *can* make words mean so many different things.'

'The question is,' said Humpty Dumpty, 'which is to be master—that's all.'

Alice was too much puzzled to say anything; so after a minute Humpty Dumpty began again. 'They've a temper, some of them—particularly verbs: they're the proudest—adjectives you can do anything with, but not verbs—however, *I* can manage the whole lot of them! Impenetrability! That's what *I* say!'

Polonius: What do you read, my lord?
Hamlet: Words, words, words.
Polonius: What is the matter, my lord?
Hamlet: Between who?
Polonius: I mean, the matter that you read, my lord. . .

'Nature's chief masterpiece is writing well.'

GRAMMAR IN A NEW KEY

Most books on the subject of language begin by reiterating the truism (which is nonetheless true) that people first learn to use their native language by conscious and unconscious imitation. This process is obviously a rather crude one and the result is usually dubious. But, as children grow older, their skill in handling the language naturally expands and improves, particularly after they have started to school. But, in spite of this learning process, people at this early age rarely attain a very high degree of accuracy. As a result, their language continues to be vague, uncertain, and often confusing—and they sometimes say what they do not intend to say. If, like Humpty Dumpty in his talk with Alice, we could use words just as we pleased, there would be no need to study language at all; but, alas, the Humpty Dumptys have to communicate with the Alices, and the Alices often misunderstand them. Hence the necessity of a more detailed, accurate, and sophisticated study of our native language in college. Of all the areas of linguistic study, that of grammar is the most basic, the least understood, and the most imperfectly used by the student who aspires to a college education. For this reason, a fresh approach to modern English grammar is vitally important.

I

Beginning with first things first, we may ask, what really is grammar?—for, until a realistic answer to this important question is devised, there is little point in studying the subject at all. Most college composition books make some attempt to define this word. Some say, for example, that grammar is a description of how a language works, others that it is the science of communication in words, or that it deals with words and their relationships to one another. There is nothing factually wrong with such generalizations as these, but they are too broad and vague to provide any real insight into the subject. In this book the meaning of grammar will be presented in a different way.

One method of clarifying meaning is to use a comparison with something that is better known or more easily understood. This is called explanation by 'analogy.' The most useful comparison for our purpose is with the subject of mathematics. It may seem odd to say that grammar—a tool that we all use every day of our lives—is not as fully understood as mathematics; but this is true for two reasons. First, it is possible to use grammar automatically to fulfill certain basic communication needs without ever fully understanding it. Second, ordinary language is a sprawling thing that is used for a multitude of purposes: to inform, to explain, to encourage, to excite, to amuse, to lull, to anger, etc., and this complexity creates many confusions.

But for the mathematician the situation is very different and much simpler. Knowledge of his subject cannot be acquired without instruction, and it has one and only one purpose: the solution of problems. For this reason, the person who uses the language of mathematics must understand its nature thoroughly. In other words, mathematicians cannot be half right in their kind of language. It may also seem surprising that we use the word 'language' to describe the subject of mathematics. But it is indeed a kind of language (a more restricted one, to be sure), which employs methods similar to those of the language of ordinary speech and writing to express certain kinds of ideas.

Anyone who has studied mathematics knows that it makes use of two types of symbols—numbers and 'signs,' which differ sharply in the way they represent ideas. Some of the more familiar 'signs' are: $+$, $\times$, $\div$, $/$, $\sim$, and $\sqrt{\ }$. There are also the various letters of the alphabet, such as x and y, which are used in algebra as 'signs' for unknown quantities. Unlike numbers, 'signs' express their meaning by a kind of shorthand notation, by which mathematicians avoid the cumbersome business of having to write out in full certain ideas that require frequent repetition. It is, for example, much more economical in time and energy to jot down + than to write out the words 'added to,' to write ÷ than 'divided by,' and to write √⎺ than 'the square root of.'

Probably the most important single fact about ordinary language is that it also has two kinds of symbols, both of which work together to express the total meaning of any utterance. This fact is not widely known; yet, if the basic distinction between these two ways of expressing meaning is not fully understood, it is impossible to understand the nature of grammar. These two kinds of symbols we shall call the 'vocabulary' elements and the 'grammatical' elements. The vocabulary elements include the thousands and thousands of words or parts of words that can be found, not in sentences, but in random lists, dictionaries, spelling-books, and the glossary sections of foreign-language textbooks. Following is a brief list of this kind:

table	happy	soon
walk	throw	mis-
street	apple	un-

This part of the language is often called our vocabulary. The first kind of language that a child learns is in this area—such words as: *mamma, bottle, baby,* and *dolly.* As children grow up and expand this knowledge, they are said to have increased their vocabulary. And when we do not understand the meaning of one of these symbols, we usually look it up in a dictionary. There we find 'definitions' of what the symbol stands for in the non-language world. The study of the relationship between these kinds of symbols and their meanings is sometimes called 'semantics.'

The second kind of symbol—the grammatical symbol—differs basically from the vocabulary symbol, and in describing this difference we shall find the analogy with mathematics most useful. Like the 'signs' in mathematics, all grammatical symbols have one thing in common: they do not represent directly the ideas that they stand for. Rather, they operate like a system of shorthand, or like a code, for which the study of grammar provides a cipher or key. For example, when we want to use a grammatical symbol to add the idea of 'past time' to a word, such as *walk* in the list above, we do not say or write 'walk in the past.' Instead, we use the shorthand-like symbol *-ed*, which stands for 'earlier than,' just as the mathematical symbol $>$ stands for 'greater than.' Again, we might take the vocabulary symbol *chair*. If we wished to add to this word the idea of 'more than one,' it is almost certain that we would say *chairs*. When this form of the word is used, the idea of more-than-oneness has not been expressed by vocabulary means (we have not said 'more than one'): we have used instead a grammatical symbol, the simple letter *-s*, which is a kind of shorthand for the idea of 'more than one.'

To illustrate this point in a more complex way, following is a list of vocabulary elements which might appear in a simple sentence:

1. Henry   3. build
2. house   4. old

And let us suppose that we want to express these additional ideas:

5. that *old* qualifies our idea of the man Henry,
6. that *build* expresses an assertion,
7. that the building is continuing at the present time,
8. that Henry is the builder,
9. that the result of the building is the house,
10. that there is only one house,
11. and that a completed statement is intended.

The resulting sentence would be:

Old Henry is building a house.

What makes it possible to condense all of these complex ideas into six words? The answer, of course, is grammar: in the sentence above the ideas numbered 5-11 have been translated into the code of grammatical 'signs.' By using a different set of such signs with the four words which convey the vocabulary meaning—*Henry, house, build,* and *old*—it would be possible to express some very different ideas, such as:

An old building housed Henry.

The nature of the grammatical symbols can be revealed most dramatically when the vocabulary elements in a sentence are blanked out and only the grammatical symbols are expressed. Following are a few sentences of this kind:

A ——al —— will be ——en about our —— into ——s.
Do ——ed ——s ——ly —— at the ——ion?
This —— of ——'s ——s that —— are ——ing to the ——s.

These sentences would probably be 'Greek' to most people. Actually, they are full of meaning, but it is a kind of meaning which is mysterious to the uninitiated precisely because of the fact that the grammatical elements are a type of code symbol. Now the question arises: How does one find the key to the meanings in this kind of sentence? As a rule, we do not consult a dictionary, although a few of these symbols are explained there. The only way fully to understand them is, of course, through the study of grammar. This brings us back to the question posed at the beginning of this chapter: What is grammar? After what has been said, the answer must be: GRAMMAR IS THE STUDY OF A SYSTEM OF LANGUAGE CODE SYMBOLS AND THE MEANINGS THAT THESE SYMBOLS EXPRESS. This grammatical apparatus is called the 'structure' of the language, and the kind of grammar that describes it is called 'structural grammar.'

There are three types of grammatical symbols, which both the spoken and written language have in common. These are called the 'major grammatical devices.' The first, and least well known, is the device of WORD ORDER, which involves the fixed position of the words in a sentence; second, and best known, is the device of INFLECTION, which involves changes in the spelling and pronunciation of a word; the third is the FUNCTION WORD, a kind of grammatical word, which differs basically from the vocabulary words described above.[1] Punc-

---

[1] For this threefold division of the major grammatical devices, we are indebted to Charles Carpenter Fries, *American English Grammar* (New York, 1940).

tuation, which of course is used only in the written language, may also be considered a grammatical device, but it is a minor one, because the uses of the various marks of punctuation are not completely standardized in modern English, and therefore cannot always be depended on to convey grammatical meaning with complete exactness.

The meanings expressed by these grammatical devices, in contrast to those expressed by any one of the vocabulary symbols, are the most frequently used ideas. A person probably would not mention the vocabulary symbols *chair, house, build,* or *old* more than once or twice a day under ordinary circumstances, and *Henry* would probably get into the conversation even less often unless a gentleman of that name were a close friend or relative. But the ideas of 'performer of an action,' 'time of an action,' 'result of an action,' 'qualification,' 'how many?' and other ideas usually expressed in our language by grammatical symbols are used by everyone hundreds of times a day. Because these symbols are in such frequent use, it is very convenient that they can be expressed by the shorthand-like method of the grammatical devices instead of the more cumbersome longhand of the vocabulary elements. If we did not have grammar, our plight would be almost as ridiculous as that of the Laputians in *Gulliver's Travels,* who, disdaining language altogether, insisted on carrying around with them all the things they expected to talk about during the day!

In other respects, however, these two areas of meaning do not differ significantly. One cannot take a list of ideas and sort them into two distinct columns, one marked 'vocabulary' and the other marked 'grammatical.' Distinctions between them can be made only according to the means by which they are expressed in a given sentence—whether by a vocabulary symbol or a grammatical symbol. This point is borne out by the fact that in any language there is a borderline area in which certain ideas may be expressed by either type of symbol. In English, for example, the idea of something happening in the future may be, and usually is, expressed by a grammatical symbol. When we say, 'She will go,' we use a special grammatical word (*will*) to express this idea. But futurity may also be expressed by vocabulary means: we may say, 'She goes tomorrow.' Here we have expressed the idea by using the word *tomorrow,* an idea which the grammatical form of the verb (*goes*) does not express at all. Again, more-than-oneness is usually expressed grammatically in English: in 'We have miles to go,' the *-s* added to *mile* is the grammatical sign of more-than-oneness. On the other hand, in the phrase 'many a mile' the idea of plurality is expressed not by a grammatical device but by the vocabulary element *many.*

Furthermore, languages vary among themselves as to what meanings should be expressed by grammatical symbols. The Alaskan Eskimo language, for example, has separate grammatical forms to express tense in nouns, as have a number of American Indian languages. One African language is said to have a grammatical method for expressing the idea of 'squareness'! And in its earliest period, our own English language (Old English) had a separate grammatical form for expressing the idea of 'twoness' (duality) in pronouns as distinct from 'oneness' and 'more than twoness' (plurality). Modern English, of course, has no way of expressing any of these ideas by means of grammatical devices.

II

A surprisingly large number of people raise the question: Why should one study grammar at all? The whole problem of the nature of grammar and the desirability of teaching it was informally and excellently discussed by Mr. E. B. White in a 1957 issue of *The New Yorker* magazine. After remarking that English usage has become 'hot news,' Mr. White continues:

> Through the turmoil and the whirling waters [of usage] we have reached a couple of opinions of our own about the language. One is that a schoolchild should be taught grammar—for the same reason that a medical student should study anatomy. Having learned about the exciting mysteries of an English sentence, the child can then go forth and speak and write any damn way he pleases. We knew a countryman once who spoke with wonderful vigor and charm, but ungrammatically. In him the absence of grammar made little difference, because his speech was full of juice. But when a dullard speaks in a slovenly way, his speech

suffers not merely from dullness but from ignorance, and his whole life, in a sense, suffers—though he may not feel pain.

The living language is like a cowpath: it is the creation of the cows themselves, who, having created it, follow it or depart from it according to their whims or their needs. From daily use, the path undergoes change. A cow is under no obligation to stay in the narrow path she helped make, following the contour of the land, but she often profits by staying with it and she would be handicapped if she didn't know where it was and where it led to. Children obviously do not depend for communication on a knowledge of grammar; they rely on their ear, mostly, which is sharp and quick. But we have yet to see the child who hasn't profited from coming face to face with a relative pronoun at an early age, and from reading books, which follow the paths of centuries.[2]

Actually, everyone agrees that all civilized people have standards of speech and writing and that the teaching of these standards is an important part of education. In the basic college composition course, for example, all students are expected to know and use the acceptable grammatical forms, and anyone would probably feel cheated if he were not helped in these matters. He is also expected to learn a great deal about the intricate business of putting words, phrases, clauses, and marks of punctuation in their proper places in order to form effective and unambiguous structures of communication. And these are all matters of grammar. For the past two hundred years many 'rules' have been passed down from generation to generation, which are supposed to solve these problems. Most of these rules are familiar to students even before they come to college. They have been told, for example, that 'the form of the verb must agree with its subject in person and number,' that 'a pronoun must be in the objective case form if it is the object of a verb or preposition,' and that 'adjective phrases must not dangle.' Rules of this kind are important, of course; but it is often not realized that they cannot even be understood unless or until a great deal is first known about 'the exciting mysteries of an English sentence' to which the *New Yorker* article refers.

[2] From an article by E. B. White, © 1957, *The New Yorker*, Inc.

One of the most serious obstacles to good writing is the tendency to compose confusing sentences, especially sentences that have double meanings (ambiguities). Most people know about such problems, but few people realize that they are problems in grammar—that bad sentences of this kind are caused by a misunderstanding of the modern English system of grammar. The following sentences are simple examples of this kind of grammatical confusion:

> He gave her dog biscuits.
> The visitors were drinking in the open air.
> He loved racing horses.
> Ask Mr. Smith who is sitting by the window.
> Clara Schumann was too busy to compose herself.

Unless they are being intentionally humorous, people write sentences like these because they are not aware that they have allowed another meaning, beyond the one they intended, to intrude. And it takes a considerable insight into the subject of grammar to see why this has happened.

In general, these difficulties are caused by a lack of awareness of the fact that the written language, in contrast to the spoken language, has grammatical deficiencies which make written communication difficult and invite ambiguities and confusions. What most people do not realize is that the spoken language has a large battery of very effective grammatical symbols that are lacking in the written language. They include, first, the various kinds of vocal intonations, such as stress and pitch. For example, we usually indicate a declarative sentence by a drop in the voice pitch, whereas at the end of a question the voice usually rises. Running words together without a pause and making an extra long pause are also important grammatical devices. Even gestures and facial expressions may clarify the meaning of a spoken utterance. These devices are usually in a writer's mind as he composes sentences, but he too often forgets that the reader, unlike the listener, cannot hear or see them, and he therefore does not make his meaning clear. The first sentence above—'He gave her dog biscuits'—is a good illustration of this kind of failure on the part of a writer. This sentence would not be ambiguous at all when spoken, for the devices of pitch and stress would make the meaning clear, but in the written language it has two meanings: (1) he gave biscuits to her dog, and (2) he gave dog biscuits to her. The writer of this sentence undoubtedly 'heard' a distinct stress and pitch pattern which expressed the meaning he intended—but, alas, his reader could not.

The process of learning to write with clarity and emphasis involves (among other things, of course) knowing how to use the relatively limited number of written devices that must take the place of the missing spoken ones. In the sentence about the dog biscuits, for example, a careful writer could have found several ways to clarify the meaning. For one thing, the words *the* or *some* (both very powerful grammatical symbols) used in the right sentence position, would have eliminated the ambiguity:

> He gave her dog *the* (or *some*) biscuits.
> He gave her *the* (or *some*) dog biscuits.

In order to use such devices effectively, it is of course necessary to understand thoroughly the whole system of coding called the grammatical devices, especially the three major devices, which will be described in detail in the next chapter.

2

THE THREE MAJOR DEVICES

The old frontiersman has captured an Indian: if we look at this statement without any knowledge of grammar at all, one thing stands out. The sentence begins with *The* and ends with *Indian,* and between these words the others are arranged in an order that cannot be altered if the sentence is to say what it is intended to say. Indeed, not one word can be moved in this sentence without creating ambiguity or nonsense or radically changing the original meaning. This example strikingly illustrates the most important grammatical device in modern English—the device of word order: the arrangement of words in fixed positions in relation to the other words in the sentence in order to express grammatical meaning.

The sentence about the old frontiersman also illustrates the two other grammatical devices in modern English. If *has captured* is changed to *captured* or *did capture,* subtle changes in meaning take place; and if *has captured* is changed to *captures, is capturing,* or *will capture,* even sharper alterations in meaning occur. The changes from *captured* to *captures* to *capturing* show that this word can have various forms to express various grammatical meanings: that is, the word may be inflected. This is an example of the second major grammatical device in modern English: inflection—the change in the form of a word to express a grammatical meaning.

The most radical change in the substitutions above was the

change from *has captured* to *captures* or *captured*—from two words to one. The additional word *has* in the original sentence, like *is, did,* or *will,* does not have the meaning it would have if it were used alone without such a word as *captured:* the *has* in 'The frontiersman has captured an Indian' is very different from the *has* in 'The frontiersman has a compass.' Indeed, when words of this type are used with other words like *captured,* they have very little vocabulary meaning at all. They are therefore called function words—words which have little meaning apart from their role as a device for contributing to the grammatical meaning of the word group of which they are a part. Recognition and understanding of these three devices—word order, inflection, and function words—are so essential to an understanding of modern English grammar as it is presented in this book that each one must be described now at greater length.

First, WORD ORDER. In the sentence *The old frontiersman has captured an Indian* we pointed out that each word had to be in a fixed position in order to convey the meaning intended. For example, the word *old* has to precede *frontiersman* in order to show that the quality of 'oldness' applies to the frontiersman; if it preceded *Indian* an entirely different meaning would be expressed. A similar use of the word-order device may be seen in the sentence

Mrs. Smith bought an antique chest.

The position of the word *antique* shows that this quality belongs to the chest and to nothing else. If this word were transposed from the fifth to the first position in the sentence—without making any other change beyond this minor shift in word order—we would have roundly insulted Mrs. Smith!

In the sentence about the frontiersman, still another type of word-order device is illustrated. The respective positions of *frontiersman* and *Indian* in relation to *has captured* show who did the capturing and who was captured. This is probably the most common type of word-order device in modern English. It can be seen even more clearly in the sentence

The policeman shot the prowler.

The relationship of *policeman* and *prowler* is shown by their respective positions before and after the word *shot*. The fact that *policeman* precedes *shot* indicates that he performed the act of shooting; the fact that *prowler* follows *shot* indicates that it was he who was shot. If the positions of *policeman* and *prowler* were reversed, how different the meaning would be!

Modern English uses many other word-order patterns to express its grammatical ideas; these will be discussed in detail later. Meanwhile, one should bear in mind that word order is unquestionably the most important grammatical device in the language. It is almost always used, along with the other devices, whenever two or more words come together. It is also the most vital, the most 'alive,' of all these devices. If a given word has grammatical devices that express contradictory ideas, it is word order that determines the meaning.

The second grammatical device in modern English, INFLECTION, is familiar to everyone if only because most English words are capable of changing their form. Such changes may occur in three places: at the beginning of the word (prefix), within the word (internal inflection), and at the end of the word (suffix, or ending). As we have already shown, a word such as *capture* can be changed to *captured* and *capturing*. A word such as *Mr. Jones* can become *Mr. Jones's*. A word such as *old* can be changed to *older* and *oldest*. In fact, there are relatively few words (like *a, the, and, upon*) which cannot be changed at least slightly. A sentence will show some of these inflections at work:

> Edward's suggestions challenged our old habits.

Here the use of the *-'s* suffix on the word *Edward* expresses a certain relationship between Edward and the suggestions; a similar relationship between 'us' and the habits is shown by the inflected form *our*, which is another form of *we*. The presence of the *-d* at the end of the word *challenged* expresses the idea of past time, and the presence of the *-s* at the end of *suggestions* and *habits* expresses plurality in both words. Thus in this simple sentence of six words, the device of inflection has been used five times.

But inflection does not occur as frequently in modern English as this example implies. Although inflection is what most people are thinking of when they speak of grammar, this device has lost much of the importance it had in the language a thousand years ago. In an Old English version of the story of the prodigal son, we read:

> he hine ġeseah ond wearð mid mildheortnesse āstyred
> (*he him saw and became with mildheartedness stirred up*
>
> and onġēan hine arn ond hine beclypte ond cyste hine
> *and towards him ran and him embraced and kissed him*)

In the eighteen words of this Old English sentence, only three (*mid, onġēan,* and *ond*) are not inflected. Because the large number of inflections could carry the burden of the grammatical meanings, word order was not very important in this early stage of the language—as the above literal translation shows. But, as the inflections of our language gradually decreased in number and importance, fixed word order came to be used instead. Therefore, when we translate Old English into modern English, many of the inflections have to be translated into a system of word-order patterns.

Similarly, when we translate from highly inflected foreign languages like Latin, word-order devices usually have to be substituted for inflectional ones. For example, in the Latin sentence

> Agricola servum bonum liberavit
> (*The farmer the slave good freed*)

each word has a special inflection that expresses one or more grammatical ideas. In fact, all of the grammatical ideas in this sentence are expressed by this device, so the meaning is not dependent at all on word order. In a modern English translation, however, there are no inflections except the -*d* on *freed,* so the fixed word-order device must be substituted for them: *The farmer freed the good slave.* The fact that in translating from Latin to English one has to move from one type of grammatical system to another explains why this language and others like it have a reputation for being 'hard.' Actually these languages are no more difficult than any others; the trouble occurs only because people undertake the study of Latin, German, and other highly inflected languages without adequate knowledge of the grammatical system of their own language. When it is once understood that grammatical meaning in English is conveyed more often by fixed position than by inflection, these difficulties largely disappear.

Languages vary greatly in their use of inflection. Modern Chinese is at the opposite pole from Latin, for it has no inflections at all! It, therefore, makes extensive use of word order as a grammatical device. For example, in the sentence

Fu ai tsi
(*The father loves the son*)

none of the words are inflected; word order alone reveals their function.

Because word order is such a powerful device, some of the inflections still remaining in the language are really not necessary to convey grammatical meaning. This fact partly accounts for the confusion about inflections that is widespread today and for the 'mistakes' that are made in using them. When inflection plays an important role in conveying meaning, people seldom make mistakes:

Charley's cap *was* there, but *mine was* gone.

The relationship between Charley and the cap is shown by the -'s; the time is established by the form *was;* and the possessive idea in the second half of the sentence appears in the inflected *mine.* On the other hand, when the grammatical ideas are clearly established by word order and the inflections are not really necessary, mistakes in the inflectional forms are more likely to occur:

You and *him* should be willing to help *she* and *I.*
The French cannot run as fast as *us.*

The italicized forms are not the ones used by careful speakers and writers: certainly in college writing they would be considered 'bad grammar.' But we have no trouble understanding both of these sentences (thanks to word order) in spite of the 'errors' in the inflected forms. Particularly in pronouns the inflections are now largely formalities—survivals from a time when these grammatical ideas could not be expressed by word order.

The FUNCTION WORD, the third major device for expressing grammatical meaning in modern English, is a far more 'alive' device than inflection; for these 'grammatical' words always contribute importantly to the meaning of any word group. Many of them are familiar to most people as 'auxiliary verbs,' 'prepositions,' and 'articles.' Although function words, unlike the other two grammatical devices, are separate words, they differ basically from vocabulary words; for, like the other grammatical devices, they do not explicitly state the ideas they express. The word *had* in the phrase *had built,* for example, expresses the idea that the building was completed in the past, but it certainly does not come right out and say 'completed in the past.' It is interesting that in the Chinese language words similar to these are called 'empty words' in contrast to the vocabulary words, which are called 'full'—a distinction which emphasizes the fact that the function word is a kind of symbol. In English, however, not all function words are 'empty' as they are in Chinese. Many of them are what might be called 'impure' function words: they partake of both the grammatical and vocabulary elements of the language—they are both 'full and empty.' Such words as *within, across, when,* and *since* are of this kind.

Other examples of function words may be seen in the following sentence:

> The voting represented the interests of the poor.

Here the function word *of* indicates the relationship between *interests* and *poor.* This same idea could have been expressed by the device of inflection (although an awkward sentence results): 'The voting represented the poor's interests.' Also in this sentence another common function word, the word *the,* appears three times: before *voting,* before *interests,* and before *poor.* In English *the* serves to mark off or limit the grammatical function of certain vocabulary elements. These vocabulary elements might, of course, also be used in other ways which would not allow *the* to precede them, as in the following sentences:

> *Voting* carelessly, the people elected weak officials.
> We are *voting* for the school tax increase.
> His discovery *interests* all scientists.
> His school work is *poor.*

If placed before the italicized words, *the* would make nonsense of the sentences.

Another example from Latin, with its emphasis upon inflection, will make even clearer the extensive role of function words in modern English grammar. Latin often uses inflections where English must use the function-word device. In the sentence

> Miles gladio interficiebatur
> (*The soldier was being killed with a sword*)

the Latin *gladio,* because of its *-o* ending, expresses the idea 'with a sword,' an idea which in modern English requires the function word *with.* Similarly, the Latin *interficiebatur,* because of its inflection *-ebatur,* expresses the complex idea 'was being killed,' an idea which in English requires two function words, *was* and *being.*

This introductory survey of the grammatical devices will be followed in later chapters by a detailed description of their use in all parts of the modern English sentence. But following are short definitions of these devices, definitions which should be memorized, for they are essential to an understanding of all of modern English grammar:

WORD ORDER: the arrangement of words in set patterns to express grammatical ideas.

INFLECTION: a change in the form of a word to express grammatical ideas.

FUNCTION WORD: a separate 'grammatical' word used to express grammatical ideas.

III

GRAMMATICAL DISTRIBUTION

I

In order to make clear the grammatical structure of the English sentence, a workable method must first be found for talking about large groups of words under various headings. Everybody knows the method for grouping words according to their spelling: the dictionary classifies them first under their initial letters and then their subsequent letters, in accordance with the alphabet. We know that *absent* will come before *bacon* and that *absent* will also appear before *account,* because *a* precedes *b* and *b* precedes *c* in the alphabet. But this method of grouping words as used in the dictionary will not help much in grammatical analysis, for words in sentences do not follow alphabetical order.

From another point of view, however, the analysis of spelling may be of some assistance; for the spelling analyst learns to expect certain letters in certain combinations and not in others. He knows, for instance, that in modern English he will not find *q* without a following *u;* and he anticipates such combinations as *gh, ph,* and *th*—indeed, combinations like *ough* are very common. On the other hand, within any syllable he is not likely to find *b* or *f* or *p* or *v* following *t* (*tb, tf, tp, tv*); nor does he expect to find a consonant following an *h* that is pronounced, nor a *g* after any consonant except *l, n,* and *r.* And we all know that it is common for vowels and consonants to alternate in English words (*decisive, nativity, recede,* etc.) and that such combinations as *phthisic* are rare indeed.

Similarly, in modern English sentences the words tend to fall into recognizable patterns. We tend to use certain words in certain places and never in others; we tend to change the forms of some words in one way and of others in another; and we tend to use some words with other words and never with still others. Thus the student of language soon learns to anticipate some combinations of words and to doubt that he will find others. In this respect he is like the geologist on a prospecting trip, who knows that certain metals always appear together in the earth. Along with uranium, he would expect to find lead and a group of rare and newly discovered metals. He knows that he will likely find gold and silver together, copper with arsenic and zinc, bromine with chlorine, sodium with potassium, and magnesium with calcium. On the other hand, he would be greatly surprised to find silver or copper with uranium, or platinum with sulphur.

In short, all analysts observe a principle of distribution in their fields: some of the elements they deal with may be expected only in certain places and with certain accompaniments; others will be found in others. When we come to words in sentences, we find that they have their own kind of distribution. We find that some words are found only in certain places with a limited group of other words; and still other words are found only in very different contexts. Certain words are capable of a set of inflectional changes which other words cannot undergo. Some words are limited to a single place or context; others are able to function in various places and to assume various forms.

Some examples make this clear. Let us consider the two italicized words in the following sentences:

> They *manage* a movie theater.
> The firm changed *management*.

If these words are considered only from the point of view of their vocabulary meaning, it would be natural to group them together, since both have to do with the idea of 'managing.' But if they are considered from another point of view, it is clear that they are very different and cannot be grouped together at all. First, it is obvious that they have different spellings: the word *management* has a *-ment* suffix, which *manage* does not. Second, their respective positions in the two sentences cannot be interchanged. Third, a *-d* inflection could be added to *manage* in order to change the time of the action, but this could not be done to *management*. On the other hand, an *-s* could be added to *management* to change the number of the word, which could not be done to *manage* to express this same idea. Fourth, *management* may be preceded by the word *the,* but *manage* cannot. By substituting other words for *manage* in this sentence, such as *own, operate, pass,* or *want,* it can be demonstrated that there are many other words which may use the same set of devices as *manage,* so we may assume that all these words belong to the same kind of group. There is also a large number of words that could be substituted for *management,* such as *foreman, director,* or *location.* These, clearly, belong to a second kind of group. These differences and similarities indicate a distinctive way of 'distributing' words, and the categories formed by this kind of distribution are called the 'parts of speech.'

From the examples above, it is clear that words are distributed as one part of speech or another, according to the grammatical devices used with them. In other words, each part of speech has a unique combination, or grouping, of grammatical devices that distinguishes it from other parts of speech. The words 'combination' and 'grouping' should be emphasized, since each part of speech has a rather large number of grammatical devices which may be associated with it. It is too bad that this is true, for grammar would surely be an easier subject if each part of speech were marked by one special device, such as a circle written over the word, or an *x* written below it. Instead, one part of speech may have as many as a dozen grammatical signs, some of which may be connected with it in one context or another. For example, it is possible for one part of speech to appear in six different positions in the sentence, to have four different inflected forms, and three types of function words. In most instances, it is only by using a combination of these devices that the word may be established as a specific part of speech.

In a given sentence, of course, a word will not be accompanied by all the possible devices that mark it as a certain part of speech, but by a selection from them. Usually two or three will be sufficient. For example, in the sentence

The trumpets will play the finale

trumpets is established as a noun by three devices: one word-order device, one inflection, and one function word; *play* is established as a verb by two devices: one word order and one function word. Sometimes, however, only one device is expressed. This is true of the word *manage* (in the example on page 21), which is established as a verb by word order alone. Since it is possible for a part of speech to be indicated by this one device, some words that belong to different parts-of-speech groups often look confusingly alike. This is true of the word *yellow* in the following sentences:

Yellow is my favorite color. (noun)
Newspapers *yellow* with age. (verb)
I like my *yellow* dress. (adjective)

It is often regarded as a grammatical curiosity that there are a few apparently identical words that may appear in sentences as five different parts of speech. *Round* is one of these:

The last *round* was the best of all.
The *round* package was for George.
We *round* the corner on two wheels.
The carousel went *round* and *round*.
The bandit fled *round* the corner.

All these *rounds* are spelled and pronounced alike; they all derive from the same word, the Latin *rotundus,* meaning 'wheel-shaped.' But from the point of view of grammar, these *rounds* are not alike at all. The first one is a noun, the second an adjective, the third a verb, the fourth an adverb, and the last a preposition. These words appear to be alike only because the device of inflection has not been used with them in these sentences. Other types of devices, however, are clearly expressed and it is these devices that establish such words as different parts of speech.

II

When a word is changed from one part of speech to another by means of a change in one or more of the three major grammatical devices, and by this means alone, this operation is called FUNCTIONAL SHIFT. Modern English uses this method very frequently. Words such as *garden, fear, paper, salt, price, smoke, dawn, wash, contact,* and *base,* to mention only a few, are shifted about freely in ordinary usage from noun to verb to adjective and vice versa, merely by changing the grammatical devices. The three 'gardens' in the following sentence illustrate this kind of shift:

We shall garden with garden tools in the garden.

This means that, contrary to what many people think, there is seldom anything in the vocabulary meaning of the word that limits it to one part of speech. Words that have been 'defined' for us as 'nouns' often turn out to be verbs, and similarly, 'verbs' often are really nouns: we read that a man has *authored* a book or *chairmaned* a committee, that his hand has the *trembles,* or that he has been to a *steak fry,* or that he has been given an *assist.* In a sense the vocabulary part of a word is like an all-purpose tool, which has many different uses, depending on the attachments (the grammatical devices) used with it at any special time.

For this reason, there is little use in learning 'definitions' of the parts of speech that are based on meaning. Since words shift about from one part of speech to another in such Protean fashion, no definition of this kind can be devised that is not full of holes. For example, the usual definition of a noun is that it 'is the name of a person, place, or thing.' But *red* is the name of a color, *north* the name of a direction, and *cement* the name of a material; yet an examination of the grammatical devices connected with these words in the following sentences will reveal that none of them are nouns:

> The *red* balloon burst, and my face turned *red*.
> We drove *north* into the *north* end of the city.
> This system of *cement* highways will *cement* friendly relations between the two countries.

Similarly, the definition of a verb—that it expresses action—might lead one to think that the word *walk* in the sentence *We went for a walk,* is a verb; but the grammatical symbols show that this word is not a verb but a noun.

While functional shift is probably the most common method used in modern English for converting a word from one part of speech to another, there is another more traditional method that is also used. This involves the use of a special kind of prefix or suffix. We could, for example, have made *round* into an adjective by using, in addition to one or more of the three major grammatical devices, the suffix *-ish*: 'The *roundish* package is for mother.' Or we could have used the prefix *a-* to convey the idea that *round* is either an adverb or a preposition.

> The carousel went *around* and *around*.
> The bandit fled *around* the corner.

Similarly, in our sentences on page 21 the suffix *-ment* was used to help convert the verb *manage* into a noun. Also *-er* could have been used for the same purpose. There are literally hundreds of these prefixes and suffixes, but two or three more examples will be enough to show how they operate. Some nouns and adjectives may be changed into verbs by adding the suffixes *-ize* or *-en*: *standard* to *standardize, rational* to *rationalize, strength* to *strengthen, weak* to *weaken,* etc. A noun may be made into an adjective by using the suffixes *-y* or *-al*: *dirt* to *dirty, condition* to *conditional.* And most adjectives may be changed into adverbs by adding *-ly*: *perfect– perfectly, smooth–smoothly, proud–proudly,* etc. More than one suffix is often used at once. The word *nationalization* contains three of these: *-al, -iza,* and *-tion.*

At first sight, these prefixes and suffixes seem to be very much like the forms which we called inflections in Chapter II; and in one way they are, for, like inflections, they express variations in grammatical ideas by changes in the spelling of words. But there is one very important difference: unlike true inflections, these prefixes and suffixes are not removable. Once added, they become a permanent part of the vocabulary meaning of the word. For this reason we shall call them 'permanent' forms. The word *standardize,* a verb form, illustrates this point. This word retains the *-ize* ending under all circumstances, whether it is in the present tense form (*standardizes*), for example, or the past tense form (*standardized*). The regular inflections used in this example are, by contrast, removable elements (the *-s* may be put on or taken off or it may be changed to *-ed*), which are added to the permanent forms, just as they may be added to any other word used as a verb. In a sense, the endings that are used to create the permanent forms are like the plaster that helps to characterize an enclosure as a room; the plaster is a permanent part of the room. The inflections are more like the furnishings which may be added or taken away, depending on whether we want to create the effect of a formal living room, a recreation room, or a study.

As we shall see later, these permanent forms are not an absolute sign that a word is a given part of speech, any more than plaster is an absolute sign that an enclosure is a room. In most instances where prefixes or suffixes are used, at least one of the three major grammatical devices is needed in addition to the permanent ending to establish the function of the word. Furthermore, this method of forming parts of speech is used less frequently today than it was in earlier periods of the language. We are more inclined today to let the major grammatical devices do the work for us. Also the major devices are always more important in establishing grammatical meaning; for, whenever the idea conveyed by them is in conflict with the idea indicated by the permanent form, it is the devices that determine the grammatical meaning of the word. For example, the word *desperation* in the expression *desperation measure* has the permanent form of the noun, but its position before a noun is one of the major grammatical devices that indicates that a word is an adjective, and it is this latter device that determines the part of speech.

All of these things will become much clearer as we progress through the next six chapters, where we shall discuss the operation of the different grammatical devices and the use of the permanent forms in connection with each part of speech. It is enough for us to know at this point that there are two ways of marking a given word as a part of speech: first, by the use of the three major grammatical devices; second, by the use of the permanent forms.

About nine hundred years ago an English monk divided the parts of speech into eight groups. These are as follows:

The verb (from the Latin *verbum,* meaning 'the word,' which suggests that this part of speech is very important).

The noun (from the Latin *nomen,* meaning 'a name' for something).

The pronoun (from the Latin *pronomen,* meaning 'for a name,' that is, a word used in place of a noun).

The preposition (from the Latin *praepositio,* meaning 'place before').

The adjective (from the Latin *adjectivus,* meaning 'added to').

The adverb (from the Latin *adverbium,* meaning 'next to the verb').

The conjunction (from the Latin *conjunctus,* meaning 'joined with').

The interjection (from the Latin *interjectus,* meaning 'thrown between').

This is not the only way words have been divided to indicate differences in their grammatical form and meaning. During the many centuries that English grammar has been studied, many different groupings have been suggested, groupings with as few as three and as many as eighteen parts of speech. Actually, it is impossible to work out a perfect system. Even the traditional one of eight parts has its weaknesses. For one thing, there are many instances of overlapping among the eight different groups: a word may have devices characteristic of more than one part of speech. For example, it may show verb inflection and adjective word order.

More than one part of speech may also use the same inflection or pattern of word order. In spite of such weaknesses, this eight-part system, because of its familiarity to everyone, is probably the best one.

Of these eight parts of speech, the verb, the noun, the pronoun, the adjective, the adverb, and the interjection carry the main burden of the vocabulary meaning. Prepositions and conjunctions are mainly function words. In the next seven chapters, the structures of the simplest sentences will be described. The first problem will involve the most basic types of utterances containing only verbs and nouns and their function words.

IV

HELP!

The title of this chapter is the shortest one in the book—yet it is a complete English sentence. From the point of view of grammar, therefore, the word *Help!* must be a very important kind of word. It is, for it represents the most vital part of speech in our language, the verb. As Humpty Dumpty remarked about the parts of speech: 'They've a temper, some of them—particularly verbs: they're the proudest. . .' Not only can words of this kind make sentences all by themselves: they occupy a crucial place in all English sentences (at least of the kind that are supposed to be written in college), and they set the limits and largely determine the order of the other sentence elements with which they are associated.

In college writing, it is quite true to say, as do most grammar books, that every English sentence must contain a verb.[1] Indeed, the

---

[1] For practical purposes we limit ourselves here to 'verb sentences.' There are, of course, 'verbless sentences' (*Ouch!, OK, Good night, What a peaceful evening, Such a silly question,* etc.), but for the student introducing himself to English grammar we think consideration of the verbless kinds should be postponed. Indeed, a wholly satisfactory answer to the question, 'What is a sentence?' is yet to be formulated, although hundreds of attempts have been made. Of these, two have been most often used in grammar books: (1) A sentence is a group of words that expresses a complete thought and (2) A sentence is a group of words that contains an unsubordinated subject and predicate. The first of these, a 'notional' definition, fails because it is wholly subjective and begs the question. There is no objective standard by which to judge the completeness of a thought, and ultimately we are reduced to the circular as-

title sentence above shows that we may have sentences without any other part of speech; but the verb cannot be dispensed with. And, in addition, the various verbal forms, apart from the verb itself, are more numerous than those of any other part of speech. A thorough acquaintance with verbs in all of their forms is therefore essential to an understanding of the structure of the modern English sentence.

I

Fortunately, this crucial part of speech is also the most easily recognized. Many verbs give themselves away by their permanent forms. Some have beginnings or endings which are often thought of as 'signs' of the verb. The most common prefixes are: *be-, en-, em-, re-,* and *with-*; the suffixes are: *-ate, -en, -ify, -ize.* There are many examples of these permanent forms, such as:

*be*devil	*with*draw	weak*en*
*be*moan	*with*stand	soft*en*
*be*rate	*with*hold	fatt*en*
*en*throne	*re*decorate	calc*ify*
*en*mesh	*re*take	ident*ify*
*en*roll	*re*duplicate	beaut*ify*
*em*broil	vener*ate*	oxid*ize*
*em*body	chlorin*ate*	harmon*ize*
*em*power	prevaric*ate*	real*ize*

And except for the *with-* words, of which there are only the three listed above, there are hundreds of others.

Although *-ify* and *-ize* are almost certainly indicative of verbs, the other prefixes and suffixes are not always the 'signs' of this part of speech: the words *be*nign, *en*voy, *em*pire, *with*out, *re*condite, sed*ate,* and gold*en,* for example, are not used as verbs. As we pointed out in Chapter III, the use of this type of prefix and suffix is only one of the ways of marking a part of speech; the decisive clues

sertion that 'a complete thought is a thought that is complete!' On the other hand, the second definition is not more than a half truth, for it rules out all verbless sentences, which, as we have already noted, may be just as 'complete' and independent as the verb sentences.

will be found in the major grammatical devices that accompany the word. Primarily, what makes the verb so easy to identify is the fact that it has so many grammatical devices connected with it. No other part of speech has so many and such distinctive inflectional forms; no other has so many and distinctive function words in alliance with it; and no other obeys a more rigid word order within its own group and within the sentence pattern as a whole. Therefore, the three major grammatical devices—inflections, function words, and word order—are the chief means by which one may gain a thorough acquaintance with the verb.

II

Apart from the so-called 'auxiliary' verbs (which will be considered later), all verbs in modern English have three forms, most of them have fourth forms, and a few have an extra fifth form. The four basic inflectional forms of the verb are as follows:

Form 1: *help*   (no ending)
Form 2: *helps*   (-*s* ending)
Form 3: *helping*   (-*ing* ending)
Form 4: *helped*   (-*ed*, -*d*, or -*t* ending)

The second and third forms of all English verbs are made in exactly the same ways. Hence, these forms do not have to be learned separately for each verb: If, for example, we know the first forms *X*, *Y*, and *Z*, we know that the second forms of these verbs will be *Xes*, *Ys*, and *Zs* respectively, and that their third forms will be *Xing*, *Ying*, and *Zing*. The fourth form of the English verb, however, is not so consistent; it varies widely among the different verbs. For this reason, it must be discussed in considerable detail.

Verbs like *help* that form their fourth form by adding -*ed*, (-*d* or -*t*) are called 'regular' verbs, because the overwhelming majority of modern English verbs have this form, as do all the new verbs that come into the language. There are thousands of these verbs, a few of which alphabetically selected are:

ask, bake, create, dodge, elude, follow, gather, hinder, incite, jingle, knock, lighten, modernize, notify, oppress, pamper, qualify, renovate, soothe, tantalize, use (pronounced 'uze'), veer, wander, yearn, zip.

There are three groups of verbs, however, which do not add -ed, -d, or -t in their fourth form. One group does not have any separate fourth form at all. The verbs in this group simply use the first form as a fourth form. These are called the three-form verbs. Many of these are very common, like the verb *cut*. We have all heard children, who tend to regularize all things in language, say 'cutted.' Other verbs which, like *cut,* have no distinctive fourth form are:

beat, bet, bid, broadcast, burst, cast, cost, cut, fit, forecast, hit, hurt, knit, let, put, quit, rid, set, shed, shred, shut, slit, spit, split, spread, sweat, thrust, wed, wet, whet.

Some of these verbs have an alternative 'regular' fourth form: for example, we may say, *She has knit* or *She has knitted a sweater; The dress fit her* or *The dress fitted her.* Other verbs like *knit* and *fit* are *shred, sweat, wed, wet,* and *whet. Spit* may have an irregular fourth form *spat.*

This last example is one of a large group of verbs which differ in another way from the regular verbs in the construction of their fourth forms. These are called, appropriately, the 'irregular' verbs; for their fourth forms are made, not by the addition of a single suffix, but by radical changes in their base forms. These changes are sometimes called 'internal' inflections because the interior spellings of the words are changed, as in *spit-spat.* Furthermore, these verbs are also irregular in the sense that these internal changes are made according to many different patterns. With some verbs it is merely the change of one letter; with others, such as *teach-taught,* the spelling of almost the entire word is changed. About fifty of these irregular verbs have another kind of irregularity in that they have an additional fifth form. The verb *go* is a good example of a five-form verb:

Form 1: *go*
Form 2: *goes*
Form 3. *going*
Form 4: *went*
Form 5: *gone*

Among the five-form verbs are the most common words in the language, such as *do, eat, give,* and *take.* Because the fourth form of irregular verbs and the fifth form of those verbs that have this extra form are not made according to any single rule, these forms must be learned separately for every verb. This is why they cause trouble in actual usage.

First and fourth forms of the four-form irregular verbs:

First Form	Fourth Form	First Form	Fourth Form
abide	abode (abided)	light	lit (lighted)
awake	awoke (awaked)	lose	lost
behold	beheld	make	made
bend	bent	mean	meant
bereave	bereft	meet	met
bind	bound	pay	paid
bleed	bled	read	read (pron. 'red')
breed	bred	rend	rent
build	built	say	said
buy	bought	seek	sought
catch	caught	sell	sold
cling	clung	send	sent
creep	crept	shine	shone (shined)
deal	dealt	shoe	shod (shoed)
dig	dug	shoot	shot
dream	dreamt (dreamed)	sit	sat
dwell	dwelt (dwelled)	sleep	slept
feed	fed	sling	slung
feel	felt	slink	slunk
fight	fought	speed	sped (speeded)
find	found	spin	spun
flee	fled	stand	stood
fling	flung	stave	stove (staved)
get	got (gotten)	stick	stuck
grind	ground	sting	stung
hang	hung	string	strung
have	had	sweep	swept
hear	heard	swing	swung
hold	held	teach	taught
keep	kept	tell	told
kneel	knelt (kneeled)	think	thought

First Form	Fourth Form	First Form	Fourth Form
lay	laid	weep	wept
lead	led	win	won
leap	leapt (leaped)	wind	wound
leave	left	work	worked (wrought)
lend	lent	wring	wrung

First, fourth, and fifth forms of the irregular five-form verbs:

First Form	Fourth Form	Fifth Form
arise	arose	arisen
bear	bore	borne [2]
become	became	become
beget	begot	begotten
begin	began	begun
bid (command)	bade	bidden
bite	bit	bitten
blow	blew	blown
break	broke	broken
chide	chid (chided)	chidden (chided, chid)
choose	chose	chosen
cleave (split)	clove (cleft, cleaved)	cloven (cleft, cleaved)
come	came	come
do	did	done
draw	drew	drawn
drink	drank	drunk
drive	drove	driven
eat	ate	eaten
fall	fell	fallen
fly	flew	flown [3]
forbear	forbore	forborne
forbid	forbade	forbidden (forbid)
forget	forgot	forgotten
forgo	forwent	forgone
forsake	forsook	forsaken
forswear	forswore	forsworn
freeze	froze	frozen
give	gave	given

[2] In the sense of coming into existence, the form is *born*, 'The woman had *borne* five children,' but 'The baby was born in April, 1900.'

[3] In baseball, the verb *fly* is regular: 'He *flied* out'; 'He has *flied* out.'

First Form	Fourth Form	Fifth Form
go	went	gone
grow	grew	grown
hew	hewed	hewed (hewn)
hide	hid	hidden (hid)
know	knew	known
lie	lay	lain 4
mow	mowed	mowed (mown)
prove	proved	proved (proven)
ride	rode	ridden
ring	rang	rung
rise	rose	risen
run	ran	run
see	saw	seen
sew	sewed	sewed (sewn)
shake	shook	shaken
shave	shaved	shaved (shaven)
shear	sheared (shore)	sheared (shorn)
show	showed	shown
shrink	shrank (shrunk)	shrunk (shrunken)
sing	sang	sung
sink	sank (sunk)	sunk (sunken)
slay	slew	slain
slide	slid	slid (slidden)
smite	smote	smitten (smit)
sow	sowed	sowed (sown)
speak	spoke	spoken
spring	sprang (sprung)	sprung
stink	stank (stunk)	stunk
strew	strewed	strewn (strewed)
stride	strode	stridden
strike	struck	struck (stricken)
strive	strove	striven
swear	swore	sworn
swim	swam	swum
take	took	taken
tear	tore	torn
thrive	throve (thrived)	thriven (thrived)
throw	threw	thrown

4 When the word means to prevaricate, it is regular: 'He *lied* about his age'; 'She has *lied* to me too many times.'

First Form	Fourth Form	Fifth Form
tread	trod	trodden (trod)
wake	waked (woke)	waked (woken)
wear	wore	worn
weave	wove	woven (wove)
write	wrote	written

There is one verb in the language which is so irregular in all its forms that it defies classification and, therefore, must be treated as a special case. This verb is usually called *be,* but there is no reason why it should not be called *am* or *are.* This verb has eight forms: *be, am, are, is, was, were, being,* and *been,* and for this reason the ordinary classification system does not strictly apply to it, but *be, am,* and *are* might be considered variations of the first form; *is* is the second form; *was* and *were* are variations of the fourth form; and *being* and *been* are easily recognized as the third and fifth forms respectively. This odd verb *be* has so many peculiarities because it is a sort of hodgepodge derived from three different verbs in the old Indo-European language from which English is descended. The important thing to remember, however, is that in modern English all these diverse forms are part of the verb *be.*

Another deviation from the normal English verb-form pattern may be found in the so-called 'defective' verbs, all of which have only one form. These verbs are *can, may, shall, will, must, ought, could, might, should,* and *would.* They are defective, however, only when they are used as function words, not when they are main verbs. This distinction will be made clear in the next section of this chapter.

III

The second major grammatical device connected with the verb is the function word, which may precede some of the verb forms to make a verb phrase—or, as this phrase is sometimes called, an 'expanded' verb. Traditionally, these function words are called 'auxiliary verbs.' We shall postpone discussing the grammatical ideas expressed by function words until the words themselves become familiar—that is, until the system of these words has been learned.

The words that may be used in modern English as auxiliary verbs are as follows:

> be, do, will (shall), have, can, could, may, must, should (would), keep, get

and the compounds:

> ought to, be to, be about to, be going to, have to, have got to, used to.

One should remember that these words, when functioning as auxiliaries, are grammatical elements, and as such may be used only with some other verb to provide the vocabulary element. This is sometimes called the 'main verb,' which has the first, third, fourth, or fifth inflectional form, depending on which auxiliary verb is used. The second form is the only one never used with a function word.

When any of the so-called auxiliary verbs do appear alone without a main verb, and when a main verb is not implied, they are of course not grammatical elements, and mean something absolutely different from what they mean as auxiliary verbs. This point may be illustrated dramatically by the word *can*. When used as an auxiliary, it means 'to be able'—*We can help,* but when used by itself as a vocabulary element with no main verb understood, it means 'put into a tin or jar.' Of course we could say, 'I can can vegetables.' Here the word appears as both auxiliary and main verb. The first *can* provides the grammatical element, the second the vocabulary element.

In speech, of course, the distinction between these uses of *can* is marked in several ways. First, when it is an auxiliary verb, the vowel is usually unstressed and indistinct; writers sometimes try to represent it by the spelling 'c'n.' Second, the stress and pitch patterns of *can* as an auxiliary and *can* as a main verb are quite different. There is a rising pitch and a stress on *help* in 'We can help,' whereas in 'We can vegetables,' the *can* receives as much stress as the first syllable of *vegetables,* and the voice pitch rises on *can,* not after it.

The indistinctness of the vowel sound applies to many of the other function words used with verbs. In speech, and often in writing, these words have greatly reduced forms: *am* becomes *'m* (*I'm*), *are* becomes *'re* (*you're*), *is* becomes *'s* (*he's*), and so does *has* (*he's gone*); *had* becomes *'d* (*we'd gone*), and so does *would* (*I'd like it*); *shall* and *will* become *'ll* (*I'll go and he'll stay*), and *have* becomes *'ve* (*we could've gone*). Because the language has these reduced forms, uneducated people tend to confuse them with other words that have the same sound combinations: so they write *theirs* for *there's*, *your* for *you're*, *its* for *it's*, and, worst of all, *could of gone* for *could've gone*.

These auxiliary verbs are so distinctive that they may be considered as indicators or 'signs' of the verb function. In other words, it may be assumed that if a word appears in combination, for example, with *shall* or *have* in such expressions as *shall help* or *have helped,* such a group of words is a verb phrase. So, if all the auxiliary verbs listed above are memorized, the task of identifying this part of speech by its form will be that much more easily accomplished. But mistakes still may be made unless one understands how a verb phrase with all its possible complexities is composed.

To those who have already heard about auxiliary verbs, this term probably brings to mind such simple forms as *will help, has helped,* or *is helping,* or possibly such three-word combinations as *has been helped.* Although this is the type of phrase most often used, actually the verb phrase may be made up of much larger groups of words. The complexity of auxiliary verb combinations is truly astonishing; auxiliaries may be piled upon auxiliaries, and the combinations and permutations among them are almost endless. This is especially so in the spoken language, in which we tend to use more complicated verb phrases than we do in writing. We often hear such sentences as, 'I didn't know that I *was going to be kept waiting*' and 'He *was about to have been tipped off.*' In writing it is best to avoid such cumbersome phrases. Yet if one is to understand the modern English verb system, its full possibilities must be considered: this means taking a look at the entire range of auxiliaries and their combinations.

First, we might examine all the forms that may be constructed by combining auxiliaries with the first form of the main verb. These auxiliaries are:

> do, can, could, may, might, must, will (shall), should (would), be to, be going to, be about to, have got to, have to, used to, ought to.

Seventeen in all! But many more than seventeen forms may be constructed, for some of these verbs are capable of inflectional changes themselves and of expansions by the use of other auxiliary verbs. For example, *do* has a second form *does* and a fourth form *did,* so we may have *do help, does help,* and *did help.* Fortunately, *can, will (shall), could, may (might), must, should (would),* and *ought* are, as we know, defective verbs and cannot change form at all. And *have got to* has only two variations in standard English: *has got to* and *had got to.* But all the compound auxiliaries introduced by *be* (*be to, be going to,* and *be about to*) may have almost as many forms as all the numerous variations of *be* itself. There are not only the simple forms—*am, are, is, was,* and *were*—but also *will (shall) be, have been, has been, had been, will (shall) have been. Have to* may have an enormous number of variations: in addition to the ordinary expanded forms, *has to, had to, will (shall) have to, has had to, had had to,* and *will (shall) have had to,* it may appear in such forms as *may have to, used to have to,* etc.

Following is a list of verb phrases composed of the first form of *help* and all the auxiliaries and their variants that are used in standard English with this form:

$$\left.\begin{array}{l} \text{do} \\ \text{does} \\ \text{did} \\[6pt] \text{can} \\ \text{could} \\ \text{may} \\ \text{might} \\ \text{must} \end{array}\right\} \text{help}$$

shall
will
should
would

am to
is to
are to
were to

am going to
is going to
are going to
was going to
were going to
have been going to
has been going to
had been going to
could have been going to
may have been going to
might have been going to
must have been going to
ought to have been going to
would have been going to
should have been going to

am about to
are about to
is about to
was about to
were about to
have been about to
has been about to
had been about to
could have been about to
may have been about to
might have been about to
must have been about to
ought to have been about to
should have been about to
would have been about to

have to
has to

help

had to
will have to
shall have to
have had to
has had to
had had to
could have had to
may have had to
might have had to
must have had to
ought to have had to } help

shall have had to
should have had to
will have had to
would have had to

have got to

used to
used to have to

It is only when we come to the variations with the third and fourth (or fifth) forms of the main verb that we can fully realize what extraordinary complexity this part of speech may have. The third form (*helping*) uses only two auxiliaries: *be* and *keep* with their normal variations: *am, are, is, was, were, will (shall) be, have been, has been, had been,* and *will (shall) have been;* and *keep, kept, will (shall) keep,* and *have (has, had, will have) kept.* This seems relatively simple, but since *be* and *keep* are themselves first-form verbs, they too are theoretically capable of having all the variations listed above for the main verb itself. For example, we could say, *was to have been helping, ought to have been helping,* and *is going to keep helping.* Furthermore, *be* and *keep* may themselves be combined to form the expression *be kept helping,* so that we may also have *is to be kept helping, should have been kept helping,* and *ought to be kept helping.* Fortunately, some of the forms possible with this combination are not ordinarily used, so the list is not quite so overwhelming as it might otherwise be.

The auxiliary verbs used with the fourth (or fifth) form of the main verb (*helped, sung, taught,* etc.) are *be, have,* and *get,* as in *am helped, have helped,* and *get helped.* The last form may be re- garded by some people as poor usage, for the acceptability of *get* as an auxiliary is still rather controversial. There are, however, many contexts in which the use of this word seems quite natural to educated persons—such as, *get started, get acquainted, get married, get frightened,* and *get arrested.* When all the possible variations of *be, have,* and *get* are considered, the verb picture of extreme com- plexity continues. *Have,* being a first form like *be* and *get,* may be accompanied by most of the auxiliaries used by that form, so such verb phrases as *could have helped, ought to have helped,* and *might have helped* are not unusual. We have already seen the many varia- tions of the verb *be* that are possible with the third form of the main verb. The same possibilities exist with the fourth form. *Get* may be accompanied by all the first-form auxiliaries and also by the third-form auxiliary *keep* with all its possible variations, such as *will have to keep getting helped.* From all that has been said, the potentialities of the modern English verb forms should now be apparent. If we were to list all the possible auxiliary verb combina- tions suggested in this discussion, the total would be approximately eight hundred!—certainly, a number far greater than most people imagine.

IV

So far this chapter has been devoted to a description of the forms of the verb, without reference to the grammatical ideas which these forms express. It is now time to look at this other equally important side of the picture. Each part of speech has not only its own dis- tinctive set of forms made up of the various inflections, function words, and patterns of word order but also its own distinctive set of grammatical ideas which these forms express. These ideas are so distinctive for the major parts of speech that if the form of a word leaves us in doubt as to what part of speech it is, we may often find a clue in the grammatical ideas expressed by the word: does it show number, tense, or degree, for example? The grammatical ideas ex- pressed by the verb are TENSE, ASPECT, MODE, and VOICE.

The most important of these is TENSE. The problem of time has engaged and baffled the profoundest philosophers, so obviously it cannot be solved here. Most people regard time as a sort of stream, or continuum, with points or sections along the stream. The 'right now' is a point in that stream; the past is a large block preceding the 'right now'; and the future is another block of varying proportions following the 'right now.' There is an old joke which suggests that young people think of the future as a much larger block than the past and that old folks see the past as much larger than the future. But most people would agree that the time from the present back to the building of the pyramids, or the fall of Rome, or the Spanish Armada, or the American Revolution is a rather sizable block. In any event, we know that time may be cut into many divisions, each one of considerable dimensions. Indeed, it can be cut into more parts than even our eight hundred verb variations could hope to express. As a matter of fact, these variations express surprisingly few of the possible divisions of time; yet they do express more time ideas than most students have been led to believe if they hazily remember 'past, present, and future' from their previous studies. Something of the spread of tense ideas the verb may express can be illustrated by the following series of variations:

> had helped
> had been about to help
>
> helped
> was about to help
> was going to help
>
> has helped
> has been about to help
>
> is helping
>
> is about to help
> is going to help
>
> will have helped
> will have been about to help
>
> will help
> will be going to help

Now if we look at this list and consider the points along the time-stream, it is clear that they range from a point relatively far in the past to one relatively far in the future (from a time before another past time to a time beyond another future time, with *is helping* in the middle, expressing the 'right now'). And it is obvious that each time differs a little from the others as we advance along that imaginary stream. Traditionally, grammarians have sought to simplify this spread of tense ideas by grouping them into a past-present-future sequence. But this kind of grouping fails to suggest adequately the range of tense ideas which our verb variations can express.

It would be almost impossible to describe all these tense ideas in terms of their form. There are, however, a few tense forms the names of which should be familiar to all students, since these terms are used in most grammar books and some of them will appear in later chapters of this book. The term 'present tense' is applied to the first form of the verb when it is not accompanied by an auxiliary verb, as in (*I*) *help,* and to the second form, as in (*He*) *helps.* All students should be warned that this term rarely means what it seems to say, for these forms express actual present time with only a very limited number of verbs: (1) the verb *be;* (2) those verbs whose vocabulary meanings express ideas of feeling, seeing, hearing, smelling, understanding, believing, wanting, liking; and (3) all verbs that describe the operation of the senses or the mind, such as (*I*) *grasp, get, follow, catch on to* (*your meaning*). With all other verbs (the great majority), the present tense forms usually express ideas of 'continuous action,' including the present, as in *He drives to work;* and 'universal truths,' such as *Warm air always rises.* Sometimes these forms may even express future time, as in *I go to Boston next week.*

The term 'past tense' is applied to all fourth forms not accompanied by auxiliary verbs, such as (*He*) *helped.* The term 'perfect tense' is used to describe the fourth (or fifth) form accompanied by the auxiliary verb *have,* as in *have helped* and *have gone.* Both the past tense and the 'present perfect' tense describe past time—the latter being used to indicate any time in the past right up to the present moment, the former when a more or less definite time in the past is meant, as in *John helped his brother when he was sick.* The 'past perfect' form (*had helped*) is used to describe an action that took place before a specific time in the past; the 'future perfect' form (*will have helped*) is used to describe an action that will take place at any time before a specific time in the future.

The 'future tense' is a term used traditionally to describe the first form of the verb accompanied by the auxiliary verbs *will* or *shall* (*will* or *shall help*); but, as anyone can see from the examples already given, the language has many other forms for expressing future time, such as *is helping, is about to help, is to help,* and *is going to help.* Finally, the term 'progressive tense' is applied to the third form of the verb accompanied by the various forms of the auxiliary *be,* such as *am helping, was helping,* and *will be helping.* These progressive forms always describe an action in progress at a given time in the present, past, or future. The present progressive tense is used almost universally in modern English to express actions which are being performed in the present.

The verb, of course, is the only part of speech in English which can convey the idea of tense by grammatical means. If we wish to express the ideas of past and future, for example, in connection with some other part of speech—such as the noun—we must say *past* (*president*) or *future* (*president*). This, of course, is a vocabulary rather than a grammatical way of expressing these ideas. Since grammatical tense is so intimately connected with the verb, we can always test a word for 'verbness' by seeing if it expresses a tense idea, or if the form may be changed to express tense. This test is particularly useful when a verb appears without any inflections or function words to distinguish it. In the sentence *I help mother,* we can tell quickly that *help* is a verb because it will allow a change to past tense—*I helped mother*—without destroying the basic meaning of the sentence.

The term ASPECT is unfamiliar to most people. Yet ideas of aspect have appeared many times during the discussion of the various tense forms, for some of these forms not only indicate points along a time-stream but also convey other rather more subtle suggestions. Some tell us that the helping process, for example, is beginning or about to begin (*is about to help* or *is going to help*); others tell us the process is a continuous one (*has been helping* or *will be helping*); still others that it is a completed one (*has been helped* or *will be helped*). Sometimes the aspect of the verb tells us that the speaker is regarding the process as a whole without considering its beginning or end, or how long it lasts (*helps* or *will help*), or that the process is a repeated one (*keeps helping*). These types of aspect are called 'inceptive,' 'imperfective' (or 'durative'), 'perfective,' 'terminative,' and 'iterative' respectively.

The term MODE (sometimes, 'mood') is more familiar than aspect. Most college students have heard it used in previous grammar courses. In brief, mode has to do with a set of ideas expressed by a verb form concerning the speaker's attitude toward what he is saying—whether he thinks the process he is speaking or writing about is certain, uncertain, probable, possible, desirable, or whether he completely denies the process, or whether he has a determined attitude toward it. In other words, it suggests he knows something is happening, or thinks it might have happened, hopes it will happen or has happened, insists that it happen, suspects it isn't happening, knows it isn't happening. Three types of mode may be seen in these examples:

> They *were* helping us.
> *Help* us!
> *Would* he *were helping* us!

The first is a statement of what the speaker assumes as a fact, the second expresses a command, the third implies a denial that the helping process exists at all, and the wish that this were not true. Traditionally, verb variations that express matters of fact have been called the 'indicative mode'; those that express commands the 'imperative mode'; those that suggest uncertainty, desirability, or denial of fact have been called the 'subjunctive mode.' Although these are useful categories, they tend to obscure the range of attitudes from certainty to denial of fact, which the following list suggests:

is helping
may help
would help
should help
could help
might help
help!
do help
(if he) were helping
would (that he) were helping
were (he) helping

The forms of the verb used to express mode are, unluckily, not quite so clear-cut as the tense forms. The form for the imperative mode, however, is clear enough. It is simply the first form of the verb as used in the title of this chapter. It cannot be inflected or accompanied by any function words. If we command something in the future, the idea must be expressed by vocabulary means, for example, *Leave the house at ten o'clock.* The imperative form for the verb *be* is *be:* as in *Be quiet* and *Be good.*

The means for expressing the subjunctive mode in the modern English verb is very complex. Old English had a large system of subjunctive verb inflections; now only a few survive, as in *Long live the king!* and we all probably remember the verb form *be* in the giant's cry in 'Jack and the Beanstalk':

> '*Be* he alive or *be* he dead,
> I'll grind his bones to make my bread.'

We also still use the old subjunctive first form of the verb (where the indicative mode uses the second form) in subordinate clauses following verbs expressing the ideas of asking, determining, desiring, and doubting, as in

> Her husband urged that she *stay* at home.
> She desired that her son *win* the tournament.

Another inflectional form used to express the subjunctive idea of 'contrary to fact' is still very much alive in the language today. This is the use of *were* where the indicative mode would use *was,* as in

Were he only here! or *If only I were you!* But we more often express subjunctive ideas with a group of function words called the 'modal auxiliaries.' These are *can, could, may, might, must, ought to, should,* and *would.* As can be seen from the examples already given, the reversal of normal word order is another possible device.

The final idea expressed grammatically by the verb is called VOICE. The differences in the verb variations in the two columns below express differences in voice:

he kills	he is killed
he was helping	he was being helped
he will have lost	he will have been lost

The forms in the left column express active voice; those in the right column passive voice. Usually the distinction in meaning between the two voices is quite obvious. This is especially true when the verb clearly expresses an action. Then the active voice indicates that the noun (or pronoun) preceding the verb performs the acting, and the passive voice shows that this noun is being acted upon. But in some instances, this distinction is not so pointed, logically. In the following sentences each pair has approximately the same meaning, although the first is in the active voice, the second in the passive:

The war began	The war was begun
The cake is baking	The cake is being baked
These cars will sell	These cars will be sold

Because ideas of voice are not always perfectly distinct, it is better for practical purposes to think of voice in terms of form. The passive voice variations are made with *be* or *get* plus the fourth or fifth form (fifth form of five-form verbs) of the main verb, as in *is* (or *gets*) *helped, has been done,* and *will be told.* The passive forms may also include any of the modal auxiliaries, as in *may have been helped* or *could have been helped.* (Discussions of the 'passive turn' may be found in Chapter VI, p. 63 and in Chapter X, p. 135n.)

These are the major ideas which the variations of the English verb forms express. When we consider that there are at least fourteen tense differentiations, six aspect differentiations, nine mode variations, and two voice variations (and the discussion of these subjects has been by no means exhaustive), it is not difficult to see why there is a need in modern English for hundreds of verb forms.

v

Many of our most common verbs are often accompanied not only by the grammatical devices we have discussed but also by a number of such small words as *across, by, down, in, off, on, out, over, through, to, up,* and *upon.* These words usually follow the verb—especially one-syllable verbs—to form such expressions as *put across* (an idea), *get up, jot down, call off, catch on, peter out, put over, put out, blow up, side with,* and hundreds of others. Some authorities regard these words as 'modifiers' of the verb. But there is another interpretation which seems to square better with the facts: namely, that they are a part of the verb itself (the basic vocabulary part)—just as if they were suffixes. In fact, these additional words and the verbs they follow may be thought of as being hyphenated to form single compound words. The basic unity of the two words may be demonstrated by the fact that so many of these combinations may be taken bodily and made into another part of speech; and, as such, the two words usually are hyphenated. We speak of *pick-up trucks,* a *falling-out, knock-down-drag-out fights,* a *break-through,* etc. When used in this way, *up, out,* etc., are not separate parts of speech and not function words, but part of the basic vocabulary meaning of the verb itself. It is important to know the status of these words when they are used with verbs, for under different circumstances they function quite differently. And since they will be encountered soon in these different roles, these last comments on the form of the verb may serve as a link between this chapter and the two that will follow.

V

S'S, ARTICLES, AND APOSTROPHES

Next to the verb, the noun is the most important part of speech, for the typical modern English sentence is built around verbs and nouns. Except for commands like *Stop, Look, and Listen,* all English sentences must include a noun or its substitute, a pronoun. The reason for this is that the basic English sentence pattern is noun (or pronoun)–verb; and this pattern must always be filled out, even when there is only one idea to be expressed, as in sentences like *It rained* or *It thundered.* Moreover, the noun is the most frequently used part of speech. Often a large number of nouns surround a single verb, like the electrons in an atom encircling their nucleus. Because of these peculiarities of the language, it is absolutely vital to understand the forms and uses of this part of speech.

I

The noun has a wide assortment of permanent forms, many of which are made from verbs: *manage–management* (the example used in Chapter III); *manage–manager; prosper–prosperity; perform–performance; apply–applicant; break–breakage; survive–survival.* Others are made from other parts of speech, usually adjectives. The list of the permanent noun suffixes is as follows:

-acy (supremacy, diplomacy)
-age (breakage, appendage)
-al (survival, approval)
-ance, -ence (performance, dependence)
-ant (applicant, assistant)
-ard (dullard, drunkard)
-dom (wisdom, freedom)
-er, -or (worker, actor)
-ery (bravery, snobbery)
-hood (childhood, adulthood)

-ing (working, helping)
-ion, -sion, -tion (union, pretension, direction)
-ism (truism, communism)
-ity (triviality, purity)
-ment (agreement, resentment)
-ness (witness, happiness)
-ship (salesmanship, hardship)
-th (wealth, health)
-ty (anxiety, cruelty)
-ure (failure, departure)

These are called noun suffixes, but one should never assume that all words that are formed in this way are nouns and only nouns. Three of these endings are also used to form adjectives; these are *-al, -ant,* and *-er.* The suffix *-ing* is a particularly shifty one, since it may be used to form adjectives and nouns, and also is the ending, of course, of the third form of the verb. These noun suffixes, like the verb prefixes and suffixes discussed in the last chapter, are no more than guideposts, as it were: they show that we are going in the right direction, but they do not prove that the destination has been reached. This proof can come only through knowledge of the major grammatical devices that characterize the noun.

II

The modern English noun, unlike the verb, has very few inflected forms. Unlike Old English, which had thirteen possible inflectional endings for the different classes of nouns, modern English has only three: *-s, -'s,* and *-s',* and a few exceptions to these which are holdovers from the past.

The most common noun inflection is the simple *-s* suffix (and its variant *-es*). The addition of *-s* to a noun expresses of course the idea of plurality, of more-than-oneness, as in *boy–boys, student–students, miss–misses,* etc. In grammatical terminology, the idea thus expressed is called 'number.' Like most other modern languages, English has only two numbers: singular and plural. Sometimes this *-s* inflection is a useful device for distinguishing nouns from other parts of speech. We may use it, for example, to distinguish a noun from a 'main verb' after certain auxiliary verbs: because of this inflection, we know that *washes* in

The old lady seldom does washes

is a noun and not a part of a verb phrase. This inflection, however, does not always mark a word as a noun, for it is also the sign of the second form of the verb. Therefore, when a word ending in *-s* has no other grammatical devices connected with it, we cannot tell whether it is a plural noun or a second-form verb. Such words as *bats, fears, gardens, rocks, stops, washes,* and thousands of others are not formally distinguished as nouns or verbs until they are 'fortified' by at least one additional grammatical device. Just what these devices are we shall see later in this chapter and in Chapter VI. In the sentence context, however, the grammatical meaning expressed by the *-s* inflection will reveal the part of speech: if the idea of plurality is expressed, the word with the *-s* ending must be a noun, for this is the only part of speech that expresses this idea by this particular device.

Although the vast majority of nouns form their plural by adding *-s*, there are a few important exceptions. The variant *-es* is used when the noun itself ends in *-s, -sh, -ch, -x, -z,* and *-o,* as in *kiss–kisses, dish–dishes, church–churches, sex–sexes, quiz–quizzes,* and *echo–echoes.* We also use the *-es* to form the plural when the singular noun ends in *y* preceded by a consonant: the *y* is changed to *i* as in *family–families.* Another exception in the formation of noun plurals is the *-en* ending. There are only a few of these: *ox–oxen, child–children, brother–brethren* (also *brothers,* of course). The third exception is the so-called internal inflection, *man–men, mouse–mice, woman–women, goose–geese, foot–feet, tooth–teeth,* etc. A fourth exception is the small group of nouns that have no inflection in their plurals: *deer–deer, sheep–sheep, fish–fish* (but also *fishes*), *cod–cod, corps–corps,* etc. Because of the nature of their meaning, a few nouns are used nearly always in the singular—some of the names of studies (*arithmetic*), names of forces (*gravitation*), states of mind (*fortitude, happiness*), and names of materials (*wool, copper*). And likewise, some nouns have only plural forms and are rarely used in the singular: *annals, athletics, dregs, goods, oats, pants, remains, tidings, vespers,* etc.

The other noun inflections are *-'s* and *-s'*. This is a curious kind of ending because it involves not only changes in the sound and spelling of the word (sound in pronunciation, spelling in writing), like any other inflected form, but also the addition of the apostrophe in writing. This inflection indicates that the word to which it is attached is a noun in the 'genitive' case. The idea of the genitive case is a much more difficult one to explain than anything encountered thus far. Up to this point, it has been possible to limit the discussion to isolated grammatical units—a simple verb or verb-group or a single noun. Now, in order to explain the meaning of the genitive form, a second unit will have to be introduced into our illustrations. In taking this step, an advance will be made from one-unit to two-unit grammatical constructions.

The use of an additional unit is necessary at this point because the genitive case idea is a 'relational' one. Case in general may be defined as a grammatical method of expressing the relationships of a noun (or pronoun) to a verb, or to another noun. The genitive case form always expresses a relationship to another noun. The precise nature of this relationship is hard to describe. In most instances, it expresses the ideas of possessing, owning, or belonging to, in the broadest sense of these terms. In such expressions as *the boy's books,* the relation is clearly one of ownership on the part of the boy. In *the cat's tail,* we cannot say literally that the *cat* owns her *tail,* but that she does possess it is clear enough. Or if we wish to reverse our point of view, we can say the *book* belongs to the *boy* and the *tail* belongs to the *cat.* As the genitive form is now used in ordinary speech, it is largely restricted to people and other living things and usually expresses the idea of possession. But expressions such as *the book's cover* and *the tree's bark* are very common, and there are a few set phrases where this form does not express the idea of possession at all—for example, *wits' end, harm's way, winter's day, today's newspaper,* and *a month's rent.*

It should be clear from these examples that the *-'s (-s')* inflection is not the only grammatical device associated with the genitive case idea. Since more than one word is involved, the word-order device too must come into the picture. Except in special situations, which will be explained shortly, the genitive case in nouns is expressed by placing a noun with the -'s (-s') inflection immediately before another noun (or adjective-noun phrase, as we shall see later) as in *cat's tail, farmers' rights,* etc. Failure to understand this genitive case word-order device is probably responsible for the occasional erroneous use of the apostrophe in non-genitive plural nouns or with singular nouns that end in -s, as in *Keats' lived in the nineteenth century.* No one who is aware of the word-order pattern of the genitive noun could make such a mistake, for *Keats* is not followed by any other noun, and no noun is understood. The apostrophe is used before the -s in the plain plural form only with figures: *2's and 3's;* with letters: *mind your p's and q's;* and with words when we are talking about them as words: *Let there be no if's or but's.*

Sometimes the context allows the noun following the genitive noun to be omitted, but the previous sentence or clause must make it very clear that this word is 'understood.' An example of this kind of omission follows:

> Shakespeare's sonnets are beautiful, but I prefer Milton's.

Again, after forms of the verb *be* a genitive noun is not always followed by another noun. In such sentences, the related noun is in the subject position: *The book is John's; The dish is the cat's.* And the genitive form may also be found at the end of the sentence after the word *of: He is a friend of John's.* This peculiar construction is known as the 'double genitive,' because the -'s and the word *of* both express the idea of possession. This usage may merely indicate a desire for emphasis on the part of the writer, or it may express a combination of the ideas of possession and of belonging to a group: John not only has a friend, but this friend is one of several.

The rules prescribing the correct position of the apostrophe are really very simple. To form the genitive singular, -'s is added to the plain singular noun form: *boy's, fish's, miss's, Jones's.* To form the genitive plural, we merely add an apostrophe to the regular plural form, provided that this form ends in an 's' or 'z' sound: *cats'*, *boys'*, *fishes'*. If it does not end in one of these sounds, we add -*'s: men's, children's.*

Except when we are talking about words as words, the -*'s* ending is a sure sign of the noun, and may therefore be used only with this part of speech. Occasionally, students who are very unsure of their grammar may insert apostrophes indiscriminately wherever they hear an -*s* ending—even in second-form verbs, as in

Mother buy's groceries every day.

In order to avoid such a serious mistake as this, one must know first that the -*'s* is used only with nouns, and second, one must be able to distinguish, of course, between nouns and verbs. (More information on the use of the apostrophe appears in Chapter XIV, pp. 204-5.)

The genitive form is the only instance in modern English in which nouns are inflected to express case distinctions. This situation is in sharp contrast to that which existed in the earliest period of the language. In Old English there were five inflectional case forms. Although almost all of these have been lost, obviously the relationships among words in a sentence still must be expressed. And in modern English, we simply use the two other major grammatical devices—word order and function words—to take the place of the lost inflections. Because the use of word order and function words for this purpose involves rather complex word-order patterns, consideration of this subject will be postponed until the next chapter.

III

Since the noun has only three inflectional forms, it is fortunate that there are certain function words which are the unique property of that part of speech. Modern grammarians have called this kind of word the noun 'indicator.' It has been so named because it is literally an indicator or marker of the noun. By far the most dependable and commonly used indicators are *the* (the definite article) and *a* or *an* (the indefinite articles) and the pronouns *my, our, your, its,* and *their.* Any one of these words marks the word that follows it as a noun, provided that we are dealing (as we are in this early chapter) with the simplest kinds of word groups involving only verbs and nouns. In such expressions as *the house, a walk, an apple, his blessing, their ideas,* the words are all marked as nouns by the preceding indicators, which, in the most literal sense, 'signal' that a noun is to follow. This is, however, a provisional definition of the indicator, since very few sentences in actual use are limited to nouns and verbs. In Chapter VIII (p. 94) this oversimplified rule will be expanded to include more complex noun groups.

There is another rather large group of words which serve as indicators in some contexts, but which also have other uses. These are *his, her, this* (*these*), *that* (*those*), *all, any, both, each, every, few, many, more, most, much, some,* and any noun in the genitive case form, for example, *Henry's.* It is easy to decide whether these words are functioning as indicators simply by substituting *the, a,* or *an* for them. If the basic meaning of the sentence is not destroyed by the substitution, the words are indicators of nouns. This test proves that in the following sentences the words *that, some, any,* and *the cat's* are indicators and that the words following them are nouns:

> *That* (the) building is a church.
> John asked for *some* (the) water.
> *Any* (a) child should drink milk.
> *The cat's* (the) dish should be washed.

In the following different sentences, however, these same words are clearly not indicators, because the substitution cannot be made:

> *That* (the) is a good idea.
> *Some* (the) like it hot.
> I like *any* (the) of those models.
> The dish is *the cat's* (the).

The indicator is an extremely useful device for marking off nouns from other parts of speech. For example, by this means nouns can be distinguished from verbs, whether the word has an -*s* ending or no ending at all. Those words listed on page 52, which we said

could be either nouns or verbs because of the dual meaning of the
-s ending, cannot possibly be anything but nouns when they are preceded by indicators: *their bats, his fears, all gardens, many rocks,
the stops, our washes.* This device is particularly important when it
accompanies nouns whose vocabulary meanings 'show action.' Since
'showing action' is an important part of the customary 'definition'
of the verb, such nouns could be easily mistaken for verbs if they
were not marked by indicators, and often are mistaken for verbs by
those who do not understand the importance of this grammatical
device. The second italicized word in each of the following sentences
is a noun of this kind:

> They take *a walk* in the evening.
> Mrs. Smith is hanging out *her wash.*
> She is always on *the go.*
> Mrs. Jones is *a has-been.*
> This chair really was *a find.*

In the English idiom, not all nouns are preceded by indicators.
Fortunately, however, this device is lacking most frequently in the
plural where the -s ending helps to some extent to mark the part
of speech, as in

> The old man keeps chickens.

But, even in the singular, there are some nouns that are seldom
accompanied by indicators. In the following sentences, the italicized
nouns are not marked by this device:

> John is chewing *gum.*
> The chimney is belching *smoke.*
> The recipe uses *flour.*

Yet these words can be shown to be nouns because the intended
meaning allows the insertion of an indicator immediately before
them:

> John is chewing (his or some) *gum.*
> The chimney is belching (some) *smoke.*
> The recipe uses (some) *flour.*

Conversely, if we take three sentences in which these same three words are used as verbs, the result is very different when we try to insert indicators before them:

> Amateurs will (the) *gum* up the works.
> Our fireplaces (the) *smoke*.
> Cooks (the) *flour* their pastry boards.

Obviously, the basic meanings of these sentences are completely 'gummed up' when the indicator is added, so it is apparent that the italicized words are not nouns. The test used in the foregoing sentences is sometimes called the 'indicator test.'

The noun indicator is a very simple grammatical device, but one should not underestimate its importance. Without it, there would be many more difficulties with confusions and ambiguities in the written language. In Chapter I we pointed out how an indicator could clear up the ambiguity in the sentence, *He gave her dog biscuits.* The fact that indicators are usually missing in newspaper headlines explains why they are often ambiguous, as in *Charity Takes Place on Grove Street.* Foreigners, whose native languages do not use the indicator, have a particularly difficult time making themselves understood in the English idiom, mainly because their teachers of English have not taught them the special importance of these words as grammatical devices.

IV

For some reason, never fully explained, the idea of 'gender' in nouns is usually given considerable emphasis in traditional books on modern English grammar. It is true, of course, that in Old English, as in many other languages, modern as well as ancient, nouns are grouped grammatically according to gender: they have special sets of inflections that are 'masculine,' 'feminine,' and 'neuter.' But no such forms exist for the English noun today. We do, however, have a group of 'feminine' endings which distinguish some nouns from their masculine counterparts. The most important of these is the *-ess* ending, although there are also *-trix, -ine,* and *-a,* as the following examples indicate: *actor–actress, god–goddess, executor–executrix, alumnus–alumna,* etc.

One reason for the confusion in this matter is that many grammarians and teachers of English have misunderstood the important difference between grammatical and vocabulary gender, calling the latter 'natural' gender. They say that such words as *man, boy, man-servant,* and *male-nurse* are masculine and that *woman, girl, barmaid,* and *woman-lawyer* are feminine because these words refer specifically to members of these sexes: they are 'naturally' masculine and feminine. This is, of course, perfectly true; but what these people fail to observe is that the idea of sex is not expressed here grammatically—that none of the grammatical devices have been used. Actually, the idea of gender, even in languages that have elaborate grammatical forms to express this idea, does not always correspond to 'natural' gender. In Latin, for example, the words for sailor and poet (*nauta* and *poeta*) are grammatically feminine; in German (as in Old English) the words for woman and child (*das Weib* and *das Kind*) are grammatically neuter. In modern English we must therefore conclude that nouns do not have gender so far as grammar is concerned.

In reviewing this chapter, three points should be remembered. First, nouns have special permanent forms which suggest strongly that they are nouns. Second, the modern English noun in the written language also has three inflectional forms: the *-s* ending (and its variants) to express the idea of plural number; and the *-'s* and the *-s'* endings to express the idea of the genitive case. Finally, there is the very important function word called the 'indicator,' and the 'indicator test' may be used to identify many nouns. This subject of the noun devices will be expanded in the next chapter, in which we shall deal with those word-order patterns and function words that define the relationships of the noun to the sentence as a whole.

VI

WHAT ARE PATTERNS FOR?

In Chapters II and III the importance of word order as a grammatical device in modern English was repeatedly emphasized. In Chapters IV and V little was said about this device because these chapters were primarily concerned with the isolated words and word groups that form only one grammatical unit. But when nouns and verbs are brought together in sentences, the patterns of word order enter the scene in their most dramatic roles.

I

From the point of view of form, sentences like the following are of the simplest type: [1]

> The dog frightened the postman.
> The people expect justice.
> Grandmother baked a cake.

It is easy to see that these sentences are composed of a verb and two nouns. But there is one more problem to be solved before their structure can be understood. Just as the nouns contribute a grammatical meaning different from that of the verb, so the two nouns contribute grammatical meanings that are different from each

---

[1] Another type of extremely simple sentence structure ('The dawn came') is discussed in Chapter X, p. 130.

other—although neither noun has any distinguishing inflection or function word to show this difference. For example, in the sentence *A dog frightened the postman,* the nouns *dog* and *postman* differ sharply not only in their vocabulary meanings, but in another way as well. This other dimension of meaning can be seen clearly if the positions of the two nouns are interchanged: obviously *dog* before the verb means something very different from *dog* after the verb. This distinction is even more apparent if the same noun is used in both positions, as in *Dog eats dog.* Although the vocabulary meanings of dog_1 and dog_2 are the same, the two animals are clearly in very different situations! It is apparent that this kind of difference in meaning is expressed by a word-order device: namely, the positions of the two nouns in relation to the verb—one noun before the verb, the other after it. The pattern can best be illustrated by a skeleton sentence in which only the grammatical devices are expressed:

	(noun)	(verb)		(noun)

A dog frightened the postman: A ——— ———ed the ———.

In such a simple declarative sentence, the noun before the verb is called the 'subject,' the noun after the verb the 'object.' The meanings of these grammatical elements are enormously difficult to pin down; many grammarians have attempted to define them without any real success. Of course, in one of the sentences above—*Grandmother baked a cake*—the subject is easily recognized as the performer of an action and the object as the receiver of that action, but this traditional definition, while applying to this particular sentence, would have to be stretched considerably to include *The people expect justice.* And it would have to be stretched even more to include some other simple subject-verb-object sentences, such as *The judge heard a commotion, Mary has a bracelet, The postman turned the corner,* and *John drives a car.* Furthermore, there are many kinds of sentences in which the meaning of 'performer' is expressed by several parts of the sentence other than the subject, and the subject has other meanings than that of performer. The truth is that 'subject' and 'object' have many different meanings, which cannot be described in general terms apart from a given sentence context. These grammatical classes, however, can be accurately defined in terms of their form—of the grammatical device by which they are expressed. In a three-unit declarative sentence,[2] any noun preceding the verb without the possibility of a mark of punctuation coming between is the subject, and any noun, not in the genitive form, which follows the verb is the object, provided that it refers to a person or thing different from the subject.

Obviously, in this type of sentence, word order is a very important device; but it determines only the relationships between the two nouns and the verb. This device does not determine finally whether a given three-unit word group actually is a noun-verb-noun pattern and not some other three-unit sentence structure, such as noun–verb–adjective, noun–verb–adverb, adjective–noun–verb, or verb–adjective–noun. And of course we must have this information before the relationships within the pattern can be established. For this reason, a minimum number of other grammatical devices, especially verb inflections and noun indicators, must usually be present in addition to the word-order device.

In addition to the subject-verb-object sentence, there is still another kind of noun-verb-noun pattern. This is illustrated by the following sentences:

> My chair is the rocker.
> Our son became a doctor.
> The student remained a pessimist.
> Benedict Arnold turned traitor.

The second noun in this type of sentence is called a 'predicate complement.' Like the object, the predicate complement always follows the verb and, in a sense, 'completes' its meaning. For this reason, both nouns in this position are called 'complements.' However, in other ways they are different: the predicate complement, unlike the object, refers to the same person or thing as the subject; in the

---

[2] Obviously, extremely simple sentences such as these are rarely used in actual discourse and even less in writing. But real situations are always enormously complex; it is therefore necessary to begin with intentionally oversimplified examples.

examples above, *chair* and *rocker* refer to the same thing, and *son* and *doctor* refer to the same person. The difference between these two kinds of complements may be seen most strikingly in two similar but contrasting sentences such as:

> Toby has a *dog*. (object)
>
> Toby is a *dog*. (predicate complement)

The predicate complement differs structurally from the object in that it occurs only with a certain kind of verb, the vocabulary meaning of which allows it to equate the complement with the subject. These are appropriately called 'linking verbs.' In American English there are relatively few linking verbs that allow noun complements. They are *be, become, prove, turn,* and *remain.* The British also use *appear, feel, seem,* and a few others. Some verbs in the passive voice form also operate as this kind of verb and are followed by predicate complements:

> Mr. Smith was made (elected, chosen, appointed) president.
>
> The soldier was held a captive.
>
> The experiment was pronounced a failure.

A predicate complement may be defined, then, as a noun that follows a linking verb and which refers to the same person or thing as the subject.

Predicate complements after the verb *be* are easy enough to recognize, but complements after *become, prove,* and *turn* may cause difficulty because both kinds of complements may be used with these verbs. For example, *Jim proved a fool* has exactly the same form as *Jim proved his statement,* but *fool* is a predicate complement and *statement* an object.[3] The structural difference is apparent only when the verb is turned into the passive voice form. If the complement can become the subject of the passive verb without seriously altering the meaning of the sentence, it is an object: *His statement was proved* . . . illustrates this point. If it cannot, then the noun is a predicate complement.

The next problem in word-order patterns involves a four-unit

[3] When verbs take direct objects they are said to be used 'transitively.'

sentence. These units are the noun-subject, the verb, and two noun-objects. The following sentences illustrate this pattern:

1. The father gave his son a lecture.
2. We feed our dog bones.
3. Jane brought her husband his slippers.
4. They found the carpenter a job.
5. The board elected Mr. Smith chairman.

It is apparent in these sentences that the two objects (with their indicators, if they are expressed) immediately follow the verb and that the second object immediately follows the first without the intervention, or possible intervention, of a mark of punctuation, or of such words as *and, or, but,* or *nor.* The pattern, then, is subject–verb–object–object. As in the three-unit sentences, this is a set word-order pattern and the respective positions of the two objects in relation to one another have enormous grammatical significance, for their order cannot be reversed without changing the meaning of the sentence or creating nonsense. *The father gave a lecture his son* makes no sense at all, and *We feed bones our dog* has quite a different meaning from our original sentence, *We feed our dog bones.*

The two-object sequence in the modern English sentence is of two kinds. The first is the indirect object-direct object sequence. The first four sentences above illustrate this type. It is very difficult to describe the 'meanings' of direct and indirect objects. It is usual to say that the direct object is the 'receiver of an action' and that the indirect object is 'that to or for which an action is performed.' But these 'definitions' are not very clear and would have to be stretched considerably even to cover the first four examples given above. The important points in connection with any structural definition of these objects are that the indirect object must precede the direct object and that both must refer to a different person or thing from the subject and from each other.

In the second type of two-object sequence, the first noun is the direct object, and the second is called an 'objective complement.'

This type of structure is illustrated by sentence five above: *The board elected Mr. Smith chairman.* Other examples are:

> The trustees named *Robert Jones president.*
> The committee appointed *John referee.*
> The scout held *the Indian a captive.*

The objective complement is used only with certain types of verbs, such as *elect, name, call, make, appoint, choose,* and *hold.* Unlike the indirect object-direct object sequence, the two objects here always refer to the same person. In the examples above, Mr. Smith is the chairman, Robert Jones is the president, John is the referee, and the Indian is the captive. There is also a formal way to distinguish between these two types of object combinations. If the two nouns function as indirect and direct objects, either word may be made the subject of the sentence if the verb is changed into the passive voice form. Thus we may say, *His son was given a lecture* or *A lecture was given to his son.* But objective complements cannot function in this way: that is, we can say, *Mr. Smith was elected chairman,* but not *The chairman was elected Mr. Smith.*

There is one more situation in which two nouns that refer to the same person or thing may come together. In this construction, however, the nouns are not restricted to the object position, but may appear in any of the positions in which single nouns are allowed. One of these nouns is said to be in 'apposition' to the other, which means literally that it is placed next to it, and its purpose is to identify or in some way explain the other noun. Here are a few examples of the noun in apposition:

> His father, *Charles,* was also in the car.
> The dog, *a coach-hound,* was riding with them.
> I gave Simpson, *the janitor,* a piece of my mind.

Nouns in apposition, like the examples above, are usually set off by commas, and, unless they are proper nouns, they may be preceded by indicators. But such nouns do not always appear immediately following the words they are in apposition to, so the term 'apposition' is somewhat misleading. We may say, *Police arrested the rebel leader, namely, George Enrico,* in which the word *namely* comes between two nouns. Other expressions, like *to wit, that is, in other words, specifically,* and *for example,* may be similarly placed between two nouns in apposition. Finally, nouns in apposition sometimes precede the words they are in apposition to, as in the sentence, '*A farmer by nature,* John worked long hours in the field.' The possibility that a noun in apposition may come between the subject and verb explains why our definition of the subject included the reservation concerning the possible intervention of a comma. Obviously, in such sentences as *His father, Charles, was also in the car,* the noun immediately preceding the verb is not the subject and our definition would not allow it to be, since a comma may, and usually does, intervene.

II

The relationship between nouns and other parts of the sentence may also be expressed by a kind of function word usually called the 'preposition.' The following sentences illustrate some of the uses of this type of word:

> The clerk sold the student a book *of* poetry.
> The officer *for* the day read the soldiers a lecture.
> The men gave the house *across* the street a painting.
> Books *on* the table give a room prestige.

Each of these sentences shows the uses of nouns as subject, direct object, and indirect object; in addition, each one contains a noun introduced by a preposition. The words *of, for, across,* and *on* are prepositions, and their primary grammatical function is to bring the nouns *poetry, day, street,* and *table* into the sentence by a device other than inflection and in addition to word order.

The combination of preposition and the noun (or pronoun) it introduces is called a 'prepositional phrase,' and the noun is said to be the 'object' of the preposition. As with the object of the verb, the object of the preposition does not have a separate object case form unless the word is a pronoun: in the sentences above, the nouns *poetry, day,* and *street* have exactly the same form they would have if they were subjects or objects of the verb. It is word order that normally gives the cue that a noun is the object of a preposition: in simple declarative sentences the normal word order is preposition–object.[4] And every preposition must have an object; for, being a grammatical device, it could no more exist without an object than an inflection could stand alone without the vocabulary part of the word to which it is attached. For example, the prepositional phrase *to the lighthouse,* is as much a unit as such single inflected words as *Henry's, waited,* or *calling.*

In contrast to inflections, however, many prepositions such as *across, down, up,* and *into* have a very distinct content of vocabulary meaning. But this fact does not rule out their functioning as grammatical devices at the same time. In the last sentence-example above ('Books on the table give a room prestige'), the preposition *on,* functioning as a vocabulary element, names the actual physical relationship between the table and the books; but, as a function word, it indicates, as do all prepositions, that a certain grammatical relationship exists between the two words. (This relationship is usually one of 'modification'—a subject that is treated fully in Chapter IX.) Function words of this kind might be called dual-purpose words, since they express both vocabulary and grammatical meanings (see Chapter II, p. 18). In this book, of course, we are primarily concerned with the preposition as a grammatical device.

A discussion of some examples in which the preposition is interchangeable with other grammatical devices will clarify its role as a function word. Indeed, this kind of interchange is sometimes so easily made that whether we use the preposition or some other grammatical device is a matter of style or idiom, not of grammar or meaning. The similarity between the preposition and the grammatical device of inflection is most apparent in the close parallel between the preposition *of* and the genitive case inflection *-'s* (or *-s'*). Examples could be multiplied almost indefinitely: *the house of the Lord, the Lord's house; the son of the banker, the banker's son; the*

---

[4] Such expressions as 'all the world over' and 'all the day through' may seem to be exceptions to this rule, but probably they should be regarded as 'poetic' or 'petrified' phrases. Also, the object of the preposition may occasionally be shifted to the beginning of the sentence for emphasis (see Chapter X, p. 134).

destruction of the building, the building's destruction; the devotion of their sons, and *their sons' devotion.* It must not be assumed, however, that this kind of interchange is always possible in modern English; for in such an expression as *a book of poetry* we cannot substitute the *-'s* inflection (that is, we cannot say *a poetry's book*). There are certain other prepositions which, although not having so close a correspondence with the *-'s* inflection as *of,* may also take the place of this ending. Here are a few examples: *rent for the first month, the first month's rent; a discovery by Professor Smith, Professor Smith's discovery; a day in summer, a summer's day.*

Comparison of modern English with highly inflected foreign languages also illustrates this correspondence between prepositions and inflectional endings. Some of these languages have numerous case endings for nouns, which express ideas that are similar to those expressed by prepositions in modern English. The Latin ablative case is a good example: *gladiō* ('ō' ending) means *with a sword; virtute* ('e' ending) means *with courage;* and *Romā* ('ā' ending) means *from Rome.*

Theoretically, a language need not have any prepositions at all. It would be quite possible to have a large number of inflectional endings to take their place. Actually, the Hungarian language does something like this. Hungarians say *house-in, house-on, house-for,* etc. But the Indo-European languages, the language group to which English belongs, have always had prepositions as well as inflectional endings.

There are also a few prepositions in modern English which correspond in grammatical meaning to one of the word-order devices. This is the device which expresses the indirect object. The following pair of sentences shows this similarity:

> The principal gave a dinner for the teachers.
> The principal gave the teachers a dinner.

Here the prepositional phrase *for the teachers* means approximately the same thing as *the teachers* alone when the latter word group is put in a fixed position between the verb and the other object *dinner.*

More often the preposition *to* is used as an alternative to this particular pattern of word order:

> The colonel handed the orders to the captain.
> The colonel handed the captain the orders.

Less frequently other prepositions may be used in this manner. For *he hit the tree a mighty blow,* it is possible to substitute *he hit a mighty blow on* (or *upon* or *against*) *the tree.* For *I asked the conductor a question,* we may substitute *I asked a question of the conductor.*

By no means all of the many prepositions in modern English can be interchanged with other grammatical devices. But they all should be regarded nonetheless as function words and as such should be memorized just as all the other grammatical devices should be memorized; for, if all the prepositions in a sentence cannot be identified, its structure cannot possibly be understood. Following is a list of the single-word prepositions:

about	around	beside	down	into	over	to	with
above	as	between	during	like	past	toward	within
across	at	beyond	except	near	regarding	towards	without
after	before	but	excepting	of	round	under	
against	behind	by	for	off	since	until	
along	below	concerning	from	on	through	up	
among	beneath	despite	in	out	till	upon	

There are, in addition, compound prepositions, which have been made up from other parts of speech in response to the increased use of this function word. They too should be memorized:

according to	as far as	because of	in spite of	out of
ahead of	as to	contrary to	in view of	owing to
apart from	back of	in place of	on account of	up to

The complexity of modern English grammar is such that some of the words in these lists, while usually functioning as prepositions, may also operate in other ways. We pointed out in Chapter IV that some of them, especially *at, by, in, off, on, to,* and *up,* when they follow certain verbs, may be interpreted as part of the vocabulary meanings of those verbs, as if the two words were hyphenated: *put-up*, *put-by*, *put-off*, etc., as in

> She *puts up* preserves.
> They have *put by* a little money.
> Do not *put off* the cleaning.

Since *up*, *by*, and *off* are parts of the verb in these sentences, the nouns following them are verb-objects rather than preposition-objects. This means that in a sentence where any word in our list comes between a verb and a noun, the function of the noun is grammatically ambiguous, for we cannot tell from the form of the sentence whether the noun is an object of a verb or the object of a preposition. However, if the vocabulary meanings are not also ambiguous, there is a method for solving this problem, which again involves word order, although in this instance the pattern is implicit rather than expressed. Here are two sentences:

> The sailors blew up the ship.
> The wind blew up the valley.

Although the apparent form of both sentences is the same, anyone who understands the vocabulary meanings of the words can see that certain changes in word order can be made in the first sentence, and that these cannot be made in the second. In the first sentence, *up* could be moved to the end of the sentence without altering its meaning: *The sailors blew the ship up* makes perfectly good sense and does not change the meaning of the original sentence in any way. However, if we try to do the same thing with *up* in the second sentence, the result will be very different. *The wind blew the valley up* makes a hodgepodge of the meaning of the original sentence. Since we know that in a simple declarative sentence a preposition precedes its object and that this order cannot be reversed, except under very special conditions, a process of simple reasoning will show that *up* in the first sentence cannot be a preposition. We may conclude, therefore, that the words in our list function as prepositions in a simple statement only if the vocabulary meanings of the other words in the sentence do not allow a change in the order of the preposition-noun combination.

If the vocabulary meanings in the sentence are also ambiguous, the structure of the sentence cannot be understood—we cannot tell whether the word in question is a preposition or part of the verb. This is the kind of situation that raises practical problems in writing. The kind of ambiguous sentence which may result when a writer is unaware that such words as *at, by, in, off, on, to,* and *up* may have more than one grammatical meaning is typified by the following 'boner' which appeared in one of our daily newspapers:

> The minister was drinking in the cool outdoor air.

The writer, undoubtedly, intended *in* to be part of the verb *was drinking* (the action the minister was performing was 'drinking in,' not 'drinking'). But any reader might give the sentence another meaning by interpreting *in* as a preposition—a meaning which might expose the writer to a libel suit! This is one of those problems, discussed in Chapter I, which are caused by a deficiency of grammatical devices in the written, as contrasted with the spoken, language. If this sentence had been spoken, the speaker would certainly have indicated the meaning he intended by variations in the pitch of his voice and by putting an extra stress on one of the crucial words in the sentence. A rise in voice pitch and an extra emphasis on the word *in,* as contrasted to *drinking,* would have assured the listener that the minister's activity was a wholesome one and far above reproach. The writer, on the other hand, does not have these devices at his disposal, and if he does not remember this fact he is likely to get into difficulties. To summarize this problem: we must keep in mind that some of the words in the list of prepositions may function in two ways when they are placed between a verb and a noun, thus giving two possible meanings to the sentence. Furthermore, we must remember that the writer cannot use speech devices to tell the reader which of these meanings he intends; so he must find additional written devices to resolve his problem, or else the sentence must be completely recast.

Something now needs to be said about the position of the prepositional phrase in relation to other parts of the sentence and to describe how the addition of this new sentence element qualifies the rules given thus far about the order of words in a simple statement. A prepositional phrase may appear in almost any part of the sentence: preceding or following the subject, after a verb, after any kind of object, and after other prepositional phrases. A sentence, such as the following, may have a great many of these phrases piled on one another:

> *In the picture* a woman *with a child in her arms* was preparing *with great difficulty* a meal *over the coals in a fireplace.*

Because of the intrusion of this additional sentence element, the basic word-order rule given earlier in this chapter must now be revised. This rule stated that a noun immediately preceding the verb is its subject and a noun uninflected for case following the verb is an object. But this rule applies only so long as the sentence is of the simplest type. When it includes a prepositional phrase in addition to the basic elements, the rule has to be 'stretched' somewhat—particularly the part that describes the subject. The following sentence shows what happens when a prepositional phrase comes between the subject and verb:

> The house *on the corner* has shutters.

Here the noun immediately preceding the verb is not the subject of the sentence; it is the object of a preposition—a fact that we know because of its position following *on,* one of the most common of the prepositions. And this would certainly seem to contradict our rule. But if *on the corner* is set off with parentheses—set aside, as it were—the familiar basic sentence pattern emerges: subject–verb–object, with *house* as the subject because of its position preceding the verb. The rule, then, regarding the position of the subject should be revised to read as follows: after setting off all prepositional phrases, a noun immediately preceding the verb is its subject. There are other word groups that may also come between the subject and verb, and, of course, these too must be set off before the rule can be applied. But these involve more complex types of sentence structures and will, therefore, not be considered until Chapters XI and XII.

To sum up what has been said about prepositions: a preposition is a function word used to introduce a noun or pronoun into a sentence by means other than inflection and in addition to word order. The noun or pronoun thus introduced is called the object of the preposition and usually occupies a position immediately following it. This discussion does not complete the subject of the preposition in modern English grammar. The role of the prepositional phrase in relation to the whole sentence is treated from another point of view in Chapter IX, pp. 118-19.

VII

SUBSTITUTES THAT ARE NOT ALWAYS SUBSTITUTES

Unlike the football coach with eleven 'regulars' on his team and dozens of substitutes, the users of language have thousands of 'regulars' (nouns) but a very limited number of substitutes (pronouns). Therefore, these few pronouns have to be worked very hard. For example, such words as *she, he, it,* and *who* are used far more often than *chair, house,* and *Mr. Smith.* In the sentence,

Mr. Smith, who is always prompt, told his wife that he would see her at his club after she had finished her appointment with their lawyer,

there are only five nouns but eight pronouns and each of the pronouns, except *who* and *their,* is repeated several times. Because pronouns are limited in number and are used so frequently, they are very easy to identify.

We have all been told that pronouns are 'substitutes' for nouns, and in a sense they are. Yet, not all words classified as this part of speech are literally substitutes. For example, *someone* and *anybody* do not really take the place of any nouns. Nor does *I,* in the strictest sense, stand for a noun. When Bill Jones calls himself 'Bill Jones' (thus using nouns instead of a pronoun), he is not saying the same thing as when he uses 'I,' for he is really thinking of himself as another person. Furthermore, this 'definition' of the pronoun, if taken too literally, would include many words which are obviously not pronouns. For example, *the boy* is certainly a substitute for *little Billy Jones*. So is *Mrs. Jones's son*. Yet, none of these words are considered pronouns by grammarians. Actually, any synonym is a 'substitute' for another word, and most of these would hardly be considered pronouns either. In the last analysis, the definition of the pronoun as a substitute for a noun is not entirely satisfactory, because it defines a grammatical category in terms of vocabulary meaning: a pronoun is a substitute for a noun mainly in the sense that they both have the same vocabulary meaning. In the sentence above, for example, *Mr. Smith* (a noun) and *who, his,* and *he* (pronouns) all refer to the same person.

Grammatically, however, pronouns are not so clearly substitutes for nouns. For one thing, many pronouns express grammatical ideas not expressed by nouns. For another, the forms of most pronouns are quite different from those of the noun. Unlike nouns (but like verbs), some pronouns are extremely irregular in their inflectional forms; unlike nouns, they do not use indicators; and finally, unlike nouns (and verbs too), they are a limited group. In the three and a half centuries since the time of Shakespeare, the English language has added thousands of nouns and verbs to its vocabulary, but the pronouns of modern English and those of the great dramatist are substantially the same.

The limited size of the pronoun group makes it possible to talk about these words individually—to list the various kinds and discuss their forms and the grammatical ideas they express. Pronouns may be divided into six kinds: personal, interrogative, relative,[1] demonstrative, reciprocal, and quantitative.

I

The personal pronouns consist of the various forms of *I, you, he, she, it, we,* and *they.* In all, there are thirty-one of these forms, and

---

[1] A discussion of the relative pronoun, which is similar to the interrogative, will be postponed until Chapter XII, where the more complex sentence structures are considered.

in the chart below they are organized according to the grammatical ideas they express:

		singular				plural			
		Case				Case			
Person	Gender	subject	genitive	object	reflexive	subject	genitive	object	reflexive
First	_____	I	my, mine	me	myself	we	our, ours	us	ourselves
Second	_____	you	your, yours	you	yourself	you	your, yours	you	yourselves
Third	masc.	he	his	him	himself				
Third	fem.	she	her, hers	her	herself	they	their, theirs	them	themselves
Third	neut.	it	its	it	itself				

(Number; singular / plural headings span the table)

As this chart indicates, the personal pronouns express four distinct grammatical ideas. We call them 'personal' pronouns because they express the idea of person. That is, their forms allow us to discriminate among three persons: (1) the person speaking (*I* and *we* and their variants), (2) the person spoken to (*you* and its variants), and (3) the person (or thing) spoken about. In terms of the idea of person, all nouns are third person: as we observed above, when Bill Jones refers to himself as 'Bill Jones' instead of 'I,' he suggests that he can speak of himself as though he were another person—he can talk about himself as he can about Ed Smith. When you and I draw up a legal contract, we speak of ourselves as 'the party of the first part' and 'the party of the second part' respectively, because we think of the agreement, not so much as one between you and me, as between two parties under the law. When a judge says, 'The court finds you guilty as charged,' he is distinguishing between himself as a man and as an instrument of the law; he might well say as judge, 'The court finds you innocent of the charge,' and think as a man, 'I have a hunch you're very guilty indeed.'

Although the personal pronouns are the chief means by which the idea of person is expressed in modern English, we do have one other method—in some of the forms of the verb: almost all of the forms of the verb *be* repeat the idea of person expressed in the subject:

> I *am* happy.
> You *are* happy.
> He *is* happy.

Also, nearly all English verbs have one form which distinguishes the third person from the first and second when the subject is singular and the verb is in the present tense. This is the second, or *-s*, form (help*s*, goe*s*, swim*s*, etc.). We say *I help* and *you help*, but *he, she,* or *it helps*. This *-s* inflection and the different forms of the verb *be* are remnants of a time when the English verb had many inflections to correspond with the person of the subject. Students of Latin know that pronoun subjects are, as a rule, not used in that language at all, because the verb forms express person: the *ego, tu,* and *ille* in the following sentences would normally be left out:

> Ego amo patriam meam
> (I love my country)
>
> Tu amas patriam tuam
> (You love your country)
>
> Ille amat patriam suam
> (He loves his country)

This is possible because the verb forms *amo, amas, amat* include the *I, you,* and *he* meanings. In modern English, on the other hand, the pronoun-subject is almost always expressed, and we look to it, not to the verb, for the idea of person. It is because of this fact that people make 'mistakes' in verb forms. They sometimes say, for example, 'He *don't* live here,' instead of, 'He *doesn't* live here,' because the idea of person has already been established with *he;* the *-s* form of the verb (*does*) simply repeats this idea and, therefore, is not essential to the meaning. Indeed, as we have said before, many of the practical difficulties with English 'grammar' stem from situations in which it is not really necessary to repeat an idea already established by another grammatical device. In fact, most people are thinking of precisely these unnecessary distinctions in form when they refer distastefully to 'English grammar.'

Three of the personal pronouns (*he, she,* and *it*) and their variants express ideas of gender. These third person singular pronouns are the only examples in modern English where differentiation in gender is expressed by a major grammatical device, the difference between the masculine, feminine, and neuter pronouns being indicated by a sharply different inflectional form. Actually, the form is changed so radically that they are different words. In modern English the gender form of the pronoun usually squares with our notions of the sex of things: we normally use *he* to stand for members of the masculine sex, *she* to indicate the feminine sex, and *it* to indicate the neuter gender, which means no sex at all (see Chapter V, p. 58). But these lines are not always clearly drawn. We often refer to a number of sexless things with the pronoun *she:*

> She's a fine boat.
> She's a beautiful hot-rod.

We not uncommonly refer to a male baby as 'it,' and to his hands as 'its little hands,' when 'its' sex is perfectly clear. Less often, we appropriate masculine gender to things to which we wish to impute grandness or majesty: of the fish that got away, we reminisce, 'He was enormous'; of the mountain we hope someday to climb, we remind ourselves, 'He is a killer.'

The fact that the language has no 'common' gender form (one applying to both sexes) for this third person singular pronoun often creates a pitfall for both speakers and writers. We have all become tangled up at one time or another in sentences like *Each child will put on his or her galoshes.* In such contexts, the lack of a word that will apply to members of both sexes is an example of how a language in a practical sense may be grammatically defective. Most of us get around this problem by speaking of such groups only in the plural (*The children will put on their galoshes*) where a common gender pronoun does exist (see Chapter XIV, pp. 218-19, for a detailed discussion of this problem).

The other two grammatical ideas associated with the personal pronoun, number and case, have already been discussed in connection with nouns. But these ideas must now be considered from another point of view. In regard to number—all the personal pronouns, with the exception of those in the reflexive case form, express this idea in a very different way from nouns. Instead of simply adding an -s inflection to the singular form, the entire word is changed: *I* becomes *we; my* becomes *our; me* becomes *us; he, she,* and *it* become *they; his, her,* and *its* become *their;* and *him, her,* and *it* become *them.* In modern English there is no distinction between singular and plural in the second person (except in the reflexive case where we have both *yourself* and *yourselves*). But in Old English there were complete sets of singular and plural forms: *thou, thy, thine, thee* and *ye, your,* and *you.* The singular forms and the form *ye* are familiar from our reading of the older English poets or of the Bible or prayer book, but they have all disappeared from usage today. The real need for a distinction in number in the second person is reflected in the regional plural form *you-all.*

The idea of case as expressed by the personal pronouns requires considerable explanation. As was pointed out in Chapter V, nouns have only one inflected case form—that of the genitive. All other case distinctions are expressed, of course, by word order and function words. The direct object, for example, is expressed merely by placing the noun after the verb:

I like the *man.*

Another kind of object is expressed by placing the noun after a preposition:

I have nothing *against the man.*

In contrast, most of the personal pronouns have special inflectional forms to convey these object-case ideas. If a pronoun is substituted for *man* in the sentences above, we must say, 'I like *him* (not *he*)' and 'I have nothing against *him* (again not *he*).' In other words, the object inflectional form must be used in addition to the word-order and function-word devices if these ideas are to be expressed 'properly.' *I, she,* and *they* also have distinctive object case forms. Actually, there is rarely any practical need for inflectional distinctions between the subject and object forms of pronouns. The meaning of the sentence is quite clear whether we use *he* or *him, we* or *us,* for the word order has already established the grammatical ideas. Indeed, it is because these differences in pronoun case forms are no longer necessary to convey grammatical meaning that people have so much trouble finding the 'right' form (see Chapter XIV, p. 225, for the rules regarding the uses of these pronouns).

There is one special case idea which is found only in the personal pronouns. This is the reflexive case. As its name implies, it is used when it can 'reflect,' or refer back to, another word preceding it in the sentence. *Myself* is the first person singular reflexive pronoun and calls for an *I*, or form of *I*, as a reference; *ourselves* is the first person plural reflexive and calls for some form of *we; yourself* is the second person reflexive and calls for a *you* earlier in the sentence; *himself, herself, itself,* and *themselves* are third person reflexives and demand some forms of *he, she, it, they,* or a noun to refer back to. Since reflexive pronouns have to refer back to nouns or pronouns that appear earlier in the sentence, obviously the normal place for this type of pronoun is in the complement territory or in a prepositional phrase, as in

> I hurt *myself.*
> You gave *yourself* the biggest share.
> He was going to do everything for *himself.*
> She is *herself* again.

These forms may also be used in the appositive position to stress or intensify the preceding noun or pronoun. When they are used in this way, they are sometimes called 'intensive' pronouns:

> I *myself* will do the work.
> They handed it to John *himself.*
> The visitors were the Joneses *themselves.*

In recent years the reflexive form has been developing another kind of use. We have all heard people say,

> They invited John and *myself.*
> Mr. Smith and *ourselves* will bring the rest of the tickets.

In these sentences the function of *myself* and *ourselves* is clearly not reflexive, for there are no other nouns or pronouns in the sentence to which they could refer back. Here they are used exactly as if they were personal pronouns in the object and subject cases respectively: they are exact substitutes for *me* and *we*. The whole idea of reflexiveness has been lost. This growing tendency to substitute these reflexive forms for the personal pronoun forms is probably the result of one of two things: an uncertainty about the proper form of the personal pronoun, or the feeling of need for emphasis. 'They invited John and *me* (or *I?*).' In order to be on the safe side, many people tend to say, 'They invited John and myself.' Concerning the need for emphasis, there are places in a sentence where the little words like *we* and *me* seem weak from a stylistic or rhetorical point of view. It is in these places that there is a tendency to substitute the stronger forms of the reflexive pronoun (see Chapter XIV, p. 226).

II

The interrogative pronouns, as their name suggests, are used in asking questions. They are *who* (and its variants *whose* and *whom*), *which,* and *what*. None of these have forms to express person or number. *Who* is the masculine-feminine pronoun; *which* and *what* are neuter. *Who* has three case forms:

subject: who
genitive: whose
object: whom

Deciding whether to use *who* or *whom* is a puzzling problem to most users of the language—and for two reasons: first, separate forms of this pronoun are not necessary to express case distinctions in modern English; second, the word order of the interrogative sentence is different from that of the declarative sentence. In the following pairs of sentences, the first is a statement, the second a question:

1. John made a perfect score.
   Who made a perfect score?

2. To Mary we shall give the first prize.
   To whom shall we give the first prize?
   (Whom shall we give the first prize to?)

3. They liked her very much.
   Whom did they like very much?

4. The visitor turned out to be he.
   Who did the visitor turn out to be?

If the pronoun retains the same position in the question as it had in the statement, there is little difficulty with the form of *who*. Few people would say, 'Whom made a perfect score?' or 'To who shall we give the first prize?' But whenever the pronoun changes its position, there may be trouble. In the alternate question in Group 2 above, where the *whom* is separated from the *to* by the whole sentence, it is more difficult to decide which form to use. And when the basic word-order pattern is inverted, as in Groups 3 and 4, the difficulty is even greater. Because of this problem, most users of English today, even well-educated ones, avoid the interrogative *whom* except when it directly follows a preposition (see Chapter XIV, p. 227).

The other interrogatives—*what* and *which*—fortunately do not have either genitive or objective case forms. The genitive form is lacking for logical reasons, for, as we have seen, the idea of possession is not often used in connection with inanimate objects. If we do wish to express this idea with inanimate objects in a question, the preposition *of* is normally used to take the place of the missing inflectional form. Thus the following conversation might take place: 'This is the book's jacket.' 'The jacket *of what?*' 'The book.' *What* and *which* express the other case ideas exactly as nouns do— by word order and function words.

III

There are four demonstrative pronouns: *this, that, these,* and *those.* These words clearly indicate number by differences in inflectional form; the first two are singular, the second two plural.

Like *what* and *which,* the demonstrative pronouns express case distinctions by the devices of word order and function words. The only practical problem in connection with these pronouns concerns the form that should be used before such words as *kind, sort,* and *type.* The use of the plural demonstrative before these words is a very common mistake, as in *these kind of apples* instead of *this kind of apples.*

The reciprocal pronouns, *each other* and *one another,* express the genitive case just as nouns do, by adding the -*'s* inflection: *each other's, one another's.* Reciprocal pronouns imply a mutual relationship. 'John and Bill help each other' is a shorthand way of saying that John helps Bill and Bill helps John. It is so convenient a device that we use it when we have in mind many more than two: 'All the students in the class help one another.'

Finally, there is a larger group of pronouns which, though they vary in form and in inflection, all either indicate, or imply, a quantity. For this reason, they are called quantitative pronouns. They are also called 'indefinite' pronouns, and many of them are indefinite in meaning: *few, many, much, several,* and *some.* But there is nothing indefinite about *all, none, both,* or *neither;* so 'quantitative' is probably the more accurate term for them all. If we exclude the numerals (*one, two, three,* etc.), which are practically innumerable, we have only twenty-six quantitative pronouns. None are inflected to show case or number, but some do form a genitive case exactly as nouns do. These are:

another	(another's)	neither	(neither's)
anybody	(anybody's)	nobody	(nobody's)
anyone	(anyone's)	one	(one's)
either	(either's)	no one	(no one's)
everybody	(everybody's)	somebody	(somebody's)
everyone	(everyone's)	someone	(someone's)

The vocabulary meanings of these words are usually singular, so an inflection is not necessary to express plural number.

Five other quantitative pronouns too express a singular idea, but these do not normally have genitive cast inflections; they are:

anything   much
each   nothing
everything   something

Four quantitative pronouns express a plural idea only, and they too
do not have genitive inflections:

both   many
few   several

The remaining five pronouns of this group do not clearly express
either singular or plural number, their number being dependent
upon the context. Compare the following sentences:

all: *All* of the sugar *is* gone.   *All* of the guests *are* here now.
any: *Any* of it *is* too much.   *Any* of the men *are* capable enough.
enough: *Enough* of it *is* on hand.   *Enough* of them *are* on hand.
none: *None* of the stuff *is* here.   *None* of the boys *are* going.
some: *Some* of the paste *is* lost.   *Some* of the apples *are* rotten.

In the left column, of course, these words are singular in meaning;
in the right, they are plural.

The pronoun *one* is in a class by itself and must, therefore, be
given special treatment. As a matter of fact, there are three *ones:*
(1) the numeral, (2) the indefinite pronoun meaning 'any person,'
and (3) the word that literally stands in place of a noun. The use
of the word as a numeral does not require any explanation, but
the second and third uses do require extended comment.

In its second meaning—that of 'any person' or 'people in general'
—the word *one* might be called the 'official' impersonal pronoun
of the language. This use is illustrated in such sentences as:

One can't be too careful.
One's dog is *one's* best friend.

Although this word is usually designated by grammar books and
teachers as the impersonal pronoun, we find that in actual speech
and writing it is probably the word least often used to express this
idea. American speakers, at least, tend to regard it as too formal
for ordinary daily use. Instead, we are more likely to use the per-

sonal pronouns, *you, we* (as in '*We,* the *people* . . .'), or *they,* and sometimes the indefinite nouns *a man, a person,* or *people.* The first sentence above would more likely appear as one of the following:

> *You* can't be too careful.
>
> *We* can't be too careful.

The second sentence as

> A *man's* dog is his best friend.

In this book *we* is often used as an indefinite pronoun. The use of *they* as an indefinite pronoun is familiar to everyone in the expression *they say.* Sometimes the use of *you* as an impersonal pronoun may verge on the slangy, as in the sentence

> Now take *your* grocery business—that's something I'd like to get into.

This usage is avoided in all except the most informal speech and writing.

The word *one* in its third use operates as a sort of dummy word in any place where we do not want to repeat a noun, especially where we wish to use an adjective modifier, as in

> I'll take the pink dress, you take the blue *one.*
>
> Are these *the ones* you want?

There is a real need for a pronoun of this kind, since personal pronouns are useless in this situation (you cannot say, *the blue it*). When *one* is used in this way it is an exact substitute for a noun. But the form of this word is not like that of a pronoun. In fact, the grammatical devices used with it are exactly like those of a noun. This word can form a plural with -*s,* and a genitive with -'*s;* it may appear in all the positions that a noun may occupy, and it may also have a noun indicator, as in both sentences above. Whether we should call this word a noun or a pronoun has not been decided by the grammarians themselves. The important thing is to know that it has characteristics of both parts of speech.

Finally, something should be said about pronouns in general. In the foregoing discussion of the five different types, it may have seemed that there are more differences than similarities. Indeed, as a part of speech pronouns are a rather miscellaneous group. Yet they do have certain characteristics in common. In the first place, most pronouns are dependent upon the noun reference for their vocabulary meaning, and in this sense they are substitute words. Second, in simple statements they all occupy the same sentence positions as nouns. In the third place, all pronouns except *one* differ from nouns in that they operate without indicators. We say *the man, a dog, the windows, my parents;* but we do not say *the either, a which, the they,* or *my both.* So, with the exception of *one,* we may regard it as a test of the pronoun that it is indicator-less. If any of the words listed as pronouns is used with an indicator, it is considered a noun; for example:

> *Nobody* came to visit this morning. (pronoun)
> *A nobody* came to visit this morning. (noun)

> He robbed *many* but gave to *few.* (pronouns)
> He robbed *the many* but gave to *the few.* (nouns)

> He is *someone* I love. (pronoun)
> He is *the someone* I love. (noun)

Since pronouns with all their forms total only about ninety words and, next to the verb, have the most distinctive set of grammatical forms, there should be little trouble in recognizing them. And once the grammatical ideas that they express are fully understood, all the practical problems that arise so often with this part of speech should be easily solved. These problems are treated in detail in Chapter XIV (pp. 216-30).

VIII

DOWN THE LADDER OF ABSTRACTION

All languages have a regular method for dividing large groups of things into smaller ones. Indeed, it would be very inconvenient if they did not. How unfortunate, for example, if there were no way of dividing the large category of 'houses' (particularly for real estate agents and their customers) into *red houses, white houses, small, large, colonial, Victorian,* etc.! This need is especially pressing in English and in the other languages to which it is related, because the meanings of most of the nouns and verbs in these languages are 'general'—that is, they represent group ideas which include a very large number of items. Think of all the possible meanings that are encompassed by such words as *house, chair, going,* and *coming,* or even by less general words like *democracy.* Since English has so many of these general words, it is fortunate that it has a very convenient grammatical method for reducing or cutting down these large group ideas. For single words the method works like this: if one wishes to reduce such a large classification as *house* to the much smaller category of *red house,* or *going* to *going quickly,* he simply links the word *house* to the word *red* or the word *go* to *quickly* by one or more specific grammatical devices. These devices will indicate two things: (1) which word is the 'reducing' word and (2) which word is the one to be 'reduced.' This grammatical process is commonly called 'modification.'[1]

---

[1] We should note that this grammatical method is not the only one that may be used for the purpose of limiting or cutting down large language

Under the heading of modification, there are various kinds and shades of meaning, which schoolbooks often attempt to describe; but, unfortunately, no 'definition' of this idea is really workable. Even a fairly precise one, such as the one given above, can be misleading. For example, a search for words that 'limit,' or make more concrete, might lead one to conclude, with a good deal of logic, that the verb *writes* in the sentence *Mrs. Jones writes* is a modifier, —for surely it 'limits' our idea of Mrs. Jones. Yet, alas, no grammarian would ever call this word a modifier, for the grammatical devices used with it never designate any kind of modifier. Similarly, many noun-objects might seem to be modifiers. For example, if the word *poetry* were added to *Mrs. Jones writes,* the verb *writes* would certainly be made more definite; yet *poetry* is not what grammarians call a modifier either. Actually, it can be demonstrated in some sentences that each word 'modifies' every other word! It must be kept in mind, therefore, that grammarians use the word 'modifier,' not to apply to any word which satisfies a 'definition' of modification, but only to those words which perform this function by the use of a special set of grammatical devices and permanent forms. This chapter and the next one will be devoted to a description of these structural devices.

I

The subject of modification involves two more parts of speech— the adjective and the adverb. A few modern grammarians treat all modifiers as a single part of speech, lumping adjectives and adverbs together as elements that are 'secondary' or 'subordinate' to the basic sentence pattern. There are some good reasons for doing so. In this book, however, we shall retain the traditional method of keeping these two parts of speech separate; but, since they are much alike

categories. Suppose we wish to speak of a large expensive house: we might use the single word *mansion* instead of a word group *large house.* Or if we wish to narrow down the idea of *walking quickly* or *walking slowly*, we might use the single words *run* or *crawl.* This is clearly not a grammatical method, for it exchanges the original vocabulary elements (*house* and *walk*) for brand new ones, which bear no resemblance in form to the originals: in other words, no grammatical devices have been used.

in form and function, what is said about the one will often apply equally well to the other. In some grammars, adjectives and adverbs are distinguished from each other according to the part of speech they modify: adjectives are said to modify nouns; adverbs to modify all the other parts of speech except conjunctions and interjections. These definitions are sometimes useful as means of setting up tentative boundaries between the two classes of words. However, if we stick to them too literally they will lead to some strange contradictions. For sometimes words which modify nouns have adverb forms and those which modify verbs and adjectives have adjective forms, and sometimes modifiers do not modify any specific word at all! It is more accurate, therefore, to make the distinction between these two types of modifiers in terms of the grammatical devices used with them.

The grammatical form of the adjective is not easy to describe, because it has so few of the major devices that are most easily understood—such as the simple inflectional tags or function words that clearly mark some of the other parts of speech. Fortunately, however, the adjective does have a large group of relatively distinct permanent forms. Following is a list of the most common suffixes out of which these forms are made:

> *-able* (or *-ible*) as in fashionable, fallible
> *-al* as in coastal, special
> *-ant* (or *-ent*) as in hesitant, dependent
> *-ary* as in ordinary, contrary
> *-ate* as in separate, desolate
> *-ed* as in clouded, heated
> *-en* as in golden, wooden
> *-ful* as in healthful, restful
> *-id* as in sordid, rancid
> *-ing* as in singing, dancing
> *-ish* as in faddish, mannish
> *-ive* as in attractive, massive
> *-like* as in ghostlike, deathlike
> *-ly* as in lovely, friendly
> *-ous* as in curious, luxurious
> *-some* as in lonesome, handsome
> *-y* as in cloudy, healthy

Although they are useful as 'sign-posts,' the permanent forms cannot provide enough information to determine finally what part of speech a given word may be. Some of the above endings, like those for the noun and verb, are not the exclusive property of any one part of speech. Thus *-ly* is a very familiar ending for adverbs; *-y* is often a noun ending, as in *baby* and *candy;* many *-ant* words, such as *attendant,* usually are nouns; *-ate* was included in our list of verb suffixes. Actually, as pointed out in Chapter III, no word in modern English is limited by its permanent form to any one part of speech. For example, adjectives with any of the endings above may be converted into nouns by the use of the noun indicator, as in *the beautiful, the curious,* and *the fashionable.* Some of these adjectives may be made into nouns by merely adding the plural inflectional ending: *perishables, nationals,* etc. These permanent forms of the adjective put one on the trail, so to speak; but the final goal can be reached only by an examination of the major grammatical devices.

Unlike the pronoun with its many variations in inflectional form, the adjective is the least inflected of all the inflected parts of speech. Logically, one might think that the adjective should have inflections that would match those of the noun, since both parts of speech refer to the same person or thing in the outside world: when we say *my rich uncle,* both *rich* and *uncle* refer to the same person. But what happens to *rich* when the form of *uncle* is changed, as in *my rich uncles* and *my rich uncle's house?* Obviously nothing at all. The form of *rich* does not change to match the forms of *uncle.* In other words the form of the adjective does not 'agree' with that of the noun. In Old English, as in Latin and modern Russian, the adjective had an extremely complex set of forms to show 'agreement.' The complete loss of these forms within a relatively short span of years is a spectacular example of language evolution.

Although the English adjective is no longer inflected to show 'agreement' with the noun it modifies, there is one situation in which inflection of this part of speech may regularly take place. If we have two well-to-do uncles, we may say *my richer uncle;* or, if we have three such lucky relatives, we may say *my richest uncle.* The

grammatical term for the idea expressed by these -er and -est inflections is 'comparison.' One uncle is not only rich, but possesses a
greater degree of wealth compared to some other uncle. This is an
example of the 'comparative' degree. The next uncle is rich in a
degree greater than two or more other uncles. The idea thus expressed is called the 'superlative' degree. When an adjective is not
compared at all, it is said to be in the 'positive' degree. Adjectives
in both the comparative and superlative forms may also express the
idea of the highest possible degree, as in *She is the kindest person*
and *the finer things of life.*

Almost all relatively short adjectives express comparison by adding the inflectional endings -er and -est to show the comparative
degree and superlative degree respectively. Anyone can think of
many examples: *warmer, warmest; happier, happiest; taller, tallest;
narrower, narrowest;* and *stupider, stupidest.* There are several
adjectives, however, whose comparative and superlative degrees are
formed irregularly. The most important of these are:

Positive	Comparative	Superlative
bad, evil, ill	worse	worst
far	farther, further	farthest, furthest
good, well	better	best
late	later	latest, last
little	less, lesser	least
much, many, some	more	most
old	older, elder	oldest, eldest

Although the -er and -est endings are closely associated with the
adjective, their mere presence is not conclusive evidence that a word
is an adjective. Many adverbs also use these inflections to show
comparison. Furthermore, -er is a very common noun suffix, usually
indicating the idea of 'agent' or 'doer,' as in *plumber, carpenter,*
and *worker.* The difference between nouns and adjectives ending
in this suffix can be seen in the sentence:

The lion *tamer* (noun) wants a *tamer* (adjective) lion.

The -er and -est inflections are not the only devices the language
has to express ideas of comparison. There are several function

words associated with the adjective which also express these ideas. The most familiar are *more* and *most,* which are used to express the comparative and superlative degrees with adjectives of three or more syllables. These function words are placed in a position immediately preceding the adjective, as in *more beautiful* and *most ridiculous.* They serve to mark the word as a modifier (adjective or adverb), provided they are substitutes for the *-er* and *-est* inflections. Like the endings that show comparison, *more* and *most* are not the exclusive property of adjectives. Adverbs too use this method to indicate the idea of comparison (see Chapter IX, p. 110). *More* and *most* may also appear in a position preceding a noun, as in *more money* and *most people,* or they may stand alone as pronouns, as in *I want more* and *Most prefer steak.* In such situations these words do not mark the following words as adjectives (or adverbs), since they are not substitutes for the *-er* and *-est* endings.

When combined with *less* (*lesser*) or *least,* a modifier expresses a lower degree than the positive form. *A less happy child* (comparative degree) certainly expresses a lower degree of happiness than *happy child,* and the *least happy child* (superlative degree) a degree lower than that possessed by at least two other children, or the lowest degree one can imagine. There are two other sets of function words used with modifiers which express a slightly different kind of comparison. These are *as* (modifier) *as* and its negative *not so* (modifier) *as:*

He is *as* happy *as* a lark.

It is *not so* cold here *as* in Chicago.

Not so . . . as is clearly a synonym for *less than. As . . . as* indicates what might be called equality of comparison: the modification is not greater or less, but equal to that which applies to some other word modified. The presence of *as* before and after a word is a certain sign that the word is a modifier. Many modifiers expressing the comparative degree, whether inflected or preceded by function words, are also often followed by the word *than:*

It is colder *than* ever.

John is more intelligent *than* his brother.

This word, apart from other functions it has, may be regarded as an adjective-adverb function word, and its presence almost always indicates that the preceding word is an adjective or an adverb.

The subject of comparison usually raises the practical question: May all adjectives be compared? Teachers sometimes say that the meanings of certain words logically forbid comparison. The words most often cited are those expressing 'absolute' ideas, such as *unique, perfect,* and *full.* Comparing these words may be illogical, but anyone who takes a good look at the living language will realize that people have been saying 'most unique' and 'most perfect' for a long time; 'my cup is fuller than yours' is not unusual, and the expression 'a more perfect union' from the Preamble to the Constitution is a classic in the language. And what people say matters a great deal when it comes to making rules about grammar. Since there is, to be sure, a certain disregard of logic when words of this kind are compared, these examples show that the influence of form is very powerful among the users of English: for the logic of the adjective form (its ability to express comparison) has triumphed over the logic of meaning. There are some adjectives, of course, which are not normally compared. A few examples are: *such, both, separate, half, eating, future, daily, standing,* and *falling.* It is possible, however, that in tomorrow's English some of these words will develop comparative and superlative forms. Even today one occasionally hears such slang expressions as, 'He is the eatingest man I have ever met.' And a certain automobile is being advertised as 'the winningest car.'

II

Although these inflections and function words may be 'signs' of the adjective function, in modern English there is a much more precise way of indicating that a word is an adjective and of pointing to the word modified. This is done through patterns of word order. A few common examples of adjectives accompanied by the nouns they modify—*large screen, stone house, bad example, thick wall, thin paper, tall clock, narrow mind*—show that in each instance the noun is preceded by the adjective. One way, therefore, of indicating that a word is an adjective, modifying a certain noun, is to place this word immediately before the noun. Adjectives in this position are called 'attributive' adjectives. When the single-word adjective is in the attributive position, no grammatical device may come between the adjective and the noun it modifies—not an indicator, not a conjunction, nor any kind of punctuation. The only place for the indicator is before the adjective: *the large screen, a thick wall, this bad example,* etc. This kind of word group—(indicator)-adjective-noun—is called a noun phrase.

The device of placing a word in the attributive position is by far the most common way of showing that it is an adjective. The description of the single-word adjective in this important word-order pattern may be clarified by means of diagrams similar to those we have used before, in which blanks represent the vocabulary elements. Here are the four possible patterns for the adjective-noun phrase.

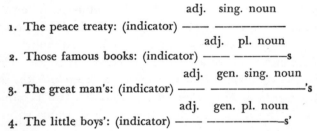

The statement that an indicator cannot come between an attributive adjective and the noun modified may seem to contradict what we said in Chapter V: that an indicator before a word marks it as a noun. This earlier rule was, of course, a provisional one, since it applies only to sentences in which there are no modifiers. In other words, it was a beginners' definition; and, like some beginners' rules in other subjects such as algebra (where trains may start at sixty miles an hour!), it applied only in a hypothetical situation. Now a final rule may be made: the presence of an indicator signals that what follows is either a single noun or a noun phrase: *the dark* (*the* signals a noun) and *the dark day* (*the* signals an adjective-noun phrase).

A simple rule may also be formulated for distinguishing an attributive adjective following an indicator (*dark* in *the dark day*) from a noun in this same position (the *dark*). Any word that satisfies the following conditions is an attributive adjective:

1. It must be followed by a noun.
2. The intended meaning of the sentence must not allow any grammatical device (an indicator, a function word, or a mark of punctuation) to come between this word and the word following.

By applying this rule it can be demonstrated that the word *dark* in the following sentence is an attributive adjective:

Her *dark* clothes are inconspicuous.

(1) The form of *clothes* shows that it is a noun. (2) The meaning intended does not allow the insertion of an indicator between *dark* and *clothes* (we could not say 'dark *the* clothes'). Conversely, a word which does not satisfy these conditions cannot be an adjective. In the following sentence, similar to the one above, the second part of the rule is not satisfied:

In the dark clothes are inconspicuous.

The word *dark* satisfies part 1 of the rule (it is followed by a noun), but the meaning allows the intervention of an indicator or a comma between the two words:

In the dark (the) clothes are inconspicuous.
In the dark, clothes are inconspicuous.

Therefore, *dark* in this sentence is a noun.

In simple sentences, the likelihood of mistaking such a noun, followed directly by another noun, for the adjective part of an adjective-noun phrase arises most often in two situations. First, it may happen as in the sentence above, where the first noun is an object of a preposition. This kind of mistake is especially likely to happen when the vocabulary meanings of the two nouns, in addition to the lack of grammatical devices, might also lead one to interpret the first word as a modifier of the second, as in the following sentences:

In *the city soot* is a menace.

On *the dock workers* were unloading the cargo.

Across *the country boys* are now playing football.

It would be natural for any reader of these sentences at first to interpret *city soot, dock workers,* and *country boys* as adjective-noun groups. It is only when the eye reaches the verb that one can know for sure that this interpretation was incorrect; he then has to go back over the sentence and revise his first impression. In order to avoid this kind of grammatical misrepresentation, which confuses the reader and forces him to waste his time rereading the sentence (and in longer, more complex, sentences quite a bit of puzzling may be involved), the writer should be very careful to supply at least one of the grammatical devices which mark each word as a noun. The use of an indicator or a comma between each pair of nouns makes the meanings of all these sentences immediately clear:

In the city, (the) soot is a menace, etc.

(More information about punctuating this kind of sentence may be found in Chapter XV, pp. 269-70.)

Second, a noun might be mistaken for the adjective part of an adjective-noun group when two noun-objects of a verb stand side by side without an indicator between them, as in,

Mary taught *the child manners.*

The application of our rule to this sentence will show that *child* is not an adjective (in spite of its position); for, although no grammatical devices come between the two words, the meaning does allow an indicator in this position (taught the child *her* manners). This is in contrast to the sentence

Mary teaches business English

in which the meaning does not allow an indicator to intervene, so *business* is clearly an adjective. There are some sentences of this kind, unfortunately, in which the vocabulary meanings of the words are such that the reader cannot tell whether the word is an adjective or a noun, and which are, therefore, completely ambiguous in writing. A few examples are:

> She showed her baby pictures.
> He gave her dog biscuits.
> She taught the group singing.

These sentences are excellent illustrations of the ambiguity which may result when the writer does not provide each sentence element with a full set of distinct grammatical devices. Whichever meaning is intended is clear enough in the spoken language because of variations in pitch and stress, but it is not clear at all in writing. These sentences could be clarified in one of two ways: first, by using an indicator, as in 'She showed her *the* baby pictures,' and 'She showed her baby *the* pictures'; second, by using a preposition and changing the word order, as in 'She taught singing *to* the group.'

The likelihood of mistaking two nouns for an adjective-noun phrase is caused by the fact that we so often shift nouns to the adjective function, as in *baby pictures, dog biscuits,* and *group singing.* Functional shifts are, as we know, common in modern English, but this particular one—from noun to adjective—is the most common of all. Several pages could be filled with illustrations. A few examples are: *dog house, fish pond, bird song, rent control, robbery victims, farm policy, Ford factory, physics course,* and *lawn care.* It is clear from these examples that the shift from noun to adjective has been established by the simple device of placing the noun in the attributive position before another noun. If the positions of the two words are reversed, the one that was originally the noun becomes the adjective. There are many of these reversible pairs: *dog house, house dog; bird song, song bird; office policy, policy office; box lunch, lunch box,* etc. Because the adjective function is established by the attributive position, nouns in this position are called 'attributive nouns,' although in a sense they are no longer nouns but adjectives. However, in all respects except word order they retain the grammatical form of nouns. Unlike adjectives, they are never compared: we cannot say the *dogger house* or the *most robber victim.* Furthermore, unlike adjectives, and like nouns, attributive nouns may be inflected for plural number, as in *the parts factory, the studies program,* and *the farm aims policy.* Also, like nouns, these words are modified by adjectives, as in *rural improvement policy* and *electrical parts factory.* For these reasons, grammarians are not in complete agreement as to whether these words should be called nouns or adjectives. But there is no doubt that the idea conveyed is that of modification.

The attributive noun does, however, modify in a way somewhat different from that of the attributive adjective. If we look carefully at the meaning of the latter, we shall see that it refers to some quality existing in the person, place, or thing modified, as *red house, ornamental plant, beautiful dress.* On the other hand, the attributive noun modifies a word usually by relating it to some object outside itself: a *beach house* is a house in a certain relationship to a beach; a *bedroom suite* is a group of furniture for a bedroom; a *street dress* is a dress for the street. The difference in meaning between the attributive noun and the regular adjective is apparent when we compare such expressions as *antique dealer* and *antique vase.* In these phrases the same word is used as an adjective in both, but the meanings are very different indeed. This difference is also illustrated by the old joke about how much dog is there in a dog biscuit. There is none, of course, because the attributive noun *dog,* unlike a traditional adjective in this position, is used merely to explain that the biscuit is 'for dogs' and has nothing to do with any quality in the biscuit itself, such as its being dry or hard or small or tasteless. This pun is possible because two slightly different meanings are expressed by the same grammatical device (a fixed position immediately preceding a noun).

These examples show that the attributive noun is a kind of parallel to the prepositional phrase. What has happened is that the preposition has been omitted and the noun that was once its object has been shifted to a new position in front of the noun modified. For example, *house on the beach* becomes *beach house.* This is a striking illustration of the fact that the same idea may be expressed in English by more than one grammatical device. The attributive noun, although a relative upstart in the history of the language, is coming to be preferred more and more over the prepositional phrase to express the idea of modification. Almost every time one listens to the radio, reads the newspaper, or looks at a label on a bottle, he will hear or see some new expression of this kind that has not been thought of before. Americans are particularly fond of this construction because it is a kind of grammatical shortcut. It is easy for a radio announcer or journalist or advertising copy writer, whose time or space is limited, to say *cold comfort* instead of *comfort for a cold, a forgery victim* instead of a *victim of forgery,* a *budget cut* instead of a *cut in the budget.* In more formal writing, too, this construction is being used more and more frequently.

III

The second large group of adjectives that may be classified according to their positions are the predicate adjectives. These are so-called because they normally occupy the predicate position—that is, the position after the verb. Predicate adjectives always follow a special kind of verb which allows the adjective to modify the subject. These are the linking verbs, some of which were discussed in Chapter VI. The most common of these are: *be, become, seem, feel, smell, look, appear, taste,* and *sound.* Examples of predicate adjectives may be seen in the following sentences:

> The book is *heavy.*
> She seems *happy.*
> The candy smells *good.*

In addition to these common linking verbs, there are others that are sometimes followed by predicate adjectives. There are more of these than most people realize. Some of them are: *keep, get, prove, go, turn, turn out, come out, continue, grow, stay, sit, stand, hold,* as in:

> He keeps *healthy.*
> The experiment proved *successful.*
> She went *crazy.*
> The clothes came out *clean.*

Because of similarity in form, predicate adjectives may be confused with nouns (either predicate nouns or direct objects) that may also appear after some of these verbs. This confusion is most likely when the noun is uninflected. *She smells smoke* (noun object) has the same form as *She smells sweet* (predicate adjective). This confusion may be cleared up only by reference to the vocabulary meanings of the words. If the meaning allows the use of an indicator before the word following the verb, this word is, of course, a noun. But if the word may be compared, it is an adjective. When the vocabulary meaning is ambiguous, as in *She played fair,* there is no way at all of determining the grammatical meaning of the word, and the sentence is therefore completely ambiguous.

Predicate adjectives may also appear after certain verbs in the passive voice form. This usage is illustrated in such sentences as,

> George was made *happy* by our congratulations.
> Mary was called *silly* by her best friends.
> Her hair was cut *short* by the barber.

In each of these, the adjective in the predicate modifies the noun subject. When the verbs in such sentences are changed to the active voice form, the nouns modified by the adjectives, as well as the adjectives themselves, appear in the predicate position, and the adjectives follow the nouns:

> Our congratulations made *George happy.*
> Her best friends called *Mary silly.*
> The barber cut her *hair short.*

Other examples are:

> She painted the barn *red.*
> I have never seen her room *clean.*
> I have always considered his service *excellent.*
> They made his life *miserable.*
> I heard the child *calling.*

This special type of predicate adjective is sometimes called an 'objective adjective' or 'adjective of result.'

This pattern may be a puzzler when the word modified is an uninflected noun, for under these circumstances the inflectional and word-order pattern (indicator —— ——) is the same as it is when an adjective is in the attributive position: *her hair short* has the same pattern as *her short hair*. Yet, in the first phrase the third word is the adjective and in the second phrase the second word is the adjective. There are at least two ways to distinguish the adjectives from the nouns in this pattern: those which may be compared are adjectives and those which may take an *-s* inflection are nouns. But most important is what happens when, in a sentence using this pattern, the verb is converted into the passive voice form: if the last word remains in the predicate when this 'passive turn' is made, this word is the adjective. Thus, if *She cut her hair short* is changed to *Her hair was cut short*, *short* remains in the predicate, so we know that this word is an adjective.

IV

The attributive and predicate positions are the major ones for single-word adjectives, for the vast majority of them will be found in these places. There are, however, three other positions where the adjective may appear. They are:

First: the appositive position, directly following the noun modified. Some of the adjectives belonging to this group are part of what are called 'petrified expressions.' These are fixed expressions that have been handed down from earlier periods of the language. Included in this group are such phrases as: *attorney general, accounts receivable, chapter ten, heir apparent, body politic,* and *evil incarnate.* Some single-word adjectives with *-ing* and *-ed* (*-en*) endings regularly appear after the noun, as in the sentences:

> Put it aside for the time *being*.
> The money *received* will go to the Red Cross.

And some adjectives with the prefix *a-*, such as *alone* and *afire*, regularly follow the noun or pronoun modified. We also find adjectives in the appositive position after certain quantitative pronouns, notably *someone, something, nothing,* and *nobody,* as in *someone else* and *something valuable.* Sometimes adjectives that modify a noun by giving it a name are placed after the noun, as in *Operation Icebox* and *Hotel Vista.* Other kinds of adjectives may appear in this position, usually for the purpose of emphasis or literary effect, or for other special purposes, such as advertising slogans: 'The Cracker Supreme!' Since this is an abnormal position for most adjectives—that is, the normal adjective-noun word-order device is missing—other grammatical devices must be used to avoid ambiguity. We can use either inflection to distinguish the noun part of the phrase as in 'soldiers three,' or a permanent form to distinguish the adjective as in 'house beauti*ful*.'

Second: the front-shifted position. An adjective in this position, like the attributive adjective, precedes the word modified; but, unlike the latter, the front-shifted adjective precedes the indicator (when one is expressed), as in *Enraged, the boxer struck his opponent below the belt.* Also, unlike the attributive adjective, those in the front-shifted position may precede a pronoun, as in *Enraged, he struck . . .* Front-shifted adjectives may be divided into two groups. The first is composed of those words which normally appear in this position whenever an indicator is used. These adjectives include *such, both, many,* and *all,* as in *such a hot day, both the boys, many a man,* and *all the men.* Such word groups may appear in any sentence position. The second group, on the other hand, appears in only one position—before the subject, as in

> *Undaunted,* the loser decided to try again.
> *Crying,* the man left the horrible scene.

The front-shifted adjective of this second kind, like the adjective in the appositive position, usually has a permanent adjective ending to distinguish it from the other parts of speech which may appear in this position. There is always a slight difference in meaning between adjectives in this front-shifted position and these same words when they are in the attributive position. The following sentences illustrate this difference:

> *Furious,* the speaker stamped out of the room.
> The *furious* speaker stamped out of the room.

It is hard to describe this difference. But it is apparent that the adjective in the first sentence makes a statement about the speaker— he is furious; the one in the second suggests an attribute of longer duration—the speaker may have been furious for a long time, even permanently furious.

Third: the end-shifted position. Adjectives in this position are distinguished by the fact that they hang in the air, as it were, like an afterthought at the end of the sentence. They are called end-shifted because they are moved from their normal position close to the subject, which they modify, to the end of the sentence, as in

> She fell to the ground *unconscious.*
> He stood before the hostile crowd *undefeated.*

Adjectives may be end-shifted only when they have permanent adjective endings or when the vocabulary meanings make it clear beyond all doubt which word is modified. If neither of these conditions is met, the inexperienced writer may be led into writing such a ludicrous sentence as the following:

> When his friend defeated him, John stared down at the grass *green with envy.*

A 'boner' of this kind points up the complexities of adjective word order. Not only are sentences with adjectives often difficult to analyze but also to construct. In fact, the proper placing of adjectives probably poses the most perplexing problem faced by all users of English. This point appears much more dramatically when the problem of placing group modifiers is dealt with in Chapter XV.

v

After this general description of the adjective in terms of the three grammatical devices, something must be said about one special type of adjective. This is the verbal adjective. These forms have already been encountered in Chapter IV as the third, fourth, and fifth forms of the verb. They are also often referred to as 'participial' adjectives. Third-form verbal adjectives are illustrated in such expressions as *a rolling stone* and *the falling snow.* Fourth- and fifth-form verbal adjectives usually end in -*ed* (-*t*) or -*en,* as in *polished brass, burnt offerings,* and *fallen arches;* less often the 'irregular' verb forms with internal inflections are used, such as *a stung beekeeper, sprung rhythm,* and *a dug well.* These forms themselves are easy enough to recognize, but there is always danger of confusing verbal adjectives with those parts of the verb itself that have the same form. For example, *rolling* may be a verbal adjective, as it is in *a rolling stone;* but in the sentence

Workmen were rolling away the stone

rolling is not an adjective but part of the verb phrase *were rolling.* Similarly, in the sentence

A tree had fallen across the road

fallen is part of the verb phrase *had fallen* and is thus not an adjective, as it is in *A fallen tree blocked the road.* Fourth-form verbal adjectives should also not be confused with the simple past tense of the verb. In *I polished the brass,* we know that *polished* is a verb, not a verbal adjective, for at least two reasons: first, its position immediately following the subject (*I*) is a verb position; second, there is the possibility of expanding the single word into several distinctive verb forms, such as *have polished* or *shall polish.* This problem is considered at greater length in Chapter XI, pp. 153-5.

One characteristic development in our language is the tendency to drop the endings of verbal adjectives, leaving the word order as the only means of conveying the adjective meaning. Such expressions as *skim milk, swim suits, mix bowls,* and *plunge necklines* are very common. Indeed, this change is accelerating to such an extent that yesterday's *frying pan* is today's *fry pan.* But this development is not entirely the result of modern carelessness in handling the language, as some people assume; for the inclination to drop these verbal adjective endings has been going on for at least a century. In fact, some verbal adjectives lost their endings so long ago that we do not even recognize them as verbals today. One of these is the word *grade* in *grade school:* the fact that it was originally *graded* would surprise almost everyone. This tendency to drop the endings of verbal adjectives is a continuation of the general tendency to simplify the inflectional system which has been going on throughout the history of the language.

The major points of this chapter may be summed up under six heads:

1. The adjective has a large number of relatively distinct permanent forms, which sometimes make it possible to shift this part of speech out of its characteristic positions.

2. Many adjectives are inflected to express the ideas of comparison. Except for a few irregular forms, these inflections are *-er* and *-est*. These same suffixes are also used by adverbs.

3. There are several function words (also shared with the adverb) used with the adjective, all of which express some aspect of comparison. They are: *more, most, less,* and *least,* and *as . . . as, so . . . as,* and *more (less) . . . than.*

4. Most single-word adjectives may be found in two positions: (a) in the attributive position immediately preceding a noun and following an indicator (if one is used) and (b) in the predicate position after a linking verb, after certain verbs in the passive voice, and after certain objects of the verb to express the idea of 'result.'

5. Adjectives also appear in three other places in the sentence: (a) in the appositive position following a noun or pronoun, (b) in the front-shifted position preceding a noun indicator or a pronoun, and (c) in the end-shifted position at the end of the sentence.

6. A special group of adjectives are called verbal adjectives because they possess the forms of the third, fourth, and fifth forms of the verb (*-ing, -ed* or *-t,* and *-en*).

IX

PERIPATETIC PERFORMERS

The other type of single-word modifier is the adverb. The literal meaning of this word would suggest, of course, that it is directed toward or modifies the meaning of the verb. This is, to be sure, the central point in most definitions of this part of speech. But it is not the only point: under certain circumstances, adverbs may modify most of the other parts of speech. This large area includes adjectives, other adverbs, prepositions, pronouns, and even a certain type of noun. Adverbs may also modify the total meaning of groups of words, large and small, often including an entire sentence. Furthermore, some words that are traditionally classed as adverbs do not, strictly speaking, really modify at all. The so-called 'conjunctive adverbs' are of this type: such words as *however, indeed, moreover,* and *nevertheless* seem rather to express a relationship between sentences than to modify. Actually, adverbs are such a miscellaneous group that it would almost seem as if some of them had been so classified because the grammarians could find no other place to put them! Because of this heterogeneous nature of adverbs, an exact definition of this part of speech is not only difficult to formulate, but would be even more difficult to apply. For this reason, it is very important to arrive at a workable description of the adverb from the point of view of its form.

I

A great many adverbs may be readily identified by the fact that they end in the suffix *-ly*. Adverbs of this type are formed simply by adding the *-ly* to an adjective base, as in *quickly, suddenly, helplessly, fully, badly, lately, brightly, fortunately, conditionally, prettily,* and thousands of others. This is the most characteristic of the permanent adverb forms, but it is not an exclusively adverbial one, for adjectives also may end in this same suffix. However, it is not difficult to distinguish the *-ly* adverbs from the *-ly* adjectives. One simply has to remember that an *-ly* adverb is formed only when the suffix is added to an adjective. Adjectives ending in *-ly,* on the other hand, are formed from other parts of speech, usually nouns, as *heavenly, lordly, worldly, orderly, daily, hourly, weekly, monthly, yearly, fatherly,* etc. The words *kindly, lowly, deadly,* and a few others, are exceptions to this rule, for the *-ly* here does not convert the adjectives *kind, low,* and *dead* into adverbs, but merely creates other adjectives with a slightly different vocabulary meaning.

Some of the *-ly* adjectives, especially those having to do with time, such as *weekly* and *hourly,* are also used regularly in standard English as adverbs. Examples of this use are seen in such sentences as:

They pick up the papers *weekly*.

He tended the furnace *daily*.

Furthermore, many of the others, including *kindly,* are often used as adverbs in the more colloquial levels of standard English, as in

She spoke *kindly* of you.

He acted *fatherly* to the child.

Now pile the papers up *orderly*.

One reason for this usage is the obvious fact that the *-ly* suffix is regarded as a 'sign' of the adverb: because it is used so widely to form this part of speech, many people feel instinctively that it conveys the idea of 'adverbness' under all circumstances.

In addition to the *-ly* suffix, there are thirteen other endings that will create permanent adverb forms. These are *-day, -long, -meal,*

-place, -side, -time, -ward, -wards, -way, -ways, -wise, -where, and *-s.*
There is also one prefix, *to-.* For example, we may say:

> He rushed *headlong* down the stairs.
>
> She always worked at things *piecemeal.*
>
> He reads the paper *backwards.*
>
> He looked *outside.*
>
> We must push *onward* into the jungle.
>
> The crab moves *sideways.*
>
> He measured the box *lengthwise.*
>
> He looked *everywhere.*
>
> She works *mornings* and *evenings.*
>
> He will leave *tomorrow.*

At the time this book is being written there is a widespread vogue
for using the suffix *-wise* to form adverbs from nouns. Every day
we hear such expressions as:

> It's a fine day *weatherwise*
>
> This will help us *taxwise.*
>
> The candidate did the right thing *votewise.*

The popularity of this grammatical form is probably caused by its
great convenience. By using this four-letter suffix we avoid the stiff
and cumbersome circumlocutions, *in respect to* and *in regard to.*
It is impossible to predict, of course, whether this form will continue to be widely used, but it seems now that it has become a permanent part of the language.

One of the interesting and important things about the permanent forms of the adverb is their grammatical stability; we do not
tend to shift them readily to another function. This is not to say,
of course, that they can never change function. It is obvious that
some words with adverb suffixes may undergo a shift to the adjective function. We may say, for example, *a piecemeal solution, an
outward thrust, a lengthwise measurement, headlong flight, outside
plumbing,* etc. Yet it is surprising how many words operate only
as adverbs. Such words as *everywhere, besides, elsewhere, otherwise,
likewise, always, outdoors, backwards,* and *sometimes* are rarely

shifted in normal English. And adverbs that end in the *-ly* suffix never operate as any other part of speech. If the permanent forms of nouns, verbs, and adjectives are compared with those of the adverb, it will become apparent that the adverb has many more forms which operate as true 'signals' of its function.

II

There are, however, a number of adverbs which do not have any of the characteristic adverb forms. Fortunately, this is a limited group and may be easily memorized. This list is as follows:

about	instead	on
above	how	out
almost	however	over
already	home	quite
also	indeed	rather
back	forth	right
before	late	seldom
behind	less	since
below	least	so
better	long	somewhat
but (only)	low	soon
down	more	still
even	much	straight
ever	near	then
far	never	there
fast	north (etc.)	thus
hard	nevertheless	too
here	not	up
in	now	yet

If these words always performed as adverbs, the chapter could end at this point, but alas, they do not. Many of them may be adjectives, nouns, verbs, and prepositions as well. We must therefore take a look at the grammatical devices that distinguish adverbs from other parts of speech. Unfortunately, the three major devices for the adverb are less distinctive than those for the other parts of speech. We have already pointed out that the same inflectional endings to express comparison are shared by the adverb and the adjective: *-er* for the comparative degree and *-est* for the superlative. Actually, very few adverbs use this device at all. Adverbs ending in -*ly* do not often express comparison in this way, and most of the words in the list above cannot be compared. It would be futile, therefore, to try to identify adverbs by their inflectional forms. Furthermore, the same function words are shared by adverbs and adjectives. Word order, then, is really the only one of the three major devices that sets the adverb off from other parts of speech. Altogether, an adverb may occupy ten different positions in the sentence. Of course, not all adverbs may occupy all of these positions. Some of them favor some of them, some favor others, depending on their vocabulary meanings and the contexts.

These adverb positions may be divided into two groups. In the first are those positions that, in the normal word order of simple statements, may be occupied by adverbs only:

1. Between the subject and verb:

> Her dress *almost* caught fire.
> She *fearfully* opened the door.

2. Inside an expanded verb group:

> He may *almost* succeed.
> She has *never* been married.

3. In the (indicator)-adverb-adverb-adjective pattern:

> She preferred the *bright* blue material.
> This is a *very uncomfortably* cold day.

4. Between a verb and another adverb, or first in the sentence before another adverb:

> *Very* often hard work is completed *too* fast.

5. Between any noun, pronoun, or verb and a preposition:

> The house *right* on the corner is being painted.
> The baby has been crying *ever* since noon.

Or before a prepositional phrase that comes first in the sentence:

> *Just* behind the house was an old barn.

6. Between a preposition and a word or word group that comprises its object:

> They kept going under *even* the worst conditions.
> You are right in *only* the first instance.

7. Immediately preceding certain of the quantitative pronouns:

> *Almost* everyone agreed.
> His story was believed by *very* few.

It is obvious that most of these are 'in-between' positions; hence the ability to recognize these words as adverbs is dependent upon being able to recognize the other grammatical units in the sentence.

The second group of adverb positions are not exclusively adverbial. Also in contrast to most of those in group one, these are all 'outside' positions. They are:

1. At the beginning of the sentence, preceding the subject and all its modifiers:

> *Unfortunately,* the best seats were taken.

Most adverbs in this position have a permanent adverb form, like the word *unfortunately,* or they belong to that group of adverbs that cannot shift their function, such as *moreover, however,* and *instead.* These forms distinguish adverbs from front-shifted adjectives.

2. At the end of the sentence outside the subject-verb-object pattern:

> He considered the picture *carefully*.

This position may be occupied by two other parts of speech. One is the predicate adjective:

> He considered the picture *good*.

When a word in this position does not have a distinctive adverb or adjective form, as in *He pulled the cord hard,* it is almost impossible to tell whether it is an adjective or adverb, and for all practical purposes there is no reason why anyone should try to do so. This position may also be occupied by a noun:

> He considered the picture *a fake*.

Here, the indicator, of course, tells us that *fake* is a noun. If a word in this position has neither an indicator nor a distinctive permanent form, the possibility of ambiguity again arises. In the sentence

> He called Checkers *home*

the meaning is completely ambiguous unless we know whether 'he' owns a house or a dog by the name of Checkers.

3. Adverbs may follow intransitive verbs—those verbs which because of their meaning cannot take an object:

> She writes *poorly.*
> She sews *well.*

This position may also be occupied by an adjective, if the verb is a linking one:

> She became *angry.*

The fact that both adverbs and adjectives may occupy these end-of-the-sentence positions causes difficulty in grammatical usage when the writer or speaker is required to choose between an adjective or adverb form. They ask: 'Should I say *looks well* or *looks good; run quick* or *run quickly; hold tight* or *hold tightly?*' This problem is discussed at length in Chapter XIV (pp. 230-5).

Another characteristic of the adverb is its mobility, for often adverbs may be shifted freely from position to position without affecting the meaning of the sentence. In other words, the writer often has a wide choice in placing adverbs, depending on the rhetorical and stylistic effects he wishes to achieve. This is in contrast to the word-order status of all the other parts of speech. Yet it does not contradict what we have said about set word order as a grammatical device, for an adverb is movable only when it modifies large groups of words or whole sentences, or when the exact direction of modification is not clearly felt. Under these circumstances, it is natural that the adverb modifier need not be set in a definite position. The movability of the adverb is illustrated by the position of the word *soon* in the sentence

> The little boy will be down to breakfast *soon.*

From the point of view of style, the best place for the word is probably at the end of the sentence, but it may appear in many other positions without seriously affecting the meaning of the total utterance:

> *Soon* the little boy will be down to breakfast.
> The little boy *soon* will be down to breakfast.
> The little boy will *soon* be down to breakfast.
> The little boy will be *soon* down to breakfast.
> The little boy will be down *soon* to breakfast.

This illustration shows that the adverb *soon* may occupy six different positions in this simple sentence. The only positions it may not occupy are those immediately before the nouns *boy* and *breakfast*. Since the adverb is the only part of speech which is freely movable, we may conclude that any word that can be shifted about in this way is an adverb. In fact, this is such a distinguishing characteristic of the word that one grammarian has abandoned the term *adverb* and renamed this part of speech 'the movable.' This is an ingenious idea, but the term is not an exact one, since not all adverbs are movable in this way. Some of them do modify specific words and occupy set positions. The position of the adverb in the following sentences illustrates one of these:

> She made the *bright* blue curtains.
> A *half* finished project is annoying.

This, of course, is position 3 in the list of true adverb positions. All adverbs appearing in this position are immovable. If, for instance, we changed the position of *bright* to,

> She made the blue curtains *bright,*

a very different meaning would result. Some adverbs appearing before prepositions (position 5) also cannot be moved without radically changing the meaning. If we moved the adverb *right* in the sentence

> The house *right* on the corner is being painted

to the end of the sentence, what a difference in meaning would result! Similarly, in the sentence

This book is more for advanced students

the meaning would be sharply changed if *more* were moved to the position following the preposition *for*. It is extremely important to understand the difference between the movable modifiers and those that are 'set' in a special position, for the misplacing of a movable modifier in a set position, or vice versa, may completely change the meaning intended or, at least, create ambiguity and confusion.

III

As a final check on whether a word is an adverb, a process of elimination may be used. When any of the words in the adverb list is clearly marked by the devices of any other part of speech, it is obviously not an adverb. A few examples will illustrate this method.

First: A word accompanied by one or more noun devices may be eliminated as an adverb:

> The *here* and *now* should be our only concern.
> This is a contest between the *ins* and the *outs*.
> He should have come before *now*.

Noun function words (indicators and a preposition) are used with *here, ins, outs,* and *now*. A noun inflection is used with *ins* and *outs*. *Here* and *now* occupy the subject position in the first sentence, and *ins, outs,* and *now* occupy a noun position following prepositions. From all this information, we may conclude with certainty that the italicized words are nouns, not adverbs.

Second: All words accompanied by the grammatical devices of verbs may also be eliminated as adverbs. In the following sentences all the italicized words are in verb positions, three have verb inflections, and three are accompanied by verb function words:

> We *backed* the best candidate.
> Our college *will down* its rivals.
> This student *is slowing* our progress.
> They *have upped* the price.

Third: It is not quite so simple to distinguish adverbs from adjectives. We do know, however, that any word that appears in the attributive position before a noun cannot be an adverb (nor any other part of speech except an adjective). In the following sentences, therefore, the words *down, then, far,* and *after,* all of which appeared in the adverb list, may be ruled out as that part of speech because they appear in this characteristic adjective position:

> Do not speed on a *down* grade.
> My *then* husband was a doctor.
> *Far* horizons often beckon us.
> We dread the *after* effects.

Fourth: A number of the words in the adverb list may also serve as prepositions, so it is very important to eliminate this function before one decides that a word is an adverb. There are thirteen words that may be either adverbs or prepositions; they are: *about, before, behind, below, but, down, in, near, on, out, over, since,* and *up.* The problem of telling whether one of these words is an adverb or a preposition is easily solved in simple declarative sentences. If it is followed by a noun, pronoun, or noun phrase and cannot be moved from this position, it is a preposition. If it is not followed by a noun structure or if it is movable, it is almost certainly an adverb. The following sentences show three of these words as prepositions:

> Jack and Jill fell *down* the hill.
> I have never seen him *before* this.
> I have not seen him *since* the Christmas holidays.

In the similar sentences following, these same words are adverbs, for none are followed by a noun structure and *before* in the second sentence is movable:

> Jack fell *down.*
> I have never seen him *before* at our house.
> I have never seen him *since.*

Sometimes these words are followed by a noun structure, but are movable:

> They blew *up* the ship.
> They blew the ship *up.*

This situation is discussed at length in Chapters IV and VI (pp. 49 and 69). When used in this way, such words are often regarded as adverbs, but we have preferred to consider them as part of the vocabulary meaning of the verb. At any rate, they are not prepositions.

IV

A person who has been taught grammar according to other methods may ask at this point: Can't the vocabulary meaning be used to determine whether a word is an adverb? The answer is yes and no. It is true that the most common definition of this part of speech is given in terms of vocabulary meanings. It is said that 'an adverb is a word that indicates time, place, manner, degree, amount, purpose, result, and means.' Sometimes such a definition is useful. The idea of 'manner' comes very close to being an exclusive adverb idea. This is the basic idea of most of the adverb permanent forms, especially the -ly forms. For example, *quickly* means 'in a quick manner,' *fearfully,* 'in a fearful manner,' and *righteously,* 'in a righteous manner.' The endings -*ways* and -*wise* also convey these ideas of manner. But most of the other ideas included in the traditional adverb definition may be expressed by many other parts of speech. In some of the examples already given, 'time' words like *now* and 'place' words like *here, in,* and *out* function as nouns; *back* and *down* are verbs; and in Chapter VIII we pointed out that the idea of 'result' could be expressed by the adjective. The idea of time, in particular, may be expressed in the vocabulary meanings of every part of speech we have studied so far except the pronoun. A few examples will make this point clear:

> *Tomorrow* will be pleasant. (noun)
> The *early* bird gets the worm. (adjective)
> We *postponed* the trip. (verb)
> I haven't eaten *since* morning. (preposition)
> I am going to market *now*. (adverb)

Other time words such as *today, tonight,* and *yesterday* often function as nouns as well as adverbs. This is also obviously true of some words expressing the idea of place, such as *home*. For example, in the sentence *He walked home* the word *home* is an adverb, but in *Home is where the heart is* it is a noun. From all these examples it is apparent that in the last analysis it is the grammatical devices, not the vocabulary meanings, that determine whether a word is an adverb or some other part of speech.

V

When modifiers appear in a series, with each one modifying the word following, the various items in the series represent different 'levels' of modification, the higher levels always being expressed by adverbs. These various levels are like the stories of a pyramid-shaped building. The noun (also sometimes the verb) is comparable to the first story, since its meaning covers the largest territory. The adjective is like the second story, still broad but more restricted in size than the first. The adverb stories are then piled above, each smaller than the other. The noun is called the primary unit, the adjective the secondary, the adverb the tertiary. If there is an adverb modifying another adverb, this is called the quaternary. Examples of typical

four-level structures are: *very uncomfortably cold weather* and a

   4   3   2   1

rather dark green color. It would be possible to have five levels as

   5 4 3   2   1

in *a not very cleverly concealed move.*

A noun and its modifiers, however, do not always represent the 4–3–2–1 order of modification. Sometimes, when there are two modifiers, both may be adjectives. In terms of their levels this scheme would be numbered 2–2–1. Examples of this kind of modification may be seen in *a beautiful big house* and *a dark stormy day.* When both modifiers are secondaries, it is often possible to put a comma, or such words as *and* or *but,* between the two words. Of course each of the two adjectives could be modified by adverbs, as in *a very beautiful great big house.* Here there are two structures of modification based on one noun. This would be numbered 3–2–3–2–1.

Sometimes the highest modifier in a 3–2–1 structure is a secondary in both form and meaning. This occurs usually when the middle member is an attributive noun as in *scented bath powder, dangerous flight conditions, trained dog act, rising price threat,* and *heavy equipment manufacturer.* The highest member in a 3–2–1 structure may also be a secondary in form when the middle member is a verbal adjective as in *high priced car, cheerful tempered person,* and *low lying land* (see p. 234 for another discussion of these forms).

Sometimes adverbial nouns too function as tertiary modifiers, as in *smoke filled room, heaven sent blessings, tailor made suit, stone ground floor, vine covered cottage,* and *stamp redemption plan.* It is also possible for nouns to be 'quaternary' adverbs, as in *food stamp*
$$\overset{4}{}\quad\overset{3}{}$$
redemption program, or to go to even higher levels of modification,
$$\overset{?}{}\quad\overset{1}{}$$
for which there is no name, such as *Connecticut State Highway*
$$\overset{6}{}\quad\overset{5}{}\quad\overset{4}{}$$
Department Operated Ferries! All of these adverbial nouns, of
$$\overset{3}{}\quad\overset{2}{}\quad\overset{1}{}$$
course, belong in the general class of attributive nouns, which were discussed in Chapter VIII as adjective modifiers. In the examples above, all the modifiers except *operated* are attributive nouns.

There are also levels of modification with the verb as a primary, but these groups do not usually reach such high levels as the noun groups. Here the secondary is an adverb and the tertiary is usually a 'degree' adverb, as in

$$\overset{1}{}\quad\overset{3}{}\qquad\qquad\qquad\overset{2}{}$$
He decided very (so, too, rather, somewhat, etc.) quickly.

VI

Before the subject of modification is completed, something must be said about the prepositional phrase as modifier. In Chapter VI the preposition was described as a function word which relates a noun or pronoun (its object) to another word. An examination of this part of speech from another point of view will reveal something about the precise nature of this relationship. The preposition is regarded by grammarians as a device for turning a noun or pronoun (its object) into a modifier. In the sentences following the italicized prepositional phrases modify the nouns preceding them:

> They sold the house *on the corner.*
> The parks *in our city* are beautiful.
> The floor *under the table* is scuffed.
> The book *by the telephone* is an atlas.

These are all adjective phrases and occupy a position following the noun or pronoun modified.

As we pointed out in Chapter VIII, the function of the preposition is similar to that of the word-order device which turns nouns into attributive modifiers. The following pairs of phrases illustrate the close correspondence in meaning between the two constructions:

Prepositional Phrases	Attributive Nouns
house *on the beach*	*beach* house
furniture *for the bedroom*	*bedroom* furniture
boy *from the grocery*	*grocery* boy
rug *in the hall*	*hall* rug

Prepositional phrases also function as adverbs, modifying verbs or adjectives:

> He worked *with a chisel,*
> She ran *up the stairs,*
> Our mother is beautiful *in spirit.*

Other adverbial phrases modify the whole sentence, as in

> This nonsense is not believed *by everyone.*

Like single-word adverbs, the positions of adverbial prepositional phrases are not always fixed. For example, we can say,

> He pried up the lid *with a knife* (or)
> *With a knife* he pried up the lid.

A few adverbial phrases, like adjective phrases, are interchangeable with an attributive construction. Compare these sets of phrases:

room filled *with smoke*	*smoke* filled room
suit made *by a tailor*	*tailor* made suit
redemption plan *for stamps*	*stamp* redemption plan

To sum up what has been said about the adverb in this chapter: (1) It has about a dozen permanent forms, one of which (ending in -*ly*) is a distinctive 'sign' of this part of speech, provided that the ending is added to an adjective base. (2) It may be compared by using the same inflections and function words used by adjectives. (3) It may occupy seven characteristic adverb positions, and three others which are shared with other parts of speech. (4) It is the only kind of word which may be moved about freely within a given sentence, without seriously affecting the meaning. (5) One can rarely tell from the vocabulary meaning of a word that it is an adverb. (6) It is sometimes necessary to resort to a 'process of elimination' before it can be determined finally that a word is an adverb. (7) One of its important functions is to express the higher 'levels of modification.' (8) Finally, a noun or pronoun may fulfill an adverbial or adjectival function by the use of a preposition.

X

THE CART BEFORE THE HORSE

The basic word-order patterns described in Chapters VI and VIII are the fundamental and by far the most common sentence patterns in modern English. But they are not the only ones; for, under certain circumstances, variations frequently occur. These variations always involve some kind of inversion of the common basic patterns. In other words, we 'put the cart before the horse.' The inverted patterns may be divided into two groups: first, those that signal a different kind of sentence from the simple statements thus far treated; and second, those that allow emphasis on certain sentence elements for rhetorical effect, without in any way changing the grammatical meaning. These new patterns will be considered in that order.

I

Thus far we have been concerned almost exclusively with what grammarians call declarative sentences—sentences that make statements. These statements may range from statements of fact, like

> We won the homecoming game.
> Barbara is getting me a ticket to the dance.

to statements of doubt and denial of fact:

> We may get tickets to the dance.
> We will not take a lunch with us.

But, in all instances, the intention of the speaker is to give information. Most writing is in declarative sentences; but there are other kinds with a different primary aim. Some, for instance, are intended not to give information but rather to ask for it; others are intended not to give information but rather to show our feelings about something; and still others are intended not to give information but to get someone to do something we want done. These kinds are known traditionally as 'interrogative,' 'exclamatory,' and 'imperative' sentences, respectively. They are more common in spoken than in written English, it is true; but they are far from rare in writing.

First, how are questions signaled? In speech any sentence may be used to ask a question: all that needs to be done is to raise the voice pitch at the end of it. In writing we indicate this raising of the pitch by a question mark. If each of the following sentences is spoken first as a statement, then as a question, the difference in the pitch pattern of the voice is readily apparent:

You have your books.	You have your books?
The house is vacant.	The house is vacant?
She is giving us tickets.	She is giving us tickets?

More often in speech, however, and much more often in writing, we rearrange the word order when we make declarative sentences into questions:

Do you have your books?

Is the house vacant?

Is she giving us tickets?

The pattern of all these inversions involves the front-shifting of part, or all, of the verb ahead of the subject. This front-shifting follows three patterns:

(1) The whole verb may be shifted, but only if it is a simple form of *be* or *have:*

Is your brother a lawyer?

Have you the information?

In earlier periods of the language this device was not limited to *be* or *have* but extended to all the verbs, as it still does in many modern European languages. Shakespeare has a character ask,

Rides the king out tonight?

And there is the question in the old nursery rhyme:

> Pussy cat, pussy cat, what *did* you there?

(2) In modern English, however, the strength of the normal sub-ject–verb order is so great that another pattern has been established for asking questions with unexpanded verbs. We put a form of the auxiliary verb *do* ahead of the subject and leave the main verb in its normal place after the subject. The following pairs of sentences show how this is done:

Statement	Question
He *does* his work.	*Does* he *do* his work?
You *brought* me the book.	*Did* you *bring* me the book?
The king *rides out* tonight.	*Does* the king *ride out* tonight?
Englishmen *like* roast beef.	*Do* Englishmen *like* roast beef?

The pattern of this kind of interrogative sentence is: auxiliary verb *do*–subject–main verb–complement. As with other auxiliary verbs, variations in the form of *do* carry the burden of expressing all of the grammatical ideas associated with the verb (for example, in the second sentence past tense is expressed), and the main verb is always in the first form. The positions of the modifiers are not affected by this reversal in the basic word-order pattern, as can be seen in these expansions of the fourth sentence:

> Do most Englishmen like rare roast beef often for supper?
> Do Englishmen like their roast beef rare most of the time?

This type of interrogative word-order pattern is so 'standard' in modern English that it is often used even with the verb *have*. *Do you have the information?* is more common than *Have you the in-formation?* And *Did he have his lessons?* is much more common, even in writing, than *Had he his lessons?* Small children, aware of the strength of this pattern, even use it sometimes with simple forms of the verb *be: Did he be a good boy?*

(3) If the verb in the declarative sentence is expanded into a phrase, the first auxiliary is shifted ahead of the subject:

Statement	Question
You *are talking* nonsense.	*Are* you *talking* nonsense?
You *have been given* a demotion.	*Have* you *been given* a demotion?
He *will be leaving* the country.	*Will* he *be leaving* the country?
He *could have been giving* us the slip.	*Could* he *have been giving* us the slip?

It is clear from these sentences that other auxiliaries (if they are present) and the main verb remain in their usual positions and all members of the verb group retain their original forms. This third pattern is the most common of all the interrogative word-order patterns. Analyzing interrogative sentences that follow these three patterns is very simple, if the forms of the auxiliary verbs have been memorized. When one of these forms appears first in a sentence, we know that the subject will follow, then other auxiliary verbs if they are present, and then the main verb: auxiliary–subject–(second auxiliary)–main verb. Pattern 1, in which the main verb is first, provides the only exception to this rule.

Sometimes special interrogative words are used to signal a question. These may be divided into three classes: adverbs, pronouns, and adjectives. When adverbs are used the pattern is exactly the same as the three described above, with the interrogative adverb preceding the first auxiliary verb.

> When *were* you in Paris?
> Where *did* he put his money?
> Why *has* Henry *given* us a slight?
> How *could* he *have done* such a thing?

In these sentences, two devices have been used to signal the question: the interrogative adverb and the front-shifting of the auxiliary. When pronouns and adjectives are used interrogatively, however, the word-order patterns are different. When used as subjects, *who, which,* and *what* alone signal the question; the normal subject–verb–complement order of the declarative sentence is retained:

> Who *is* her leading man?
> What *has caused* this spot?
> Which *could be* the best route?

When the interrogative adjectives *which, what, whose,* and *how many* function as modifiers of the subject, the same order is kept, too:

Whose uncle *gave* us the money?
Which cousin *lost* his eyesight?
What calamity *could cause* this despair?
How many people *are coming?*

On the other hand, when interrogative words are complements, or modifiers of complements, the order of the sentence elements is changed radically, for the interrogative word must come first to signal the question, and this means that the complement must be moved from its normal position late in the sentence. In addition to this change, the auxiliary verb is front-shifted to buttress the signal. Thus two changes in normal declarative word order have been made:

What does he do?
Which stories did he write?
Whose name is he calling?
What player did they name captain?

In the first sentence the interrogative word itself comprises the entire complement. In the others the interrogative word modifies a noun complement. In all the sentences, however, the order is the same: complement–auxiliary verb–subject–main verb. In the fourth sentence a second object follows the main verb.

Interrogative sentences of this type may also involve a change in another important sentence pattern: namely, the order of the preposition and its object. The object may be moved from its normal position following the preposition and front-shifted whenever the object is an interrogative word, or when a word of this kind modifies the object, as in

What are you thinking about?
What girl are you thinking of?
Whom is he talking to?

This violation of normal word order is repugnant to some people. So, in order not to break up the prepositional phrase they place it in its entirety at the beginning of the sentence:

Of what are you thinking?
Of what girl are you thinking?
To whom is he talking?

But this type of word order has its disadvantages too: the interrogative word loses its force in this weak second position and, worst of all, a stiff, awkward sentence usually results.

II

In the exclamatory sentence the primary intention is to express surprise, indignation, excitement, or some other intense feeling. In speech, just as any sentence may be made a question by vocal pitch pattern, so may any sentence be made exclamatory if a normally unstressed word or word group is given unusual emphasis. In writing, such stress may be more or less indicated by the exclamation point and the italicization of the stressed word or words:

John *didn't believe* it!
Have *you* wrecked the plan!
John *is* tall!

The first and the last of these sentences follow normal declarative patterns; the middle one follows a normal interrogative pattern. In speech, probably most exclamations are indicated by vocal devices.

But in writing, the vocal pitch is lost—even the italics and exclamation points are rather weak substitutes—and the exclamatory effect desired is more effectively gained by a shifting of the elements of the sentence and by the use of exclamatory signal-words *how* and *what*. Sometimes the exclamatory word alone suffices to give the signal:

How he could tell stories!
What a thunderstorm hit us!

But often the complement needs to be stressed, and in this instance both the signal-word and a rearrangement of the sentence elements are used:

How funny he is!
What jokes he can tell!

What a whopper he told you!
What a fool we elected senator!

In the first two examples, the pattern is exclamatory word–complement–subject–verb. In the last two, where there are double objects, one of the objects is front-shifted ahead of the subject and verb, the other remaining in its normal position after the verb. In all of these examples, the exclamatory word is a modifier of the complement. Written English has few devices for expressing exclamations, as compared with its devices for questions. For the exclamation is, on the whole, an element of the spoken language, and an element which has so little intruded into the written language that few methods are needed for its expression.

III

The imperative sentence has as its primary intention to elicit a response from the listener or reader, and ranges from a demand ('Pay me or else!') to a simple request ('Please hold the line a minute'). This sort of sentence is unique for two reasons: More often than not it does without a subject, and its verb invariably is in the first form. Unlike interrogative and exclamatory sentences, imperative sentences cannot be made merely by vocal pitch and stress: the declarative sentence *Henry makes his own bed* may be made either a question or an exclamation merely by changing the pitch and stress pattern:

Henry makes his own bed?
Henry makes his *own* bed!

To make this sentence imperative, however, several other changes are necessary even in speech:

Henry, make your own bed.

Most important, the whole sentence must be changed from third to second person: this is done by changing the form of the verb from *makes* to *make* and the form of the pronoun from *his* to *your,* and by setting off the original third person subject with a comma. (This word in imperative sentences is called a 'noun in address.') A new second person subject *you* may also be added, as in

> Henry, you make your own bed.

The tense form of the verb must also be changed if the original declarative sentence is not in the present tense.

The imperative sentence follows an absolutely fixed word-order pattern (with the exception of the noun in address, which may come either at the beginning or end of the sentence, and serves only as a signal to attract the attention of the person addressed): first the verb and then the complement (or complements) with modifiers coming wherever they would appear in a declarative sentence, and with the possibility of *you* preceding the verb. Sometimes, of course, there may be no complement: then the order is verb–modifiers. The following sentences illustrate these patterns:

> (you) Tell the story, John. (verb–direct object)
> (you) Tell them the story, John. (verb–indirect object–direct object)
> Now, (you) be good, girls. (adverb–verb–pred. adj.)
> (you) Tiptoe quietly into the room. (verb–adverb–prep. phrase)

The only auxiliary verb that can be used in the imperative sentence is the verb *do;* and its presence does not destroy the basic pattern:

> Do tell me the news.
> Do try the door again.

In most instances, this fixed pattern makes the imperative sentence an easy one to analyze.

Sometimes, however, it may pose a problem when the verb is followed directly by an object without any noun indicator, as in

> Cash checks at this window.

The difficulty arises because the first two words in this sentence have the same form as the first two words in a certain kind of declarative sentence, such as

> Cash buys goods at lower prices,

in which *cash* is the subject and *buys* the verb. Under these circumstances, we usually have to depend on the vocabulary and grammatical meanings of the other words in the sentence in order to
decide whether it is declarative or imperative. Sometimes sentences
of this type are wholly ambiguous. If the word *goods* is omitted from
the last sentence above, the meaning becomes obscured. And the
sentence

Ice cakes quickly after cooling

is quite ambiguous; it could be taken either as a statement concerning the condition of one's windshield on a winter day or as a
direction in a cookbook. This kind of double-talking sentence could
be avoided by introducing a few extra grammatical devices. For
example, indicators inserted in the proper places would completely
resolve the ambiguity:

(The) ice cakes quickly. . . (declarative)
Ice (the) cakes quickly. . . (imperative)

In addition, if the sentence is intended to be declarative, a change
in the position of the adverb *quickly* would clarify this fact, for the
more inflexible word order of the imperative sentence would not
allow this change in normal standard English.

IV

All of the word-order variations thus far described are used to
convert a declarative sentence into another type. There is, however,
another kind of inversion which does not change the type of the
sentence, the purpose of which is to draw attention to, or place
emphasis upon, a member of the pattern by pulling it from its
normal place—or, conversely, under other circumstances to de-
emphasize it. The strength of the patterns is so great in modern
English that, whenever we vary a sentence from the expected
sequence, we call attention to one of the parts. An analogy may
make this clearer. If we lived in a town where every house had
a large front porch, a front porch would not especially draw our
attention. But if someone built a house with no front porch at all,
but rather a large back porch, his porch would probably be noticed

by everyone in town; he would call attention to his porch by putting it in an unexpected place. And he would call attention to the front of his house also because of its porchless appearance. So, in a language in which the subject, verb, and complement are expected to fall in that order, we can call attention to one of the members by changing this order. Of course, if nobody recognized the housebuilder's porch as a porch, it might not draw attention, and it also would be extremely confusing. So the shifted member (or members) of a sentence must be clearly marked as one part of speech or another by other grammatical devices whenever the standard word-order patterns are altered in any way.

There is one type of declarative sentence that is very easily inverted. All of the following short sentences may be turned around without any effect on the basic meaning of the statement:

The roses are lovely.	Lovely are the roses.
The storm was fearful.	Fearful was the storm.
The water was murky.	Murky was the water.

Each of these sentences is obviously composed of a noun subject, a verb, and a predicate adjective; and the two parts that have been reversed are clearly marked as nouns (by indicators) and adjectives (by permanent endings) respectively. It is generally true that all sentences which do not contain a noun complement (either direct or indirect object or predicate complement) have a relatively flexible word order. This applies not only to the predicate adjective type of sentence above, but even to simple sentences containing only a subject and a verb. For example, it is quite possible to change *The dawn came* to *Came the dawn* and *The birds flew* to *Flew the birds* without impairing the meaning of the word group. It is true that the usual order in normal discourse is subject–verb, but since these units may be reversed without any serious effect upon the grammatical meaning, the subject-verb word order in these two-unit sentences is not a true grammatical device. This is why this type of sentence was not discussed in Chapter VI among the simplest sentence patterns, in spite of the fact that this one would seem to be the simplest of all.

When any of these subject-verb combinations is preceded by a modifier, inversion takes place very frequently. In fact, in such sentences as the following it is a question whether subject–verb or verb–subject is the 'normal' one.

> Then came the dawn.
> On the table were the remnants of our party.
> Thus began all our troubles.
> Now comes the amusing part of the story.

When sentences of this type contain not a simple verb but a verb group, the auxiliary verb is usually the only part of the group that is placed before the subject:

> Once again had war broken out.
> At no time had Henry been sleeping.
> Upon no such eventuality had the outcome depended.
> Never have I seen such weather.

It is interesting that in all these sentences except the first one the use of the 'inverted' word order is not optional, but required: the English idiom does not allow such a sentence as *At no time Henry had been sleeping.* Indeed, the inverted word order is standard for all sentences introduced by any kind of adverb expressing negative ideas like those in the sentences above. This is also true when a negative 'connective' is used, such as *nor* or *not only.*

There is one common function word which normally calls for the inversion of the subject-verb pattern in sentences without object complements. This is the word *there.* When this word is placed before the verb, the normal word order is verb–subject. This is a very widely used idiom:

> There are three answers.
> There will be trouble with the neighbors.
> There was no response to our query.

Not all verbs may be used in this idiom. The most common is *be,* but a few others, such as *seem, exist, remain, come,* and certain verbs in the passive voice, such as *is felt,* may also be so used. Examples of these words with *there* may be seen in the following sentences:

> There seemed no escape from the cave.
> In the old days there existed savage tribes in this area.
> There remained two possibilities.
> There came a strange light in the sky.
> There is felt to be a lack of co-operation.

It should be noted that the familiar subject-verb order is not impossible in this idiom, provided that the position of *there* before the verb is retained:

> Trouble there will be.
> Three wise men there were.

But this word pattern seems too 'poetic' for ordinary discourse and is definitely an abnormal one for this particular idiom. However, when it does occur, it is obvious that the subject receives enormous emphasis.

It should be noted that the function word *there* is not the same word as the adverb *there*. The difference between the meanings of the two words is illustrated by the sentence:

> *There* are three books *there* on the table.

The order of the words in this sentence tells us immediately which is which, but sometimes either *there* may appear in the position preceding the verb:

> There is a dollar on the table. (function word)
> There is the dollar on the table. (adverb)

In speech, of course, the adverb is easily distinguished from the function word, for the adverb is more heavily stressed when the sentence is spoken aloud.

In declarative sentences containing a noun (or pronoun) complement of any kind, the purpose of inversion is to maneuver the complement into the first position and thus give it a great deal more emphasis than it would have in its normal place at the end of the sentence. But it is not nearly so easy to manipulate the basic word-order pattern of sentences with noun complements, since this pattern is a vital grammatical device that determines which word is the subject, which the verb, and which the complement. And if one tampers with this order, there is real danger of creating ambiguities or nonsense. In Chapter II it was pointed out that noun-verb-noun sentences, like *The policemen shot the robber,* cannot possibly be inverted without completely changing the meaning. But there are three situations in which partial inversion may take place if emphasis on the object is desired:

(1) When the subject or object is a type of pronoun that has distinctive subject and object case forms. These are *I, we, he, she, they, me, us, him, her,* and *them.* Since the inflectional forms of the pronoun provide all the information we need about the subject and object functions, the grammatical meaning of the sentence does not depend entirely on word order. Therefore, it is possible to front-shift the complement for emphasis without impairing the basic meaning of the sentence. For example, in the sentence

<blockquote>The actress he admired</blockquote>

the form of *he* establishes it as the subject, and therefore it may be assumed by a process of elimination that *actress* is the object. When one of these pronouns is an object, an inversion is even more likely, as in

<blockquote>Her the student admired.</blockquote>

Actually such simple sentences as these rarely occur, but inversions are quite common when there are modifiers in addition to the basic sentence elements:

<blockquote>The girl next door he admired particularly.
'Him the Almighty Power hurled headlong.'</blockquote>

The order in this type of sentence is never completely reversed; that is, there never is an object-verb-subject order. The reason for this is the great power of the normal word-order pattern: If any group of words appears in the noun (pronoun)-verb-noun (pronoun) order, no matter what the forms of the pronouns may be, we interpret the first word as subject, the second as verb, the third as object. In other words, if we saw the sentence

<blockquote>Her admired he</blockquote>

we would interpret *her* as the subject and *he* as the object and con-clude that the writer had made a serious grammatical blunder in selecting the forms of the pronouns.

(2) An object is sometimes front-shifted when it is an emphatic pronoun or when it is modified by an emphatic adjective, as in

> *That* dress I liked best of all.
>
> *That* our government won't tolerate.
>
> *Such* antics our school will not condone.
>
> *Some* of these things the workmen have already completed.
>
> The bed *itself* my mother didn't see.

This kind of inversion cannot occur unless the vocabulary meanings of the words will allow only one interpretation of the grammatical relationship. (For example, the meanings of the words *dress* and *liked* in the first sentence above would not allow us to interpret *dress* as anything but the object.) Otherwise, in spite of the emphatic word, the scrambled word order would make it difficult to tell which word was supposed to be the subject and which the object.

Objects of prepositions also are sometimes front-shifted for em-phasis under these same two conditions which allow us to change the position of direct objects. All three of the following inverted sentences use emphatic words and inflected pronoun forms, which help to clarify their meaning:

> That theory I really believe in.
>
> Him I could look at for hours.
>
> Such a fool I wouldn't listen to.

These sentences are, of course, an exception to the rule that in simple declarative sentences the object of a preposition must always follow the preposition. But in spite of the fact that this important word-order device is lacking, the structure of such sentences is not difficult to understand. When the subject and verb are once identi-fied, the first noun (or pronoun) will emerge as the prepositional object by default, since there is nothing else it could be.

(3) A third device that sometimes allows the front-shifting of the complement is that of parallel structure. This device will be dealt

with more fully later. For present purposes, it may be defined briefly
to show how it makes inversion possible. By parallel structure is
meant the ordering of elements in sentences in the same pattern; it
extends from similar word forms to similar sentence patterns—from
the simple parallel between the forms of *getting* and *spending* in

'*Getting* and *spending* we lay waste our powers'

to the more complex parallelism in the following snatches from
Mother Goose:

'The sheep's in the meadow.
The cow's in the corn.'

'Taffy was a Welshman.
Taffy was a thief.'

'Who put her in? Little Johnny Green.
Who pulled her out? Little Tommy Stout.'

This latter kind of parallelism does help to invert the position of
the complement in the subject-verb-complement pattern. These
pairs of sentences show how this works:

The king is a tyrant. But a fool the king is not.
Mary tolerated her first husband. Her second husband **Mary**
loved.
The critics gave Henry praise. John the critics gave scorn.

The fact that a pattern has been laid down in the first sentence of
these pairs makes it possible to understand the grammatical meaning of the second sentence in spite of the inversion. All of these
changes in word order stress the front-shifted complements (*fool,
second husband,* and *John*).[1]

---

[1] Some grammarians consider constructions in the passive voice to be a
means of front-shifting the complement to give it emphasis, as in *The house
was struck by lightning* instead of the active form, *Lightning struck the house.*
This kind of change, however, is not a true inversion; it is simply a change
from one pattern to another. Moreover, it is questionable that any very great
increase in emphasis is gained. In sentences with double objects, however, con-
version to the passive construction does provide a method for stressing the
inner object, as the following sentences show:

In the second sentence above, the inversion also gives emphasis to the verb *loved*. Now the verb, in spite of the fact that it is crucial to the English sentence, occupies a position in most of our patterns which, by a primary rule of rhetoric, is the least emphatic one. In our language, in contrast to 'periodic' languages such as German and Latin (in which the verb usually ends the sentence with a bang), this part of speech regularly occupies the weak middle position. And there are, unfortunately, few ways of circumventing this problem by altering the normal order of the sentence elements. It is this paradox which accounts for the rather common practice among writers of English of resorting to underlining or italics to attract attention to the verb.

Under certain circumstances, however, it is possible to maneuver the verb to the beginning or end of the sentence, and writers should always make the most of these strategies. As we have just shown, the front-shifting of the complement will sometimes leave the verb in the end position. There is another device for stressing the verb by inversion that is less common but should be noted briefly. It may be employed only when a sentence closely parallels the wording of the previous sentence, when it is in the subject-verb pattern, and when the verb is composed of more than one word. Under these conditions, as the following illustrations show, the main verb may be front-shifted, leaving the auxiliary verb in its normal position after the subject. This inversion may be seen in the second sentence of each example:

> I told him he would have to sweat, if he meant to pass.
> And *sweat* he did.

> We expected to find Grandfather snoring in his bed.
> And *snoring* he was.

> Of course he does not want to die.
> But *die* he shall.

> The manager gave *the office staff* a bonus.
> *The office staff* was given a bonus by the manager.

Stress on the inner object may also be gained by using a function word which allows this object to be shifted to the end of the sentence: *The manager gave a bonus to the office staff.*

Here there is not only the inverted order of the subject and main verb, but also the order of the auxiliary and main verb—a double inversion which allows emphasis on both main and auxiliary verbs and which is perhaps the most radical departure from normal order among the simple sentence types.

All of the major simple sentence patterns have now been examined—those that are regarded as 'normal' declarative word-order patterns, and in this chapter the inversions of those patterns. The first group of these inversions were those that result from the desire to use the sentence for other than statement-making purposes—to ask questions, give commands, express surprise, and the like. The second major group of inversions were those which stem from the desire to stress an element or several elements of the pattern by moving them from their expected positions and especially by moving them to the positions of major stress—the beginning and end of the sentence. The first group are sometimes called MODAL inversions—inversions made to signal the intention of the speaker or writer in respect to his use of the sentence. The second group might be called RHETORICAL inversions—inversions made to secure special emphasis on certain sentence elements. In the first group there are six patterns, in the second group about the same number, making only about a dozen in all. And, except for the interrogative inversions, these are not frequently employed, so putting the cart before the horse in English sentence structure is the exception rather than the rule.

XI

WHEELS WITHIN WHEELS

One of the central facts of modern English grammar, which this book has repeatedly demonstrated, is that all sentences must conform to a very limited number of patterns. At most, the English sentence may include four basic elements (subject, verb, and two complements) and their modifiers. And even when the order of these elements is varied, as it can be under limited circumstances, their number remains unchanged. This means that when each element consists of only one word, the resulting sentences must be very restricted indeed, for they can say only as much as the patterns will allow. This is perhaps enough for a small child. The following series of sentences will probably convey all the meanings he needs or wishes to express on these subjects:

> My mother has gone to the store. What are you doing? We worked in the garden last night. It got dark.

Although mature people often do use such simply constructed sentences (with somewhat different subject matter, however!), their thinking is usually too complex to be fitted into such elementary patterns. We live in a complex world, and we cannot talk or write about that world and our experiences in it without making qualifications, conditions, reservations, and without indicating numerous relationships within the sentence. These complexities force us to find means of escaping from the simple sentence patterns. Yet, the general patterns of the language are fixed; our listeners and readers are adjusted to these patterns and they anticipate them in what we say or write. It is not our privilege to invent new and different patterns if we expect to be understood.

I

Some means must therefore be found within the basic patterns to convey these more complex ideas. And, although it is not ideal, modern English responds to these demands rather well even within the limitations of the major sentence patterns. This is accomplished regularly by the process of EXPANDING the simple elements. One way to do this is to use modifiers: *The famous writer completed his historical novel* is certainly a more complex statement than *The writer completed his novel,* and *The writer finally completed his novel* adds an important qualification to the original simple statement. Prepositional phrases are another means of enriching the meaning of a sentence through modification. In the following pair of sentences, the second reports an event with more accuracy, with more sophistication, than the first:

> The famous writer finally completed his historical novel.
> The famous writer *from the South* finally completed his historical novel *about the Civil War.*

There is another even simpler means of expanding any sentence element. This is by the method of DUPLICATION—by inserting two or more grammatical items where there was only one before. These are called compound elements. Every part of the sentence may be duplicated, including even the entire sentence. Here are a few examples of how this may be done:

> Verb: The team *sang and danced.*
> Subject: *The tenor and the soprano* sang.
> Direct object: The team danced *the rumba and the samba.*
> Adjective: It was *a song and dance* team.
> Adverb: He worked *slowly but surely.*

Prep. phrase: They fought *on the beaches and along the hedge-rows.*

Preposition: He was pacing *up and down* the hall.

Object of prep.: They fought on *the fields and beaches.*

Genitive noun: This is *Mary's and John's* work.

Complete sentence: He carried the groceries, and she opened the door.

This list could also have included compounded pronouns, indirect objects, objective complements, predicate complements, and adjectives and adverbs in other positions.

The mention of 'compounded' sentence elements brings us to another part of speech—the function word called the 'conjunction.' As we pointed out in Chapter III, the name of this part of speech is derived from the Latin, meaning 'joined together.' The conjunctions that join compound elements are called 'co-ordinating conjunctions.' There are four of these: *and, but, or* and *nor.* Very often when there are more than two items in a compound construction, a comma replaces the conjunction between all items except the last two. This kind of compounding is usually called a series. Although the conjunction usually appears between the last two items of a series, the use of a comma preceding that conjunction is controversial. It is both more logical and more accurate to use the comma, but widespread practice leaves it out. All sentence elements may appear in a series. The following sentences will illustrate a few of them:

Noun subject: *Trains, busses, and boats* serve this area.

Noun objects of prep.: Hurray for *the red, white, and blue.*

Verb: She *argued, scolded, pleaded, and cajoled.*

Adjective: *A red, white, and blue* emblem hung from the ceiling.

Whole sentence: *He called for his pipe, he called for his bowl, and he called for his fiddlers three.*

The expansion of sentence elements by compounding does not really increase the grammatical complexity of a sentence. It merely increases its bulk, as it were. It is like a suit with two or more identical pairs of trousers—or two identical coats—or both. Compounding a complete sentence is like loading a suitcase with two navy blue serge suits, instead of one. But if the second garment were cut on different lines from the first and made of different material, complexity and variety as well as bulk would have been added to the wardrobe. And this is what happens when types of expansion other than compounding are employed. This analogy, of course, cannot be carried too far, for the ways of expanding sentence elements are much more complex than the tailoring of a suit. One of these methods is by the use of 'verbal' structures. The rest of this chapter will be devoted to a study of the verbals.

II

A review of Chapters IV, V, and VIII will serve as a reminder that words ending in *-ing* may function as several different parts of speech: as the third form of the verb, as a noun, and as a participial adjective. But, however they may function as 'parts of speech,' these words are all derived from the basic form of a verb. This is why grammarians call words of this kind verbals. Verbals are quite different from other forms derived from a verb base, such as *arrival, performance, actor,* and *selection;* for the verbal, unlike these other words, does not completely lose its verb characteristics when it is converted to another part of speech. So, in a sense, it partakes of the characteristics of two parts of speech at once. The third-form verbal ending in *-ing,* when it functions as a noun, shows this process most clearly. This form is called a 'gerund.'

In most respects the gerund is like any other noun; it may be accompanied by all the grammatical devices characteristic of that part of speech. In the sentence

Teaching is a rewarding occupation

the gerund *teaching* is the subject of the sentence, and this fact is revealed by its position, just as it is for any other noun. Gerunds may also appear in other normal noun positions to show that they are complements of verbs or objects of prepositions:

> I enjoy *teaching.* (direct object)
> She gave *teaching* her whole heart. (indirect object)

>Her profession was *teaching*. (predicate complement)
>She was devoted to *teaching*. (object of preposition)
>She loved her profession, *teaching*. (appositive)

Under some circumstances this form may be accompanied by an indicator: 'The *teaching* is excellent at our school.' It may also be inflected to show plural number: 'His *teachings* were not believed.' And occasionally it may appear in the genitive case form: 'The *teaching's* effect on the children was doubtful.' Like other nouns, the third-form verbal may be modified by adjectives, either single-word adjectives, prepositional phrases, or attributive nouns:

>*Daily* washing is unnecessary. (single word adjective)
>Washing *by hand* is hard. (prepositional phrase)
>*Dish* washing is dull. (attributive noun)

In all these ways these verbals are like other nouns, but in several respects they are not like nouns at all—even the other verb-like nouns that we have mentioned, such as *arrival* and *performance*. For, in addition to the familiar method of expansion by the use of modifiers, these gerunds may be 'complemented' by one or more nouns or pronouns following them, just as verbs may be. In the following sentences, for example, they have direct objects:

>*Washing dishes* is a dull chore.
>We enjoyed *washing the deck*.

The words *dishes* and *deck* are both objects of *washing*. A third-form verbal noun may also have an indirect object, an objective complement, or a predicate noun or adjective, if the meaning of the verbal allows these constructions:

>Her job was bringing *the men* hot coffee. (indirect object)
>She disliked calling him *Sonny*. (objective complement)
>He liked being *the boss*. (predicate complement)
>She disliked being *homely*. (predicate adjective)

Many gerunds may have, in addition to complements, several other verb characteristics. First, they may have what must be regarded as subjects. The position of a gerund subject is like that of any other subject; it immediately precedes the verbal. But its inflectional form is quite different. In serious writing the subject of a verbal, whether it is a noun or pronoun, is in the genitive case form:

> *His* selling the car was a great mistake.
> We do not approve of *Mary's* dating John.

The problem of the form of the gerund subject is discussed in Chapter XIV, pp. 205-6. In addition to these verb qualities, gerunds, unlike ordinary nouns, may be modified by adverbs. This kind of modification may be seen in the sentence:

> Washing clothes *too quickly* may leave them dirty.

The fact that the gerunds, as well as other verbals, have these verb characteristics explains why we have said that these forms may function as two parts of speech at once. What happens is that verbals, while operating as nouns (or as adjectives, as will be shown later) within the basic sentence structure, retain within their own phrases many of the grammatical meanings and forms of the verb. In fact, they retain all of the grammatical apparatus of the verb except the ability to make a completed statement or ask a completed question.

It is an interesting fact that when a gerund has all these verb characteristics, it cannot have some of the noun devices. Most importantly, when a complement of any kind is expressed, an indicator cannot be used, nor an attributive adjective. A native English speaker never says, 'I do not enjoy *the* washing dishes,' or 'I do not enjoy the *daily* washing dishes.' It also cannot have a plural form: we would never say, 'His teaching*s* the Indians were praised.' If we wish to use these noun devices as well as a verb complement, the complement must be changed into a prepositional phrase, as in *I do not like the endless washing of dishes,* thus substituting a noun device (modification by a prepositional phrase) for a verb device (being followed by a complement). However, even when the gerund phrase has all of the verb characteristics, three noun devices are retained: (1) the possibility of being preceded by a noun or pronoun in the genitive case form; (2) the possibility of being the object of a preposition; and (3) all of the word-order devices of the noun. Word order is, of course, the most important noun device, so that, although some noun devices are lost, the most important characteristic of that part of speech is retained.

III

Actually, it is not literally true that the gerund may operate as both noun and verb at the same time; for when a gerund is expanded in the ways that have been described, it is not the verbal alone that functions as a noun, but the entire word group of which it is a part. This group fits into the basic sentence pattern as a unit, exactly as if it were a single word. No matter how long this type of phrase may be—and sometimes it may be a very long one—it fits into the basic sentence pattern as subject, object, predicate complement, etc., just as any single word does. The fact that the verbal phrase functions as a unit may be demonstrated by marking it off with parentheses:

> (Washing the kitchen floor) is hard work.
> We enjoy (washing the deck of our boat).
> He was proud of (accomplishing his dangerous mission).
> Her greatest pleasure is (painting landscapes in oil).

In each of these sentences, the group of words in the parentheses operates as a unit in some kind of noun function: in the first sentence, the group is a subject, in the second a direct object, in the third an object of a preposition, and in the fourth a predicate complement.

Considered from another point of view, it is clear that the individual words in these groups play their own parts inside the group and that these activities have nothing to do with the role played by a group as a whole. In other words, the group has an internal structure of its own, to which the individual words within the phrase contribute. Some grammarians refer to these elements within a construction as 'constituents.' In modern English, there are many different kinds of internal structures, of which the verbal is only one. Simple modification groups also have internal structures. Within this kind of group, of course, the individual words may operate as adjectives, adverbs, prepositions, and objects of prepositions; the noun modified is often referred to as the 'head word' to avoid the use of the word 'noun,' which might lead to a confusion of the function of this individual word with that of the phrase as a whole. In verbal-noun structures, as we have seen, the complexity of the phrase is also increased by the addition of various kinds of complements, so that its structure takes on verb characteristics as well as those of modification.

What we have in the language, then, is a system of patterns nested within patterns; or, as they are sometimes called, 'structural layers.' The patterns that cannot stand alone may be called the 'internal' patterns, and the larger pattern, within which the internal patterns operate and which comprises the finished sentence, may be called the 'external' pattern. There are also internal patterns within internal patterns. An adjective modifying the object of a preposition is an example of a modification structure within a modification structure, as in *The man in the gray flannel suit*. This nesting of patterns is one of the most remarkable and exciting features of modern English grammar and is obvious everywhere. Perhaps it is because this nesting is so obvious that it is so seldom noticed. Insufficient understanding of this process is probably the reason why so many students who have studied grammar for many years often do not know that internal and external structures must be sorted out before a sentence can be understood grammatically.

In a language which has this system of nesting, one must be continually on the look-out for the boundaries of the internal patterns so that words belonging in that pattern will not be mistaken for elements of the external pattern. In Chapter VIII it was shown how mistakes of this kind could occur with prepositional phrases —how the object of a preposition (part of an internal structure) could be mistaken for a member of an external structure (see pp. 95-6). That is why it was recommended that all prepositional phrases be set off with parentheses as preliminary to clarifying the structure of the sentence. Similarly, with verbal forms, it is a good idea first to see whether the verbal belongs to an internal pattern, then to analyze the words belonging to this internal pattern and set them off from the rest of the sentence. After this is done, the function of the group as a whole within the total sentence can be determined. This preliminary operation will delineate the boundaries of the verbal phrase and minimize the possibility of mistaking, for example, the object of a verbal for part of the basic structure. This is particularly important when the verbal phrase is in the subject position, where one may mistake the object of the verbal for the subject of the main verb. In the sentence

> Washing the boat is fun

the word *boat,* because of its position, might be construed as the subject of the verb *is* (*The boat* is fun). Here, of course, the entire phrase *washing the boat* is the subject.

Sometimes a sentence in which the gerund phrase functions as a predicate noun in the external structure is difficult to distinguish from a simple subject-verb-complement structure in which the verb phrase includes a third form as main verb. The two following sentences illustrate this problem:

> Harold's job was washing the dishes.
> Harold's wife was washing the dishes.

The form of both sentences is obviously the same, so we cannot tell whether *was washing* is the main verb with *dishes* as its object or whether *washing the dishes* is a predicate noun phrase after the simple verb *was.* But a few rearrangements of the parts of these sentences will clarify this difficulty. If *washing* is part of a verb phrase, it may be changed into another verb form: we can say *washed,* for example, or *will wash.* In the second sentence above this can be done, but not in the first. We can say, 'Harold's wife *washed* (or *will wash*) the dishes,' but not 'Harold's job *washed* (or *will wash*) the dishes.' If, on the other hand, *washing the dishes* is a gerund phrase, it can be shifted to the subject territory ('Washing the dishes was Harold's job'), whereas the third form, when part of a completed verb, is not so easily front-shifted: 'Washing the dishes was Harold's wife' is a very awkward inversion.

IV

Thus far in this chapter the discussion has centered on the use of the third-form verbal as a noun in the external structure of the sentence. This form may, of course, also function as an adjective, sometimes called a present participle. The third-form verbal adjective may appear in any of the adjective positions, as the following sentences illustrate:

> *Whistling* girls and crowing hens always come to some bad end. (attributive position)
> A man *whistling* appeared in the window. (appositive position)
> George was heard *whistling*. (predicate position)
> *Whistling*, she picked up the morning paper. (front-shifted position)
> She ran up the steps *whistling*. (end-shifted position)

It is an interesting fact of the language that *whistling girls* has the same form as *washing dishes*. Or, to take a more striking example, *washing powders* has the same form as *washing dishes*. Yet, the vocabulary meanings of the words make it clear that the constituents of *washing powders* are adjective–noun, and those of *washing dishes* are noun (gerund)–noun. Sometimes, however, the vocabulary meanings are such that an *-ing* verbal followed by a noun could be interpreted either way, making the sentence completely ambiguous. One such example is:

Jim liked *racing horses*.

It is impossible to tell from the written words whether Jim liked a certain kind of horse—those that race (verbal adjective structure) —or whether he liked the act of racing these horses (gerund-with-object structure). In the spoken language, however, the distinction can be made quite clear by variations in the pitch of the voice. If the first meaning is intended the pronunciation of *racing* is pitched higher than that of *horses;* if the second is intended this pitch pattern is reversed and the pitch is raised on *horses*. This is one of those many situations where the spoken language is more resourceful in providing grammatical devices which will clarify the meaning. As we have said before, it is important for students of composition to grasp the significance of this fact; for it is not a mere grammatical curiosity, but a real obstacle to clear writing if it is not understood. Too often the inexperienced writer will compose ludicrous or ambiguous sentences because he does not realize that what is clear enough in his mind (where his inner ear 'hears' the words spoken) may not be clear to the reader, who either does not hear the words or hears them differently. All of the following 'boners' result from the fact that the writer was not aware that in the written language a third-form verbal followed by a noun may have two grammatical meanings:

> Henry had a morbid fear of kissing girls. (Was he afraid of girls who kiss or was he afraid to kiss girls?)
> The principal of our school made a rule against petting students. (Did he want teachers to stop petting students, or was he opposed to students who pet?)
> The faculty discussed cheating students.
> Whenever possible, our salesladies avoid boxing gloves.

It should be noted that this kind of ambiguity is resolved when an indicator precedes the verbal. If, for example, *cheating students* were changed to *the cheating students,* the constituents of the word group could only be adjective–noun; for, as we pointed out earlier in this chapter (p. 143), a gerund-complement group never uses an indicator.

Just as the *-ing* verbal noun can be expanded into a phrase, so may the *-ing* verbal adjective be expanded into what is called a 'participial phrase.' The verbal adjective does not have a 'subject' in the sense that the gerund does. (The word modified is the 'notional' subject.) But, like the gerund, the verbal adjective may be modified by all kinds of single-word adverbs and by prepositional phrases, and it may be followed by all kinds of complements. When it is expanded by prepositional phrases and/or complement(s), the third-form verbal modifier usually follows immediately after the noun or pronoun modified. The following sentences will illustrate the nature and position of this type of group adjective:

> The lady, *feeling gratitude for our help,* gave us a dollar.
> I do not know the old lady *scrubbing floors in the hall.*

In the first sentence *gratitude* is the object of the verbal *feeling* and the verbal phrase modifies the subject of the external structure; in the second, *floors* is the object of *scrubbing* and the phrase modifies the direct object in the external structure. In each instance the noun modified is *lady.*

Although this type of phrase usually appears directly after the word modified, it is often front-shifted or end-shifted. The front-shifted participial phrase, like the single-word adjective in that position, precedes the entire subject (including the indicator, if one is present) of the external sentence structure and modifies the subject. The following sentences illustrate this position:

> *Baring his fangs,* the tiger prepared to attack.
> *Briefly outlining the assignment for us,* the professor paced up and down the room.

End-shifted adjective phrases also modify the subject, but should be placed in this position only when no other noun or pronoun which could attract the phrase as a modifier immediately precedes the phrase. The following sentences illustrate the correct use of this position:

> Smith spoke briefly, *telling us the story from his point of view.*
> John cut his foot *mowing the lawn.*
> The old woman fell down, *moaning about the robbery.*

The general rule for the position of a participial phrase is that it must always be close to the word modified, unless there is only one word in the sentence that it could modify either grammatically or notionally. If this rule is not observed, all kinds of ludicrous effects may result. In the following sentence, for example,

> Blowing down the hedgerow, the dog sniffed the cold wind,

the writer intended to express one grammatical idea, but, because of his ignorance of the rules of word order, he used a signal that expresses another. He obviously intended the participial phrase to modify *wind,* but the word order he has used (preceding *dog*) conveys the idea that he wished the phrase to modify *dog*—with utterly ridiculous results! Of course, the sentence should read:

> The dog sniffed the cold wind blowing down the hedgerow.

Following are some other 'boners,' which result from placing participial modifiers so that they seem to modify some word other than the one intended:

> John saw the corpse *swimming in Lake Michigan.*
> Anybody would be arrested by the police *going seventy miles an hour.*
> The old lady wisely gave her money to her nephew, *needing very little of her vast wealth.*
> Martha thought at once of her psychiatrist, *needing mental help.*

This problem is treated more fully in Chapter XV, pp. 249-52.

The internal elements of the third-form participial phrase often observe a different word-order sequence from the one just described. This involves a complete reversal of the order of the three principal components of the phrase. In terms of grammatical meaning, what was 1–2–3 becomes 3–2–1: for example, instead of *the waiter* (word modified) *singing* (verbal adjective) *opera* (object of verbal), we could say, the *opera* (object) *singing* (verbal adjective) *waiter* (word modified). In this new arrangement, the verbal adjective is shifted from the appositive to the attributive position (it no longer follows but now precedes the word modified), and the object of the verbal is also put in an attributive position, in which it is no longer a noun-object but a tertiary modifier. The curious thing about this new structure is that it is so similar in form to the original one. Both *waiter singing opera* and *opera singing waiter* have the pattern: —— ——ing ——. This peculiarity of the language can cause ambiguity and puns. For example, *a man eating fish* could be interpreted variously as a person at the dinner table or as a dangerous denizen of the southern oceans. But this kind of pun is possible mainly because so few grammatical devices are expressed in this particular example. In most word groups of this kind the meaning may be clarified by the use of additional devices.

V

Almost everything that has been said of the third-form verbal as adjective applies equally well to the fourth (or fifth) form. These are the forms which usually end in -ed, -t, or -en, known in traditional grammar as 'past participles.' As single-word adjectives, they may appear in all the positions characteristic of that part of speech. These positions are illustrated by the word *undefeated* in the following sentences:

> Middle State has an *undefeated* team. (attributive)
> Middle State, *undefeated,* goes into its last battle. (appositive)
> The Middle State team remains *undefeated.* (predicate)
> Middle State goes into its last battle *undefeated.* (end-shifted)
> *Undefeated,* Middle State goes into its last battle. (front-shifted)

These fourth-form verbals also may be expanded in substantially the same way as the third-form verbals: they may be modified by adverbs of various kinds and by attributive nouns and prepositional phrases, and they may take a complement. Here is an example of a fourth-form verbal phrase that includes several types of expansion:

> Mr. S., *elected president unanimously three times in five years,* now decided to resign.

These fourth- and fifth-form verbals differ from the -ing form in two basic respects: they express passive, not active, voice, and past, not present, tense. The fact that they are passive in meaning limits to a certain extent the type of complement which may accompany them. Like other passive verb forms, they may be followed by only one type of complement at once: unlike the active third-form verbal, they cannot be followed by both a direct and an indirect object, nor by a direct object and an objective complement. The following sentences illustrate the four types of complements that may follow this type of verbal:

> Given *an inch,* we often take a mile. (object)
> Elected *president* three times, John wanted to retire. (objective complement)
> We liked her hair cut *short.* (predicate adjective)
> Turned *traitor,* he must now face the firing squad. (predicate noun)

There is still another way to expand all kinds of verbals. In this type of expansion, the verbal forms themselves are multiplied by the use of the auxiliary verbs *have* or *be,* or a combination of both; the first auxiliary is a third-form verbal and the others fourth- or fifth-form. This kind of expanded verbal expresses a variety of different grammatical meanings, as the following examples will show:

> Present perfect verbal: Having washed
> Present passive verbal: Being washed
> Perfect passive verbal: Having been washed
> Present perfect progressive verbal: Having been washing

The last form operates only as an adjective; the first three operate as either adjectives or nouns in the external structure. These two different uses may be seen in the following sentences:

Having accomplished his mission was a great relief to Mr. S. (noun)
Having accomplished his mission, Mr. S. was greatly relieved. (adjective)

We know that the italicized phrase in the first sentence is the subject of the verb *was* because of its position immediately preceding that verb; and that it is an adjective in the second sentence, modifying the noun *Mr. S.,* because of its position preceding this noun. The two contrasting uses may also be seen in the two sentences:

> Mrs. Jones was proud of *having been praised by the critics.*
> Mrs. Jones, *having been praised by the critics,* was very proud.

In the first sentence the phrase is a noun functioning as object of the preposition *of* by virtue of its position immediately following that word; in the second the phrase is an adjective by virtue of its position following the noun *Mrs. Jones.* As the sentences above show, these forms may also be expanded by complements, single modifiers, and modifying phrases.

The most serious practical problem that arises in connection with the use of third-, fourth-, and fifth-form verbals is the tendency on the part of many people to use them in sentences as if they were 'completed' verbs—sometimes called 'finite' verbs. Verbals have many verb characteristics, but there is one they do not have: they cannot make a completed sentence. To put it another way, they never provide the verb element in an external sentence pattern; they may operate only in an internal structure, and this kind of structure can be used only if an additional verb element—a completed verb—is provided to round out the sentence. Despite their similarity in form, there is an absolute line of demarcation, grammatically speaking, between verbal and verb. And this difference must be understood in order to avoid one of the most common and most serious errors made by students of composition—the punctuating of a verbal phrase as if it were a complete sentence. (See Chapter XV, p. 261, for further discussion of this problem.) Many people have a kind of 'sentence sense' that tells them right away that 'singing in the rain' and 'loved by her neighbors,' for example, are not complete sentences. However, judging by the great number of 'sentence fragments' of this kind that appear in student themes, not everyone has this sense. A more dependable procedure for distinguishing a verbal from a completed verb must be based on an understanding of the formal difference between these two types of words.

This distinction is easily made with the third-form verbal, for a difference in form distinguishes it absolutely from any completed verb. No simple third form (unaccompanied by auxiliary verbs) may ever function as a completed verb. Verbal phrases such as the following, then, should never be mistaken for complete sentences:

> *Pushing* the heavy door with all his might . . .
> His *taking* the dog on the trip with him . . .

Similarly, no verb phrase that begins with a third-form auxiliary may ever be a completed verb. These phrases also should not be mistaken for complete sentences:

> John *having pushed* the door with all his might . . .
> The door *having been pushed* as hard as possible . . .
> His *being named* head of the party . . .
> She *having been sewing* on the dress all day . . .

When a verb phrase is introduced by any form of the auxiliary other than the third form, it becomes a completed verb. Notice how different the following word groups are from those above:

> John *had pushed* the door with all his might. (fourth form)
> The door *has been pushed* as far as possible. (second form)
> He *was named* head of the party. (fourth form)
> They *have been sewing* on the dress all day. (first form)

Fifth-form verbals are also easy to distinguish from completed verbs. In standard English, such forms as *done, gone, seen,* and *driven* are never used as completed verbs, unless they are expanded by auxiliary verbs.

The fourth-form verbal is more difficult to distinguish from one type of the completed verb, for all regular verbs use the same form to express the simple past tense and the past participle (*-ed, -d,* or *-t*). These two uses can be seen in the following pairs of contrasting sentences:

Fourth Form as Completed Verb	Fourth Form as Verbal Adjective
He *polished* the brass.	The *polished* brass was beautiful.
The police *wanted* the murderer.	*Wanted* for murder, Scarface fled the country.
They *called* the man Scarface.	There is the man *called* Scarface.
It *required* ten dollars.	The amount *required* came to ten dollars.

When this verbal form appears in the attributive adjective position, as in the second sentence of the first pair ('*polished* brass'), its function as an adjective is immediately apparent. The completed verb in this sentence is, of course, *was*. It is also not difficult to see that *Wanted* in the second sentence in the second pair ('*Wanted* for murder') is a verbal, since no completed verb ever appears in the initial position in a declarative sentence.

The real difficulty arises when this verbal form appears in one of the middle positions, for this is the home territory of the completed verb. Sometimes when this happens the structure of the entire sentence must be grasped before one can decide whether the form in question is a completed verb or a verbal. The last two sentences in the right-hand column illustrate this problem. It is usually the discovery of another verb form which is clearly a completed verb that solves the problem. In these sentences *is* and *came* are clearly verb forms of this type. However, sometimes neither verb form is clearly one type or the other. For example, in the sentence

The tax required increased work

both *required* and *increased* could be either fourth-form verbals or past-tense completed verbs. Therefore, the sentence is ambiguous—for the same reason that other sentences we have discussed are ambiguous: an insufficient number of grammatical devices has been provided by the writer to make the meaning clear. In this sentence, both of the words in question have the same inflectional form and occupy the same middle position in the sentence, and neither has a function word connected with it. The whole problem could have been cleared up if the writer had supplied just one function word:

The tax has required increased work (or)
The tax required has increased the work.

In the first sentence the function word *has* indicates that *required* is the completed verb; and, in the second sentence, the same device in another position shows that the completed verb is *increased*.

Because the simple past tense and the fourth-form verbal have the same form, it is generally unwise for a writer to use a fourth-form verbal in a completed verb position, as in the sentence:

The students *needed* to complete the experiment were chosen from the psychology class.

Needed in this sentence is a verbal adjective modifying *students,* but it is in a position which is a normal one for the completed verb, and because the basic subject-verb-object pattern is so powerful in communicating meaning, the reader will automatically interpret *The students needed to complete the experiment* . . . as a subject-verb-object sequence. And there is nothing in the sentence to help him discover his error until he reaches the actual verb *were chosen.* Then, of course, he must reread the sentence and revise his first interpretation, but this takes time and energy and gives him a bad impression of the writer's ability. This is another example of a type of sentence which is clear when spoken but confusing when written. The fact that *needed* is intended as a 'subordinate' element may be clarified in writing by using an additional grammatical device before *needed* and by changing this word into a completed verb form: 'The students *that were needed* . . .'

Something must now be said about a kind of third-, fourth-, or fifth-form verbal phrase that operates in the sentence somewhat differently from those considered so far. The verbal phrases discussed in the preceding pages function in the external sentence pattern as nouns or modifiers of nouns. This other type is a participial phrase but it performs in a different and less essential way in the external pattern. The participle plus the word it modifies is usually called an 'absolute' construction, because it is comparatively independent (absolute) of the basic structure. A few examples will illustrate this kind of phrase:

> *The rain being over,* the game continued.
> *Robert offering no objections,* we went ahead with our plans.
> *The game concluded,* we all rushed over to the gym.

Each of the italicized constructions is unnecessary in the external structure, as anyone can check by reading the sentences without the italicized phrases. But each of these parts does have a logical connection with the rest of the sentence, for each poses a kind of condition under which the sentence operates. In this sense, the so-called absolute construction is not really independent of the sentence at all. We would not, for example, say or write:

The rain being over, tomorrow is Tuesday,

for there is no logical relationship between the parts of the sentence. Actually, absolute constructions are much like movable adverbial modifiers, as can be seen when adverbial prepositional phrases are substituted for the absolute constructions in the sentences above:

> *After the rain,* the game continued.
> *With no objections from Robert,* we went ahead with our plans.
> *After the game,* we all rushed over to the gym.

Like these adverbial modifiers, absolute constructions can be freely moved around in the sentence. One example will illustrate this point:

> *Robert offering no objections,* we went ahead with our plans.
> We, *Robert offering no objections,* went ahead with our plans.
> We went ahead, *Robert offering no objections,* with our plans.
> We went ahead with our plans, *Robert offering no objections.*

VI

No discussion of the verbal is complete without a description of the form known traditionally as the 'infinitive.' In modern English the infinitive is composed of the first form of the verb, usually preceded by the function word *to,* as in

> I wanted *to laugh;* her tendency *to cry* was distressing.

The word *to* may be regarded as an infinitive indicator, provided that the difference between this *to* and the preposition *to* is understood. In modern English the functions of these two words are quite unlike. For example, in the two following sentences the grammatical meanings of *to work* are very different:

> He went *to work.*
> He hated *to work.*

In the first, it is a prepositional phrase, with *work* as object of *to;* in the second, it is an infinitive. In the first, *work* is a noun; in the second, it is a verbal form. One way to determine whether a word group of this kind is a prepositional phrase or an infinitive is to decide whether the word following *to* is a noun or a verbal. When, as in the sentences above, not enough grammatical devices are expressed to indicate which is which, the indicator test may be useful. If the meaning of the word allows an indicator, the word group is a prepositional phrase. In the following pairs of sentences, those on the left allow the indicator and those on the right do not:

Prepositional Phrases	Infinitives
He went *to* (the) *town*.	He liked *to* (the) *dance*.
He walked *to* (the) *school*.	He walked *to* (the) *strengthen* himself.
He came *to* (the) *church*.	He came *to* (the) *apologize*.

A more dependable way, perhaps, of distinguishing between these *to's* is to understand the difference between the two meanings of this word: the infinitive indicator is a pure function word, for it has no meaning apart from its grammatical one; the preposition *to* has a large content of vocabulary meaning, defined in most dictionaries as 'expressing the relation of direction.' If the word *to* does not have this kind of meaning, one can be sure that it is an indicator of an infinitive.

The infinitive may function as a noun, an adjective, or an adverb within the external structure of the sentence. The following sentences illustrate the various uses of the infinitive as noun:

Subject:	*To err* is human.
Direct object:	He wanted *to go*.
Predicate complement:	His aim is *to win*.
Object of preposition:	He had no thought except *to win*.
Appositive:	Her ambition—*to act*—was never told.
End-shifted subject:	It is human *to err*.

This last use of the noun infinitive, the end-shifted subject, is one of the most common and requires special comment. An infinitive in the normal subject position is rather rare in modern English. The eighteenth-century poet, Alexander Pope, could write, 'To err is human,' but today one would more likely write, 'It is human to err.' This change involves moving the infinitive to the end of the sentence and replacing it in the subject territory with the 'dummy' word *it*. This use of *it* is comparable to the use of *there* in this same position. The purpose of both these words seems to be to maintain the basic subject-verb pattern of the declarative sentence; if the subject territory were left vacant, one of the basic rules of modern English would be violated: namely, that a declarative sentence may never begin with a verb.

When used as a modifier, an infinitive usually follows the word modified. In the following sentences the infinitives modify nouns:

> The man *to elect* is George.
> It's time *to retire*.

Here they modify adjectives:

> I will be happy *to stay*.
> Lovely *to see*, the garden lay behind the house.

They may also modify verbs:

> She played *to win*.
> We work *to live*.

Sometimes, when infinitives modify verbs, they may be placed after the complement:

> She played the game *to win*.

It might be said that in this sentence the adverbial infinitive phrase modifies the entire predicate *played the game*, or even the whole sentence. Sometimes, when an adverbial infinitive definitely modifies the entire sentence, it may be front-shifted to a position before the subject:

> *To live*, one has to work.

The internal composition of the expanded infinitive phrase is similar to that of the other verbals. It may be modified by both single-word adverbs and prepositional phrases, as in

> She was told *to go immediately to bed*.

In this sentence the infinitive *to go* is expanded by the use of the adverb *immediately* and the adverbial prepositional phrase *to bed*. Infinitives may also take all the possible kinds of complements— objects, both direct and indirect, objective complements, and predicate nouns and adjectives. The following sentences illustrate some of these types of expansion:

> They decided *to give us the money.*
> They decided *to call the baby John.*
> He decided *to become a doctor.*
> We all want *to be happy.*

The infinitive phrase may also have a subject. This subject precedes the infinitive indicator. If it is a noun, it is uninflected; but if it is a personal pronoun, it is in the objective case form. Infinitive phrases with subjects appear most frequently in the complement territory of the external structure and are a very familiar form of expression:

> Do you want *me to go?*
> He didn't want *us to overhear the conversation.*
> We asked *Mrs. Smith to sing.*

It is possible for an infinitive with an expressed subject of its own to appear in the subject position of the outer structure; but, when this happens, the whole phrase must be preceded by the function word *for:*

> *For her to sing tonight* would be wrong.

Under certain circumstances, some infinitives that include a subject do not use the infinitive indicator *to*. This occurs when the phrase is a direct object of certain verbs—those whose vocabulary meanings involve the senses of sight, feeling, hearing, and a few others. The particular verbs that may be followed by this type of infinitive are *see, hear, feel, watch, listen to, let, make,* and sometimes *help* and *have.* The following sentences illustrate this type of construction. The infinitive phrases are in italics:

I saw *him cross the street.*

I have never heard *her sing.*

I felt *the wounded man move.*

I watched *the prowler sneak out of the room.*

I listened to *Mary play the first sonata.*

I let *the maid go.*

You can make *us work,* but you cannot make *us like it.*

My friend helped *me pass the exam.*

We had *him play a song.*

Because this structure is so lacking in expressed grammatical devices—so 'stripped down,' as it were—there is always a possibility of confusing it with several other structures and of creating a number of ludicrous puns. All of us have heard the joke: 'Have you ever seen a horse fly?' This joke is possible because the last two words could be interpreted grammatically as either a simple adjective-noun structure of modification, with *horse* modifying *fly,* or as an infinitive structure with *fly* as the first-form verbal and *horse* as its subject. Sometimes the form of the infinitive phrase without *to* is identical with that of the subject-verb part of the external structure. This possibility is seen in the sentence

The soldiers hear the children cry.

The soldiers hear (subject–verb of external structure) has precisely the same form as *the children cry* (subject-verbal infinitive phrase). Each group could be a complete sentence, if the words were punctuated differently. It is word order, and this device alone, that provides the information needed to identify the second set of words as a verbal phrase—for this type of phrase, without the infinitive indicator, may function only as a direct object of certain verbs, and therefore must follow one of these verbs.

When the indicator *to* is expressed, any infinitive, like any other verbal, may be expanded by the use of auxiliary verbs. A 'perfect' infinitive, expressing past time, is formed with the auxiliary verb *have:*

It was foolish *to have given* money to that boy.

The man *to have seen* was Mr. Smith.

A passive infinitive is formed with the auxiliary *be:*

> The suspect asked *to be interviewed.*
> This is really a question *to be asked.*

Finally, a perfect passive infinitive is formed with both *have* and *be:*

> It was foolish *to have been frightened* by a mouse.
> *To have been ignored* three times was a disgrace.

With all these different ways of expanding the infinitive, this kind of internal word group may at times become very long and involved. It may even have other verbals and other infinitives nested within it. The following sentence shows how a complicated phrase of this kind may be constructed:

> It was foolish (to have given all that information before going to talk to the police).

All the words within the parentheses are part of a greatly expanded infinitive phrase, operating in the external structure as subject of the verb *was.* Within this phrase, the verbal is, of course, the perfect infinitive *to have given; information* is the direct object of this verbal; then comes a prepositional phrase with the gerund *going* as object of the preposition *before.* But the gerund has been expanded with the infinitive phrase, *to talk to the police,* which itself has been expanded with the prepositional phrase *to the police.* What we have, then, in this sentence is a prepositional phrase nested within an infinitive phrase, which is nested within a gerund phrase, which is in its turn nested within another infinitive phrase, which in its turn is nested within the external sentence pattern. Quite literally, we have wheels within wheels, within wheels, within wheels, within wheels. It is important to make sure at this point that this process is fully understood, for the next chapter will show how word groups may be nested within each other in more complex and curious ways than even the materials in this chapter would lead one to suspect.

XII

COMPLEXES MORE COMPLEX

In the preceding chapter we examined the many ways in which simple structures could be expanded into sentences of greater grammatical complexity. Yet, as 'complex' as these sentences were, every one of them retained the basic sentence pattern. Indeed, they were all what grammarians call 'simple' sentences, even though they were by no means simple communications; for by 'simple sentence' grammarians mean a sentence which has only one subject-verb combination. Almost all of the illustrative sentences used so far in this book have been simple sentences in terms of their grammatical structure.

I

'Charles and Alice danced and sang' is a simple sentence, but 'Charles danced and Alice sang' is structurally different. Only *Charles* and *danced* combine and only *Alice* and *sang* combine: obviously Charles did not sing and Alice did not dance—or at least the sentence does not say that they did. Here, then, are two subject-verb combinations—or, in more familiar terminology, two clauses. This is what grammarians call a 'compound' sentence: two (or more) clauses joined by a co-ordinating conjunction or by co-ordinating punctuation marks (the colon or the semicolon). Clauses that are joined in this way are called 'independent' clauses. The sentence 'Charles danced *when* Alice sang' also contains two clauses with the same subject-verb combinations as the foregoing example. But the connective between these two clauses—*when*—is a 'subordinating conjunction' and the second clause, *when Alice sang,* is called a 'dependent clause.'

The distinction between independent and dependent clauses is obscure to many people; and, since the whole problem of grammatical dependence is important, it must be discussed at some length. First, the difference between simple and compound and complex sentences is not one of length. Of the three examples above, the simple sentence is the longest:

> Simple: Charles and Alice danced and sang.
> Compound: Charles danced and Alice sang.
> Complex: Charles danced when Alice sang.

The difference is one of structure—a difference not only in the number of clauses but also in their structural arrangement. The number of clauses distinguishes the simple sentence from compound and complex sentences; the structural arrangement of clauses distinguishes the compound from the complex sentence. And it is to this problem of structural arrangement that we must now turn in a discussion of grammatical 'dependence' or 'subordination.'

Because grammatical 'dependence' is widely misunderstood, it may be profitable to discover, first of all, what it is not. For several reasons, it is not logical dependence. In the first place, practically all communication is logically dependent, if it is at all coherent: it depends upon other things said or written, or upon a clearly understood state of affairs. *He did it* is an independent clause; it is a sentence; and no grammarian would call it grammatically dependent. And yet, unless we know who *he* is and what *did* and *it* refer to, we can make very little out of the sentence. It depends, logically, upon other sentences, or upon a clearly understood situation. Even pure exclamations ('Ouch!' 'Heavens!' 'Hooray!')—which may be used independently of other words—are dependent upon surrounding circumstances for their full meaning. Dependence in this logical sense, therefore, is not what grammarians mean by the term.

Moreover, the distinction between 'dependent' and 'independent' in grammar cannot be very successfully demonstrated in terms of vocabulary meaning. In such terms, these two expressions are equivalent:

> then he left the house,
>
> when he left the house.

Both consist of a subject-verb-object combination headed by a time word indicating a connection with some other idea (both *then* and *when* suggest that some time is understood). Yet, the former of these expressions is grammatically independent, the latter dependent, and not because of their 'meaning,' but because we accept *then* as signaling a complete unit of communication and *when* as signaling only a portion of a unit. 'Then he left the house,' by a long-established convention of English-speaking people, is not taken as a portion of a larger pattern; we take it as a full pattern itself. But 'when he left the house' is understood as being included in a larger pattern. The punctuation of the following pairs indicates this difference, and if they are spoken aloud, in normal conversational voice, we can hear distinct differences:

> The clock struck midnight. Then he left the house.
>
> The clock struck midnight when he left the house.

In the former, the voice pitch drops low after *midnight,* and there is a noticeable pause. In the latter, the voice drop after *midnight* is not so low and the pause is much less noticeable.

This distinction between what is included in a larger pattern and what is free or absolute permeates all grammar. Grammatical dependence has been illustrated repeatedly throughout this book in our discussions of word-order patterns. Even primary sentence elements depend upon one another: in *John kissed Mary,* each word depends on the other two in that each is included in a pattern larger than itself, a pattern which we all know and expect. Likewise, secondary and tertiary elements—'modifiers'—depend upon the primary ones: in 'the little girl,' *little* depends upon *girl,* and in 'the very little girl,' *very* depends upon *little.* This is obviously true of phrasal modifiers as well: in 'the manager, deceived for a moment,' *deceived for a moment* depends upon *manager;* and in 'searched through his desk,' *through his desk* depends upon *searched.* That is, in each of these instances the words or phrases in question are part of a larger structural pattern.

Like phrases, dependent clauses are nested in a larger pattern. They differ from phrases in that they have a different inner structure. Notably, they are clauses—they contain subject and completed verb combinations. But they are like other nested structures in that they fit into a larger sentence pattern as a unit. By a complex sentence, in short, is meant a sentence in which one or more clauses are nested in another clause.

The outer structure in which a dependent clause nests is not always 'independent,' as students often assume, for it may be nested in still another outer framework to form a series of structural layers. In the following sentence, the underlined words are nested as a clause within the italicized group, which is in turn nested in the completed sentence:

> They knew *that I did not have the money* <u>*which the trip required.*</u>

There also may be clauses within clauses within clauses like the nine circles of Hell in Dante's *Inferno.* Three dependent clauses are nested in this way in the following brief sentence:

> John told friends *that he didn't believe* <u>*Clara knew (what he was doing).*</u>

II

Like verbal phrases, dependent clauses may be substituted in sentence patterns only as nouns, adjectives, and adverbs. Noun clauses may operate in any one of the eight noun functions: subject, predicate noun, direct object, indirect object, objective complement, object of preposition, appositive, and subject of the infinitive. These functions are indicated by exactly the same word-order patterns as are single-word nouns. The following sentences illustrate all of these types of noun clauses:

What he told us changed all our plans. (subject)

This gift is *what you deserve.* (predicate noun)

He reported *that John had won the fight.* (direct object)

He gave *whatever he did* his full attention. (indirect object)

We called our new game *what the children suggested.* (objective complement)

We gave the books to *whoever wanted them.* (object of preposition)

His decision, *that he would take the job,* was forced upon him. (appositive)

I want *whoever is causing the trouble* to leave. (subject of infinitive)

Like the infinitive, the noun clause functioning as the subject may also appear in a back-shifted position, provided that its normal position has been filled by the 'dummy' pronoun *it:*

> It has not been decided *who will lead the way.*
> It has been rumored *that Jones will retire.*

Moreover, noun clauses may be compounded in these functions just as simple nouns may: 'He reported *that we had fought, that John had won,* and *that we had later parted friends'* is an example of a compound direct object of *reported,* which is grammatically equivalent to its simple noun counterpart: 'He reported our *fight,* John's *victory,* and our *reconciliation.'*

Clauses functioning as adjectives are usually found in the appositive position after the nouns they modify—either immediately after them, as in the following sentences:

> The man *who bought these flowers* was very generous,
> The answer *which she gave* left us unconvinced,
> This is the place *where the body was found,*

or following another modifier:

> The only business remaining, *which we must consider,* is our budget.

Of course, rather often in speech and altogether too often in careless writing, the adjective clause does not follow the noun it modifies; and the result is often either ambiguous or ridiculous. The practical problem of placing clausal modifiers is treated at length in Chapter XV, pp. 253-5.

Adverbial clauses may be found wherever single word adverbs are found. They appear in fixed positions after the word modified, provided that the modification is directed specifically toward that word. The clauses in the following sentences clearly modify verbs (*ran* and *should do*):

> He ran *as he never ran before.*
> John should do *as he is told.*

In the next sentences, the clauses clearly modify adjectives (*Leaving* and *enough*):

> Leaving *before we got up,* Henry had a head start.
> He had money enough *so that he didn't have to worry.*

And, in this sentence, the clause specifically modifies another adverb (*faster*):

> He responded to the treatments faster *than I thought he would.*

But many adverbial clauses do not so clearly and unmistakably modify a single word; many suggest conditions of time or place, causes, results, purposes, concessions, and other relations to the sentence as a whole. Such clauses tend to be movable in the over-all sentence structure:

> *If it is good,* the play will be produced on Broadway.
> The play, *if it is good,* will be produced on Broadway.
> The play will, *if it is good,* be produced on Broadway.
> The play will be produced, *if it is good,* on Broadway.
> The play will be produced on Broadway, *if it is good.*

III

Obviously the word order is important in determining the functions of clauses, just as it is when single words are involved. But clauses, unlike most single words, usually employ a function word in addition. We have seen many of them in the examples already given, such as *that, what, who,* and *when.* Like the preposition, this type of function word may be broadly classified as a 'connective,' since it is the grammatical device by which one clause is joined to another. Unfortunately for the student, but for good reasons, grammarians have not agreed on a single part-of-speech name for words that perform this function. Some are called conjunctions, some pronouns, and some adjectives or adverbs, depending, as we shall see, on the role they do, or do not, play in the internal structure of the dependent clause.

These connectives are of two general types. Connectives of the first type, usually called subordinating conjunctions, are as follows:

after	because
although	before
as, as though, as if	even though, even if
for	since
if	so, so that
inasmuch as	that
in case	though
in order that	unless
in that	until
lest	when
like [1]	where
now that	whereas
once	whether . . . or not
provided that	while

Like prepositions, most subordinating conjunctions are 'impure' function words. That is, they have considerable vocabulary meaning in addition to the work they do as grammatical words. They not only serve as connectives between clauses, but they indicate specifically the nature of that connection. For example, *because* in the list above indicates a causal relationship, *if* indicates a conditional one, *in order that* indicates a purposive one, and *when* indicates

[1] After a long grammatical battle, the argument against the use of *like* as a conjunction has nearly subsided, but not completely. For generations, this use of *like* ('She cooks like her mother did') has been banned in nearly all grammar books; yet this usage has persisted—and not only among uneducated people. Certainly there are no historical grounds for condemning it; and in a language that so freely indulges in functional shift, there can be no theoretical basis for the ban. Yet 'Winston tastes good like a cigarette should' is still frowned upon by many people.

one of time. In all, these connectives of the first type express nine kinds of relationship: cause, comparison, concession, degree, manner, place, purpose, result, and time.

As grammatical devices, the function of these words is rather limited: they are merely connectives. They have no grammatical function other than to serve as a link or bridge between two clauses and indicate that the clause following is to be regarded as subordinate to the other one. In sentences using this kind of connective, each clause is a complete and distinct sentence structure and, as such, could stand alone as an utterance if the connective were omitted. This may be shown by dropping the connective *since* in the following sentence:

> We can't take the trip (since) the check didn't come.

Obviously the word groups on each side of the connective are full sentence structures, and their 'completeness' is not damaged in any way by dropping the conjunction. In fact, in sentences of this kind the conjunction sometimes is omitted if the logical relationship between the clauses is clear from the context:

> We can't take the trip; the check didn't come.

Like the compound sentence, this type of complex sentence has a structure that is extremely transparent. Both clauses have the same word-order scheme as the simple sentence. The external clause may have the declarative, interrogative, or imperative pattern; but the dependent clause usually follows the normal pattern of the declarative sentence: subject–verb–(complement).

Dependent clauses introduced by this first type of connective almost always have an adverbial function, and, like other adverbs, they often come at the beginning or the end of the sentence. In these positions, they seldom present problems in analysis, since the two clauses are intact and distinctly marked. However, the dependent clause may come inside, so that the external structure is interrupted, just as that structure may be interrupted by any adverb, whether it is a single word, a phrase, or a clause:

The play *presumably* will be produced on Broadway.

The play, *in the meantime,* will be produced on Broadway.

The play, *since it is good,* will be produced on Broadway.

Although the outer structure is interrupted by the adverbial element, its normal word order has not been changed. The subject is first (*the play*), followed by the dependent clause (*since it is good*), then comes the main verb (*will be produced*), just as we would expect in any declarative sentence. The dependent clause, of course, is NEVER broken up by any element of the external structure.

Several of the words in the list of type-one connectives have already been discussed as other parts of speech—as prepositions or adverbs or as both. These three different functions may be distinguished, of course, by the fact that the adverb functions as a single word; the preposition introduces a noun to form an adverbial phrase; the subordinating conjunction introduces a dependent adverbial clause. The word *since* in the following sentences illustrates each of these functions:

I have never seen her *since.* (adverb)

I haven't seen her *since* Monday. (preposition)

I haven't seen her *since* she won the prize. (subordinating conjunction)

Sometimes the words in this first group of connectives may also be used to introduce a single-word adjective or an adjective phrase into the sentence, thus expressing more precisely the relationship between the adjective and the word it modifies. This construction, called a conjunction-headed phrase, may be seen in the following sentences:

Take ten drops *when* needed.

He is a different person *while* on vacation.

Although making poor grades, I shall try to stay in college.

Such structures often cause difficulty for anyone who does not understand that the words following the conjunctions are adjectives. If they are not recognized as such, the writer may fail to provide a word in the sentence for them to modify, and without such a word, the adjective phrase is left 'dangling' in mid-air, as in the following commonly used sentences:

> He exercises *when* needed.
> He drives downtown *if* rainy.

This problem is treated more fully in Chapter XV, p. 257.

IV

The second group of connectives that may introduce subordinate clauses is as follows:

how, however,[2] no matter how	where, wherever
than	whether
that	which, whichever
what, whatever	who, whoever
when, whenever	why

This group also includes a few compound connectives:

as (or so) . . . as	such . . . that
more (or less) . . . than	the . . . the [3]
so . . . that	

Like connectives of the first type, those in this second group function as connectives between clauses, but they also have other curious and truly 'complex' functions in the sentence, and it is for this reason that the two types are properly separated in our discussion. It is not too much to say that connectives of the second type create a different kind of complex sentence—a more truly 'complex' kind— than the type in which the dependent clause is introduced by group-one connectives.

This second kind of complex sentence differs from the first in that the clauses are more tightly knit together and are more inter-

---

[2] *However* is a subordinating connective only when it is not followed by, and cannot be followed by, a mark of punctuation. It usually precedes an adjective or adverb and functions as a modifier of this part of speech: 'However hard he tried, he couldn't please his teacher;' 'We will solve the problem, *however* difficult it is.' The other use of this word is usually regarded as adverbial: '*However*, we shall solve the problem.'

[3] As in '*The* bigger they are, *the* harder they fall.'

dependent. We observed that if connectives of the first type were dropped, two complete statements resulted:

> We can't take the trip, *since* the check didn't come.
> We can't take the trip; the check didn't come.

But complex sentences utilizing connectives of the second type are radically different, as some examples of even the least complex kind—those involving noun clauses introduced by *that*—will reveal:

> *That we had won* was a surprise to all.
> Harry believed *that Martha had left him.*
> The reason for his failure was *that he didn't study.*

From these examples, it is apparent that some of the connectives of this second type introduce clauses that are indispensable elements in the external structure (the dependent clauses in these sentences function respectively as subject, direct object, and predicate complement); therefore, these structures—the so-called 'independent' clauses—do not form complete utterances without the dependent clausal element: for example, *was a surprise to all* in the first sentence above means nothing without *That we had won.* Furthermore, some connectives of the second type not only introduce clauses which are essential to complete the external structure, but are often themselves essential to the completeness of the inner clause. For example, in the clause *whoever loves,* the connective *whoever* is the subject and obviously the rest of the clause—*loves*—is not a complete utterance without it. Both of these kinds of interdependence between clauses are illustrated in the sentence,

Whoever loves must suffer.

Not only is *whoever* essential to the dependent clause, but the whole dependent clause *Whoever loves* is essential to the other clause. Neither clause, then, is complete in itself: one clause must incorporate the whole of the other into its structure in order to round out its pattern; the other must incorporate the connective. It is because of the lack of independence among the elements of this kind of sentence that it is more accurate to refer to the two parts of the sentence as external and internal structures rather than 'independent' and 'dependent' clauses.

The adjective clause is the most common type of internal clause introduced by connectives of the second type. It is also called a 'relative clause,' and the connectives used are called 'relative pronouns.' These are *who* (and its other forms, *whose* and *whom*), *which*, and *that*.[4] They qualify as second-type connectives because they always function as essential elements in the internal clause. They are called pronouns because they substitute, in this clause, for a noun or another pronoun in the external clause. In other words, like the personal pronouns, they are used to avoid repetition, but unlike this other type of pronoun, they have a connective function as well. The word for which the relative pronoun substitutes is called its 'antecedent.' This process of substitution may be seen in the following sentences:

> The desk *which we selected* has not been practical. (*which* substitutes for *desk*)
>
> The man over there, *who bought the flowers,* is very generous. (*who* substitutes for *man*)
>
> I asked everybody *that we know.* (*that* substitutes for *everybody*)
>
> He is the author *whose book you have been reading.* (*whose* substitutes, in the dependent clause structure, for *author,* which would have to be *author's* here)

In all of these sentences the relative pronoun functions as an essential element in its own clause. In the first sentence, *which* is the object of *selected;* in the second, *who* is the subject of *bought;* in the third, *that* is the object of *know;* and in the fourth, *whose* is a modifier of *book* (the object of *have been reading*). A relative pro-

---

4 This *that* is quite different grammatically from the *that* used as a connective in the noun clauses above (p. 167), and also from the *that* in the list of subordinating connectives of the first type. It is important to keep these three *that's* distinct: (1) The *that* of the first type ('Help us, *that* we may do the right thing') has a distinct vocabulary meaning of 'so that' or 'in order that.' (2) The *that* which introduces noun clauses ('John said *that* he would come') is a 'pure' function word, without vocabulary meaning. Both of these are called subordinating conjunctions. (3) The relative pronoun *that* has a distinct vocabulary meaning as a substitute for its antecedent, and functions as an element in the dependent or inner structure.

noun may also function as the object of a preposition in the dependent clause, as *whom* does in the following sentence:

> The man *of whom I spoke* is here now.

Where, when, and *why* may, in a like manner, be regarded as 'relative adverbs,' when they substitute for words in the outer structure:

> There are times *when* nothing goes right.
> This is the place *where* he left his glasses.
> I do not know the reason *why* he left.

Certainly the use of these words here is very different from their function as connectives of the first type. This is why they are listed in both groups.

Akin to the relative clause, in that its connective plays a similar double function, is the kind of noun clause usually called an 'indirect question.' Such clauses are introduced by many of the same words which signal direct questions. These are illustrated in the following sentences:

> What: *What you do* is no concern of mine.
> Whatever: I like *whatever he plays.*
> Who: We never discovered *who did it.*
> Whom: They didn't know *whom we selected.*
> Whoever: *Whoever carries the cities* will win the election.
> Whether: I don't care *whether he loves me or not.*
> Where: Home is *where the heart is.*
> When: We wondered *when they would go home.*
> How: *How he can do it* is the big question.
> Which: I don't know *which road leads to the cabin.*
> Whose: *Whose toys are lost* remains to be determined.
> Why: Have you heard *why he left town?*

Dependent clauses of this kind are called indirect questions because they suggest questions but do not directly state them. They suggest, 'What do you do?' 'What does he play?' 'Who did it?' 'Whom did we select?' etc. We can see how the interrogative words which serve as connectives in these sentences also serve as essential elements in the structure of the dependent clause. In the first sentence *what* is the direct object of *do;* in the second, *whatever* is the object of *plays;* in the third, *who* is the subject of *did.*

It is obvious from these examples that the word-order pattern of indirect questions differs in one respect from that of direct questions. Compare the following questions, the first put in direct discourse, the second in indirect:

Direct Discourse

He asked, 'Where is John going?'
We wondered, 'How can they do it?'

Indirect Discourse

He asked where John was going.
We wondered how they could do it.

In the direct question, the inversion of the normal subject-verb word order, described in Chapter X, takes place. On the other hand, in the indirect question, the normal declarative word order is observed: 'John was going' rather than 'is John going'; and 'they could do it' rather than 'can they do it.' [5] Indeed, within dependent clauses of all kinds the subject-verb word order is absolutely fixed, except when the word *there* or *it* is used to replace a back-shifted subject, as in 'He asked when there would be a ticket available' (compare: 'when a ticket would be available'); or when inverted word order takes the place of the conjunction *if: He would have called, had he known about the accident.*

In another respect, however, the word order of many dependent clauses introduced by group-two connectives, including all relative clauses and some indirect questions, varies from the normal subject-

[5] The tense of the verb in the dependent clauses also changes: *is* to *was, can* to *could.* This tendency of the verb in the dependent clause, in indirect discourse, to take the tense of the main verb, is called 'attracted tense' or 'sequential tense' by grammarians. It takes place in indirect statements as well as in indirect questions:

Direct Discourse	Indirect Discourse
John replied, 'I will go alone.'	John replied that he would go alone.
Helen said, 'I was not hurt.'	Helen said that she had not been hurt.
Tim predicted, 'They will lose.'	Tim predicted that they would lose.

verb-complement pattern. These variations have to do with the positions of the complement, of some prepositional phrases, and of the subject of the infinitive in clauses introduced by *who, whom, whoever, whomever, which, whichever, what, whatever,* and *that* (when it is a relative pronoun).

When one of these connectives functions as a complement in its own clause, it is shifted to the beginning of the clause. The word order within the clause then becomes: complement–subject–verb. The following sentences illustrate this pattern:

> The man *whom you met* is my uncle. (*whom* is the direct object of *met*)
> *Whatever he does* is wrong. (*whatever* is the direct object of *does*)
> I don't know *who he is.* (*who* is predicate complement of *is*)

The complement is also front-shifted when it is modified by one of these connectives:

> The man *whose house you bought* is leaving town.
> He asked *what train he should take.*

When the connective is the object in a prepositional phrase modifying the complement or when the connective is the modifier of such an object, the whole complement may be front-shifted:

> I recommend this book, *a copy of which you will soon receive.*
> I recommend this author, *a copy of whose book you will soon receive.*

In the first of these sentences, the prepositional phrase alone may be shifted or merely the connective:

> I recommend this book, *of which you will soon receive a copy.*
> I recommend this book, *which you will soon receive a copy of.*

When this type of connective is the subject of an infinitive, it again is shifted to the beginning of the clause:

> The blind boy interviewed the couple *whom he thought to be his parents.*

When it is the object in a prepositional phrase modifying the verb, the entire phrase is often front-shifted:

> The ground *on which we built the house* was sandy.
> The beggar *to whom you gave the dollar* is really rich.

Or the connective alone may be front-shifted, leaving the preposition at the end of the clause:

> The ground *which we built the house on* was sandy.
> The beggar *whom you gave the dollar to* is really rich.

Although some teachers of English disapprove of separating a preposition and its object, this pattern is widely used in speech and writing and by well-educated people. Sir Winston Churchill's reaction to the proscription against it is famous: 'This is a sort of nonsense up with which I will not put!'

Because this type of connective does not always come first in its clause, it is sometimes difficult to tell where the clause begins. The following sentences illustrate what difficulties may arise:

> The question *of which you spoke* is still before us.
> The question of *which girl we should send* is still before us.

In the first sentence, *of* is part of the inner structure; in the second, it is part of the external structure and the entire dependent clause operates as its object. The simplest way to solve this problem is to test the preposition for movability. If it can be moved to the end of the dependent clause, it is part of that clause; for instance, we can say, 'The question *you spoke of* is still before us.' If it cannot be moved, it is part of the basic structure of the outer clause; and the dependent clause is its object: We cannot say, 'The question which girl we should send of' in the second example above.

In order to understand the complicated structure of sentences using connectives of the second type, one important point must be remembered; namely, that the forms and functions of the words in the inner clause have no connection with the functions of any of the words in the external structure. Nor do they have anything to do with the function of the inner clause as a whole in relationship to the external structure. In short, once the inner clause has been identified and set off, its structure must be examined separately without regard to the rest of the sentence. For example, in

Do you know (*who is coming to the party?*)

the form of the inner clause, *who is coming to the party* (*who*, subject; *is coming*, verb; *to the party*, adverb phrase), has no connection with the fact that *who* follows *know*, or that the external clause is a question, or that the dependent clause is nested as a direct object. The analysis of this clause would be the same if, for example, the main clause were a statement instead of a question:

I know (*who is coming to the party*)

or if the clause were nested as subject rather than object in the outer structure, as in the sentence:

(*Who is coming to the party*) is not yet known

or if it were an adjective:

The writer (*who is coming to the party*) is very famous.

This observation concerning the structural separateness of the dependent clause has an important bearing on the practical problem of selecting the acceptable forms of *who* and *whoever*, a baffling problem to many people. We can see from the examples already given that the *who* and *whoever* forms are used when the words function in the inner structure as subjects or predicate complements and that the *whom* and *whomever* forms are used when they function in the inner structure as any kind of object of a verb, object of a preposition, or subject of an infinitive. But many people who know these 'rules' still select the wrong form because they are not sure which verb or preposition determines that form—one in the outer or one in the inner structure; or they do not know how to separate the elements of the two structures. Once they realize that the form of the pronoun depends entirely on its role in the dependent clause and are able to separate that clause from the rest of the sentence, the problem disappears. A simple rule for selecting the forms of these pronouns will be found in Chapter XIV, pp. 227-30.

Another common problem associated with the complex sentence involves an incorrect use of the connective *that*. The following sentences illustrate this error:

> He is the kind of man *that I hate his looks.*
> He is the kind of person *that you can't tell him anything.*

In one respect, the *that's* in these sentences are used correctly as relative pronouns: both have clearly expressed antecedents; but, in another respect, they are not like relative pronouns at all, for neither has a function in its own clause. They are stranded, as it were, outside the structures of the inner clauses, like a child left out of a family picnic. We know that these words can have no function because all the places at the 'picnic table' are filled: each of the dependent clauses already has a full subject-verb-complement(s) pattern, and *that* cannot be a modifier when it is also used as a connective. To correct these sentences, one of the elements in each inner clause must be eliminated so that a place is made for the connective, and *that* must be changed to a form of *who:*

> He is the kind of man whose looks I hate.
> He is the kind of person whom you can't tell anything.

This error probably results from the fact that *that* may operate as both a type-one and a type-two connective, thus leaving the way open to this borderline kind of use in which it is half relative pronoun and half subordinating conjunction. The error may also stem from a fear of using the wrong form of *who.*

v

Another special problem which arises in sentences with connectives of the second type has to do with finding the dependent clause or clauses in the mass of words that often comprises this kind of complex sentence. When the connective is expressed, the problem is usually a simple one, for then there are two clear-cut grammatical devices to serve as signals—the word order and the function word. But a special situation results from the fact that some of these function words are often not expressed. Fortunately, this happens only when the position of the clause in the external structure is absolutely fixed, so that we know exactly where to look for it.

First, these clauses will be found after the verbs *say, feel, see, know, indicate, decide, think, hear, declare, show, prove, tell, hope, fear,* and a few others of similar meaning. The function word which is omitted is the conjunction *that.* Examples of this kind of sentence are:

> Evidence shows (that) the same thing will occur again.
> The elderly man declared (that) the package on the counter was his sister's.
> This proves absolutely (that) he is the culprit.
> I think (that) everyone should hear the story.

These are noun clauses functioning as direct objects of the verbs of 'saying,' etc. Unsignaled clauses of this same kind may also function as subjects, but only if the clauses are end-shifted and follow such expressions as *it is said, it is thought, it was decided,* and *it proves,* as in

> It is thought (that) many people do not like these regulations.
> It is said (that) the trees take ten years to bear fruit.

Examination of the sentence *Evidence shows the same thing will occur again* will reveal how we may go about discovering the point where this kind of unsignaled clause begins. Once the second verb *will occur* has been found, we know that we have a two-clause sentence. We also know that it is a complex, not a compound, sentence, because there is no co-ordinating conjunction between the two parts. Since the subject-verb word order is rigidly fixed in all internal clauses (unless the expletive *there* is used), we may conclude that *same thing* is the subject of *will occur.* In this sentence, then, the components of the inner clause are *the same thing will occur again,* the dividing line between the two clauses coming between *shows* and *the same thing.* We may conclude then that, in complex sentences of this kind in which the conjunction *that* is omitted, the point of division between the two clauses occurs before the noun, or noun group, which comes between the two verbs or verb phrases.

The addition of modifying elements does not qualify this rule in any way. In the second sentence, for example, the prepositional phrase *on the counter* is part of the noun phrase *the package on the counter,* which, because of its position, must be the subject of the verb *was* in the dependent clause.

Under only one condition may two noun constructions come between the two verbs in this kind of complex sentence. This occurs when the verb in the external structure is *tell, inform, show, notify, write,* or *advise;* for these verbs, unlike the others, may take two objects—a noun (or noun phrase) and the noun clause in indirect discourse. For example:

> The nurse told the children their mother was on her way home.
> The doctor advised John his health was failing.

Here, of the nouns between the two verbs, the first (*children, John*) is an indirect object of the main verb; and the second (*mother, health*) is the subject of the verb in the dependent clause. The dividing line between the two clauses comes between the two nouns (or noun phrases)—*children* and *their* and *John* and *his.*

Second, clauses with dropped connectives will be found after adjectives or adverbs that are preceded by the word *so* and after nouns that are preceded by *such* or *such a.* Here again the dropped connective is the conjunction *that,* but the clause itself functions not as a noun but as an adverb. Following are examples of these constructions:

> He was so happy (that) he cried.
> There was such a commotion (that) we could not hear the judge.

Third, clauses with dropped connectives are found in a position following any noun, noun phrase, or pronoun. These are, of course, the relative (adjective) clauses, and the connectives omitted are relative pronouns. The following sentences show the position of this kind of clause in relation to the noun or pronoun preceding it:

> The house (that or which) *we liked best* was sold.
> George finally bought the suit (that or which) *his wife preferred.*

We always choose a woman (that or whom) *we know* to stay with the baby.

This isn't the lot (that) *we looked at.*

This is the best choice (that) *there is.*

The day (when) *we graduated* it rained.

Clauses of this kind may follow nouns or pronouns that function in any way in the external structure, as the sentences above show.

One thing that simplifies the problem of finding the beginning of this kind of clause is the fact that its internal structure always observes a strict subject-verb word order (except when the expletive *there* is used in the subject territory, as in the fifth sentence above). This means that the clause not only follows a noun construction, but also begins with one. The pattern, therefore, that signals an adjective clause with a dropped connective is noun (or noun phrase)–noun (or noun phrase)–verb, without the possibility of any punctuation or co-ordinating conjunction coming between the two noun elements. This pattern may be seen in such examples as *the subject the speaker chose, a man everybody likes, the day the house burned down,* and *somebody I love.* The first noun or pronoun belongs in the external structure, and is the word modified by the clause; the second is the subject in the dependent (internal) clause. Clearly it is word order, and this device alone, that shows us that the unsignaled dependent clauses (*the speaker chose, everybody likes, the house burned down,* and *I love*) are modifiers of the preceding nouns (*subject, man, the day,* and *somebody*). For it is only when this close contact is established between the subject of the dependent clause and the noun modified that the relative pronoun may be omitted. For this reason, clauses of this kind are often called 'contact clauses.'

This word combination—two nouns standing side by side without a connective, yet belonging in different clauses—often creates a real problem for the reader. This is caused by the fact that native English speakers almost automatically read words in bunches, grouping them together according to grammatical structures. For example, when we see such a phrase as *the speeding automobile,* we do not first read *the,* then *speeding,* then *automobile,* but we grasp the whole phrase as a unit with one eye-span. When two nouns come together, we are particularly inclined to read them as if they belonged together structurally, especially when no indicator comes between them, as in the sentence:

> The tree lightning destroyed in 1950 was our prize elm.

The first response of the reader to this sentence might be to interpret *tree* as an attributive noun, modifying *lightning*. In other words, he would think of the two nouns as part of the same structural group, and he would undoubtedly be extremely puzzled, since this reading makes no sense. However, if he understands the nature of structural layers, he will revise his interpretation upon reaching the second verb (*was*); for his first interpretation would be grammatically impossible, since it would leave this verb without a subject. The confusion is doubly confounded when the vocabulary meanings of the two nouns, as well as the omission of the indicator, allow an attributive noun-noun interpretation, as in these sentences:

> The city *people like to visit* is New York.
> The small apartment *houses have supplanted* is obsolete.
> The farm *machinery is used properly on* will make money.

Such sentences may require several readings before the meaning becomes apparent. They may seem far-fetched, but all of them were printed in first-class newspapers, and actually this sort of thing appears frequently both in print and in student themes. The moral is, of course, that the writer who is tempted to compose complex sentences of this kind should remember to use either the connective or the second indicator. Although the sentences above are technically 'correct' without these function words, the burden on the reader is too great when they are omitted. A well-constructed sentence does not have to be read several times, or subjected to grammatical analysis before its meaning can be ferreted out.

A final problem associated with marking off the dependent clause in a complex sentence—determining where the dependent clause ends—is usually not a serious one. The clause ends when its structure is complete, and in careful writing the end of the structure is clearly indicated. But sometimes in careless writing a sentence element, usually a modifier, is placed between the clauses in such a way that it could be interpreted as a part of either clause, as in the sentence

> The prize which he won *at first* seemed worthless.

Of course, in the spoken language the demarcation between the two structures is indicated by a distinct pause and change in the voice pitch, but the writer of the sentence above forgot that this device is not expressed in the written language and that the reader cannot 'hear' what is in the writer's head. These ambiguously placed modifiers are usually called 'squinting modifiers,' because they seem to look in both directions. A few more examples will illustrate this kind of ambiguity:

> The medicine the doctor prescribed *immediately* cured the infection.
> What Mary said *finally* had its calculated effect.
> The course he chose *in the end* didn't greatly matter.

VI

Once the clause is clearly marked off, there remains the problem of determining its function in the external pattern. It would be convenient if the connectives would solve this problem. But unfortunately they do not; *since* may introduce either adjective or adverb clauses; five others (*because, if, whenever, wherever,* and *whether*) may introduce either noun or adverb clauses; two others (*which* and *who* in all its forms) may introduce either noun or adjective clauses. And *that, when,* and *where* may introduce either noun or adjective or adverb clauses, as these illustrations with *when* reveal:

> *When he will come home* is anybody's guess. (the dependent clause is a noun clause, subject of the verb *is* in the external structure)
> There comes a time *when you cannot sleep ten hours.* (the dependent clause is an adjective clause, modifying the end-shifted subject of the external structure, *time*)
> The fire had gone out *when we came home late.* (the dependent clause is an adverb clause, modifying the external structure *The fire had gone out*)

In short, the introductory function word of a dependent clause is not a sure index of the function of the clause. Fortunately, word order and the inner structure of the clause itself usually provide the information needed.

Workable rules for distinguishing the three types of dependent clauses may be briefly put: Adjective clauses (1) must fall in the appositive position after a noun or noun phrase; (2) they must utilize the connecting function word, if one is expressed, as an essential part of the dependent clause structure, and (3) the connective must be a substitute for an antecedent in the external structure. Noun clauses (1) must be placed in noun positions in the general sentence structure, and (2) they may not be moved except as any noun may be moved. In the first sentence above, using the connective *when,* we know that the clause functions as subject in the general structure because of its position immediately preceding the verb. Adverb clauses (1) must be placed in an adverbial position in the sentence pattern (usually, but not always, at the beginning or end of the sentence); (2) they can usually be shifted to the opposite end, and may often be moved to other adverb positions.

These structural 'rules' for discovering the function of the dependent clause will apply in the great majority of instances. However, there are a few types of sentences in which they will not solve the problem. Some noun and adverb clauses with the connective *that,* for example, cannot be distinguished, since they use the same structural devices: that is, they always have the same internal structure and fit into the same position in the general sentence pattern following a noun. This similarity may be seen in the following two sentences. In the first, the clause is a noun, functioning as the object; in the second it is an adverb:

> They told the boy *that he must be prepared for the worst.*
> He stayed on deck *that he might see the maneuvers.*

The movability of the clause in the second sentence provides the only clue that it is grammatically different from the clause in the first sentence. Sometimes, however, the vocabulary meanings of the other words in the sentence are such that we cannot tell whether the clause is movable or not, as in the sentence,

The Captain granted my request, *that I might see my wife.*

The dependent clause here may be either a noun in apposition (the *request,* namely *that I see my wife*) or an adverb (in order *that I might see my wife*). Only the total context of the sentence could clear up this ambiguity.

In at least one situation, adjective and noun clauses introduced by *who* or *whom* also have the same structural devices and thus allow the possibility of ambiguity. The following sentence has two meanings depending upon whether we interpret the dependent clause as a noun or an adjective:

Mary asked the man who was sitting on the stairs.

The position of this clause after a noun, as well as its internal structure, allows it to be interpreted as either part of speech. If the clause is an adjective, then *man* is the antecedent of *who* and he is sitting on the stairs; if it is a noun, the clause is the direct object of *asked* (an indirect question) and we do not know who is sitting on the stairs, but Mary thinks that the 'man' knows. Here again the grammatical meaning of the sentence is amply clear when the sentence is spoken, and is ambiguous only when the grammatical signals of speech are missing. Such ambiguities as these can be avoided only by constant awareness of the grammatical devices and the role they play in communicating meaning.

It is obvious that the complex sentence in English raises a great many enormously complex problems for both the grammarian and the writer. When there are complexities within complexities—with each structural layer enfolding another like the numerous skins of an onion—there is constant danger for the writer of getting parts of the sentence in the wrong place or of having pieces left over, thus causing confusions, ambiguities, and at worst sheer nonsense. And yet, this kind of sentence is the staple of student writing in college and of adult writing in general. From half to three quarters of college students' sentences are of this kind, and nearly all of them use phrasal complexities as well. The complex sentence, therefore, is one 'complex' that no student can afford to be afraid or ignorant of. Until he is able to understand these involved structures, he is not in a position to talk intelligently about his own problems in speaking and writing—to understand the errors he makes or to expect to improve his skills in communication. With such knowledge and understanding, however, he can begin to assume a reasonable command of his native language.

XIII

PAST AND PRESENT

I

Compared with many other languages, English has a relatively short history; but, despite its 'youth,' it is one of the most interesting and exciting languages in western civilization. The main reasons for this are the sensational changes that have taken place in the pronunciation, the vocabulary, and the grammar of English during the last nine hundred years. The entire history of English is usually divided into four periods, whose names and inclusive dates are: Old English (450-1100), Middle English (1100-1500), Early Modern English (1500-1700), and Modern English (1700-today).

Some of these radical changes in English largely account for the present-day difficulties with its grammar. Remnants of the old language have mingled with later innovations. As a result, modern English retains some forms and constructions little changed from Old English along with new forms and constructions unknown in the earliest period of the language. A short sketch of this history of English will give some idea of these changes which have taken place through the centuries and throw light on some of the puzzling and peculiar aspects of the language today.

After the Romans withdrew from England in 410, three Teutonic tribes from the shores of Germany began crossing the Channel in a long series of raids on the southern and eastern coasts of England.

Later in the century they began settling there. These tribes called themselves 'Angles,' 'Saxons,' and 'Jutes,' and it was out of their Germanic dialects that the English language arose—so-called from the name of one of the tribes, the Angles. Thus modern English is linguistically a kind of 'cousin' to modern German (although one would not know it by superficially comparing them). English is similarly related to modern Norwegian, Swedish, Danish, and Icelandic: they are all descended from a parent Germanic language.

Out of this intermingling of dialects Old English (sometimes called Anglo-Saxon) slowly developed; and, by the time of King Alfred the Great (871-901), English had become a national language with an extensive literature of its own in both prose and poetry. Our concern here is with the grammatical history of that language, which in itself reveals such striking changes over the centuries that for us today Old English is virtually a foreign language. An example will show this at a glance:

> Fæder ūre þū þe eart on heofonum, sī þīn nama gehālgod.
> Father our thou who art in heaven, be thy name hallowed.

> Tō becume þīn rīce. Gewurðe ðīn willa on eorðan swā swā on heofonum.
> To become thy kingdom. Be done thy will on earth so as in heaven.

> Ūrne gedæghwāmlīcan hlāf syle ūs tō dæg.
> Our   daily   loaf give us   today.

> And forgyf ūs ūre gyltas, swā swā wē forgyfað ūrum gyltendum.
> And forgive us our guilts, so   as we forgive   our   detractors.

These are the first four lines of The Lord's Prayer in Old English, with a literal translation. Unassisted, we can recognize a number of the words, but most of them look strange with their different vowels and their bewildering variety of inflections. For us today, however, the most important difference is the almost total absence of fixed word order in the sentences. There is, of course, some use of this device; but it is little needed because the function words and especially the large number of inflections convey most of the grammatical meanings.

Old English is what is known as a 'synthetic' language—that is, it synthesizes or gathers into the forms of words the grammatical devices of the language; most of its words have a great variety of these inflectional forms. In the fourth line, for example, the word 'our' in Old English changes form to agree with the form of the word it modifies: 'ūre gyltas,' but 'ūrum gyltendum'; and in the same line the form of 'forgive' changes to accord with the person and number of its subject: 'forgyf,' but 'wē forgyfaỡ.' Modern English, on the other hand, is primarily—but not completely—an 'analytic' language. It analyzes or breaks down into phrases the grammatical information which in a synthetic language is gathered into a word form. Modern English is not completely analytic, however, inasmuch as it does retain many of the inflectional forms—especially those of verbs, nouns, and pronouns.

In 1066 the 'English' were themselves invaded by the Norman French under William the Conqueror. Although the French language, which William imposed upon the English, influenced the English vocabulary tremendously, it affected the grammar of English very little (if at all). Actually, English grammar had been changing steadily even though it was little affected by this foreign influence. By the time Old English had evolved into Middle English, these changes were widespread and striking. Most important were the loss of many inflectional endings and the rise in importance of word order as a grammatical device. A sample sentence from the Middle English of the poet Geoffrey Chaucer (late fourteenth century) shows that by this time most of the inflections had been lost and that word order had become almost as fixed as it is today. Thus from Chaucer's *Tale of Melibeus:* 'A yong man called Melibeus, mighty and riche, bigat up-on his wyf that called was Prudence, a doghter which called was Sophie.'

Other changes in Middle English grammar, though less important, are perhaps equally interesting. One of them was the development of the 'periphrastic genitive.' The Old English speaker said, 'then spoke *their* one'; in Middle English there developed the use of the phrase genitive common to modern English: 'then spoke one *of them.*' Another was the development of the auxiliaries we commonly use to express future tense, *shall* and *will.* In Old English *shall* meant to 'owe or be obliged,' and *will* meant to 'command or desire'; in Middle English the meanings of these words dwindled to the merely future-time signification of our present-day use of them as function words. Similarly in Middle English there developed the common use of the so-called 'perfect tenses'—*have driven, had gone,* and the like—constructions rare or unknown in Old English.

In Early Modern English these changes in forms and syntax continued. For one thing, this period witnessed a remarkable proliferation of verb function words. For instance, *do* as an auxiliary in Chaucer tended to mean to 'make or cause to':

> I wot wel she wol do me slee som day
> Som neighebor
>
> (I know well that she will cause me to slay, some day,
> Some neighbor).

Also negative statements usually did not employ *do* as we always employ it in English today ('Latyn *ne canst thou* yit but small': 'Latin you *do not yet know* very well'). Our present-day use of *do* with verbs—'I *do* not know,' 'he *does* work hard'—we owe largely to the Early Modern English period. The same is true of a number of other function words now employed with verbs: *be about to, be going to, have to, have got to,* and *get* in such expressions as 'I *am about to* leave,' 'we *are going to eat,*' 'you *have to* finish it,' 'they *have got to* remember the rule,' and 'they *got* cheated' all were developed in this period.

In the Modern English period the language has continued to change. What was presumably 'correct' in Shakespeare's day is no longer so in ours. Shakespeare often uses the 'double' comparative and superlative in adjectives ('more larger,' 'the most unkindest cut of all'), which we no longer consider acceptable. He often uses what we would say is the wrong case of pronouns and the wrong number in verbs: 'Is she as tall as *me?*' 'with the hand of *she* here,' 'My old bones *akes,*' 'Then *is* Caesar and he . . .'' etc. And young Milton writes in the opening lines of his elegy *Lycidas:* 'Bitter constraint, and sad occasion dear, *Compels* me to disturb your season due.' No one, we assume, would dare to maintain that these masters of our language did not know their grammar!

Inflectional changes that occurred in the Modern English period include the dropping of most subjunctive forms of the verb. In the Early Modern English King James Bible (1611), for example, we find that many of these forms are retained where we would not use them today: 'If a man *love* me, he will keep my words' (John 14:23); 'Though he *slay* me, yet will I trust him' (Job 13:15); 'That *were* a reproach to us' (Genesis 34:14). Also in Modern English occurred the dropping of the *-eth* and *-est* verb forms: 'The wind bloweth where it listeth' (John 3:8); 'Thou judgest false already' (Shakespeare). And, of course, along with this development went the dropping of the second person singular forms of the personal pronoun, *thou, thee, thy,* and *thine.* Another interesting development was the extension of the use of the pronoun *its;* usually in Early Modern English *his* was used as the possessive form of *it:* 'but if the salt have lost *his savour,'* for instance; the form *its* appears fewer than a score of times in the combined works of Shakespeare and Milton. Yet another interesting development was that of the 'group genitive'—'the *king of England's* daughter' rather than the earlier 'the *king's* daughter of England.' In Modern English the 'double' negative was dropped, as the double comparative was. In earlier periods of the language negatives tended to pile upon one another, as this example from Chaucer, which contains four negatives, illustrates:

> He *never* yet *no* vileyne *ne* sayde
> In al his lyf unto *no* maner wight.

In modern English but one negative would suffice:

> He *never* yet any villainy said
> In all his life to any sort of person.

One important word-order development occurred in modern English: the use of auxiliary verbs in questions. Where Shakespeare wrote, 'Ride you this afternoon?' we now normally would say, '*Do* you ride this afternoon?' or '*Will* you ride this afternoon?' or '*Are* you *going to* ride this afternoon?' Akin to this development is the use in modern English of various new verb forms. One of the most interesting is the increasing use of the so-called 'progressive' constructions. In Shakespeare's *Hamlet,* Polonius asks Hamlet, 'What *do* you *read,* my lord?' We should now almost certainly ask, 'What *are* you *reading?*' The language is not changing as rapidly today as it once did, because the popular media of communication have been an influence toward standardization. But changes still go on, as they must in any living language. One of the most interesting of all recent developments is the increasing use of the attributive noun, so that today we hardly blink at four nouns in a row: 'Indiana limestone ranch house'!

II

During the periods when most of these changes were taking place in the English language, there were either no English grammar books at all or none very widely used. Indeed, until well along in the eighteenth century (the first century of Modern English), the language may be said to have managed without any grammars. English grammar as a serious and widespread study may be dated from the 1760's. The rapid growth in wealth and power of the British middle class during the eighteenth century was accompanied by an increased demand for 'correctness' and propriety in the use of language. And this no doubt contributed to a general attempt to systematize English. Since all of the teachers and scholars then knew much more about Latin than they did about English and English grammar, and since they assumed that the 'rules' of Latin could be imposed upon English grammar, they failed from the start. For English by the eighteenth century had become a radically different kind of language from Latin and from the earlier Old English: it was no longer a synthetic language, but primarily an analytic one, and hence the rules derived from a synthetic language, such as Latin, were inappropriate. Yet, unfortunately, the English 'grammars' of the late eighteenth century became the models upon which most nineteenth-century grammars were written and taught. And these, in turn, have widely influenced nearly all introductory grammars right down to our own day.

One of the most influential of these was Bishop Lowth's *Short Introduction to English Grammar,* first published in 1762, which went through more than twenty editions by 1800 and nobody knows how many more in the nineteenth century. Lowth's book was a 'prescriptive' grammar; that is, in it he assumed that the 'rules' of modern English, like those of classical Latin, could be discovered and set down once and for all and that the speaker or writer had only to look up the 'rule,' follow it, and he would always be using 'correct' English. Among the many usages that Lowth banished from the language were the double negative and such expressions as *had rather, different than, it is me, between you and I,* etc. This kind of prescriptive grammar has never been true to the facts of the language, and its influence has been uniformly bad. Among such bad influences was the widespread assumption that there are permanent 'laws' of English grammar—that there is always a 'right' and a 'wrong' in English usage.

The fact that the rules of our grammar cannot be fixed for all time does not mean that there are no standards. Standards do exist and are extremely important, as we have been saying, describing, and illustrating throughout this book. However, they must be based upon the actual practice (spoken and written) of the users of English today. This usage, of course, varies tremendously. Naturally, a person who has had little education will not speak and write as a college professor speaks and writes. Yet this person's way of using his language is as 'acceptable' in his own environment as is the professor's way in his. There is, therefore, no one absolutely 'correct' way of using modern English: There are instead numerous ways that vary with the conditions in which they are used. For example, at a football game, when the opposition threatens our goal, the cry, 'Admit no further advance!' would be completely improper. In that situation, we would properly shout, 'Hold that line!' And it would be equally inappropriate for a carpenter, after hitting his thumb with a hammer, to speak as young Macaulay did under the same circumstances: 'The agony has abated!'

It is extremely difficult to study these language habits scientifically. Probably the most active and successful practitioner in this field is the American grammarian Charles C. Fries of the University of Michigan. In his *American English Grammar,* published in 1940, Professor Fries based all of his 'rules' and conclusions concerning modern English usage upon a study of about three thousand informal letters that he obtained from the United States government. Of course, the writers of these letters had no idea that this use would be made of them, and the writers 'include business men, electricians, foremen of large shops, superintendents of mills, heads of police departments, undertakers, Red Cross workers, nurses, and non-commissioned officers of the army of the grade of sergeant.' [1] In 1952 Professor Fries published another similar study, *The Structure of English,* based upon the tape recording of conversations amounting to more than 250,000 words. The enormous difference between this kind of scientific, factual approach and the prescriptive, authoritarian method of Bishop Lowth in 1762 is clear.

Although there are many varieties of modern English usage, we may, broadly speaking, divide them into two kinds: non-standard English and standard English. Non-standard English is not 'vulgar' or 'inferior' English: it is rather the English used by the populace in general; it is the English spoken and written by the masses. Between the grammar of standard English and that of non-standard English the line is clearly drawn; the one can never be mistaken for the other. Certain definite usages set non-standard English apart: for example, the use of *ain't;* the confusion of the fourth and fifth forms of the irregular verbs (*I seen, he has wrote,* etc.); frequent confusion between the first and second forms of all verbs (*they was, he don't, the faucets leaks*); use of objective case forms of pronouns in subject positions (*Him and John just left*); and use of the double negative (*I don't want none*). The following sentence

[1] Charles Carpenter Fries, *American English Grammar* (New York, 1940), p. 31.

is clearly non-standard and would never be taken by anyone, probably even the speaker himself, as standard English:

> Them guys all gits back to their respectable bases when he clomb the fence and catched that fly.

All these characteristics set non-standard English apart, but we should remember that this kind of English is as satisfactory and acceptable for its users as is standard English for its. When a man says, 'I ain't got no more of them apples' or 'I seen him,' it should be emphasized, there is no ambiguity or failure of communication.

Within standard English, upon which this book is based, there are at least three sub-varieties: formal English, informal English, and shoptalk or technical English. Formal English, as the name implies, is that which is used by people of education on certain special occasions and in certain kinds of writing in which various kinds of 'formality' are expected. This English is usually more impersonal than informal English; it uses a larger and more precise vocabulary, more polysyllabic words, and a more complex and rhetorical sentence structure. It is more careful in the use of grammatical forms and avoids localisms of any kind. Dr. Johnson, who was a master of both formal and informal English, provides us with a perfect example of each. In a conversation with his friend Boswell concerning the seventeenth-century comedy *The Rehearsal*, Johnson first remarked informally, 'It has not wit enough to keep it sweet'; then, after a pause, he repeated this idea, but with what a difference!—'It has not vitality enough to preserve it from putrefaction.' Finally, in keeping with the foregoing qualities, formal English tends to avoid the use of contractions, abbreviations, and other short-cuts that are often characteristic of the informal variety.

Informal English is used by the same large group that on special occasions employs formal English. Thus the two are related, but only in this one way, for informal English is both different from and far more often used than formal. It is the everyday spoken and written language of these people. A more detailed description of it is therefore called for. This is a difficult matter, for we have to attempt answers to the questions, just what is informal English and who determines its standards? And the fact that the language is constantly changing does not make these answers any easier. Just how and when was it decided, for example, that 'It is *me*' would be acceptable informal English? And by whom? Why has *ain't* never been so accepted? In order to understand these matters, we must first acquire some understanding of the complex ways by which any word or grammatical construction becomes acceptable in informal English.

Informal English is the result of many compromises among the various influences continually at work upon the language. Just what are these influences? We know that language is a social, a cultural, phenomenon: it is the way in which millions of people, acting in every conceivable situation, agree to communicate with one another. And this communication is never perfect; it is, in fact, often illogical, uncertain, and even confused. But it always, as we have said, involves compromises—compromises subject to change without notice. The most important influences occur, first of all, among those who are themselves most influential in the other areas of the given society—the 'leaders' of that society—those employed in the extremely influential communications industry, and teachers of all kinds from the first-grade teacher to the college English professor. Yet, it is apparent that a successful, but high-school-trained, businessman will not agree in all grammatical matters with the college professor or the local bishop. Nor will the labor leader who came up 'through the ranks' agree in these matters with the Harvard-trained president of his company. The linguistic tensions thus created usually result in compromises—and these are what we call informal English.

Out of this situation of change and compromise there have developed at least two discernible areas of usage in informal English: that of the casually educated and that of the well-educated, a distinction which has little to do with their social position or personal success. This distinction is based largely upon differences in the grammatical usage of the two groups. The casually educated tend to use the language more loosely and employ certain forms and constructions that the well-educated frown upon.

At the present time (1958), however, there is some evidence that in usage these two groups may be moving closer together, especially under the influence of the spoken word on radio and television and the tendency of good journalists to write more and more informally. One example of this tendency is the widespread substitution of the reflexive for the personal pronoun: 'All the work was done by Charles and *myself*' (instead of 'Charles and *me*'). Another is the growing tendency not to use the genitive noun or pronoun before the verbal noun in some positions: 'I don't like the idea of *him* going' (instead of '*his* going'). And the utter confusion, in both spoken and written informal English, between the *who* and *whom* forms is of course admitted on all sides. These influences and subsequent changes are at work in all kinds of modern English, but for our purposes they are most significant in the broad area of informal English.

Shoptalk or technical English is, as the terms suggest, a specialized kind of language in which hundreds of groups of people communicate with one another about subjects that are especially well known to them. Literary critics, doctors, lawyers, the various groups of scientists, sociologists—in fact, all of the different professions and skills tend to develop their own kinds of specialized language. These terms are often 'Greek' to the outsider, and use of them ranges from the technical language of scholars and scientists to the 'cant' of hoboes and criminals. The main difference between this kind of English and the other kinds lies in its specialized vocabulary, in which the words and abbreviations are so specialized that only the 'initiated' can understand them. What, for example, would the average person make out of a conversation between two skilled printers if their talk were based upon words like *chase, em, en, pi, pica, platen, rule, spreaders,* etc.? And not much more can be made out of the following definition of an 'organism' by a social scientist: 'a movable mathematical point in time-space, in reference to which matter-energy moves in such a way that a physical situation exists in which work is expended in order to preserve a physical system from a final gravitational and electromagnetic equilibrium with the rest of the universe'!

Then there is slang, a very special kind of language usage. It is difficult to know where to put slang, for it is used by all kinds of people, who otherwise use either standard or non-standard English. Probably we should think of slang as coming somewhere between and overlapping both standard and non-standard English. In slang the normal linguistic processes are used to produce grotesque, fantastic, or highly distorted meanings. The effects are usually novel, humorous, ironic, sarcastic, satiric, or colorful in the extreme. Because slang easily attracts attention, it is regularly used in the language of advertising. As with shoptalk, slang often goes to such extremes that it is understood only by the 'initiated.' 'Oh, *dig* that dancer!' (about a 'jitter-bugger'), 'Doesn't he *send* you?' (about a 'be-bop' saxophone player), 'Oh, that *drug-store cow-boy!*' (about a high-school boy who is a soda-fountain addict), etc. Some slang is borrowed from shoptalk and given a wider applica-tion, as in the expressions *a close-up, behind the eight-ball, he won't get to first base, he is a punk, scram,* etc. Slang may also occur when words from the general vocabulary are used in a distorted figurative sense: *a wet blanket, a good egg, raining cats and dogs, the life of the party*. Since slang always respects brevity, it often appears as a shortened form of various words: *prexy* for *president, prof* for *professor, pug* for *pugilist,* etc.

Finally, it is not often noted that there is also grammatical slang. This is the intentional misuse of the grammatical devices by ex-aggeration or distortion for humorous purposes (results often doubt-ful). Someone may say, for example, 'He *guested* the celebrity,' in which the normal inflectional method of making a noun into a verb is here used fantastically. Or the wrong inflection may be intentionally used, as in 'He *brang* his girl-friend.' Slang may also result from the exaggerated use of word order—extra-long groups of modifiers before nouns, for example: 'his recently dead but while she was alive fantastically rich old great-aunt!' And similarly with the ridiculously long group genitive: 'the man I saw you with at the game yesterday's overcoat!' And with the double and triple negative: 'I don't want nothing nohow,' the excessive use of *there:* 'Where are them there contracts,' etc.

Most of us have had experience with all of these various kinds of English usage, and each of them is acceptable and appropriate in its own place. For our purposes, however, it is standard English that we must be most concerned with; for this is the kind with which the great majority of students will think, speak, and write throughout their lives.

Obviously written English, especially serious written English of the kind employed in college themes and dissertations, must be more formal and 'conservative' than the spoken language. In terms of grammar and sentence structure, it will differ in some ways from informal speech. The sentences should be more tightly constructed and more logically ordered; inflectional forms should be more consistent and conform more closely to a set of standards generally agreed upon by our best writers; and above all there must be no ambiguities such as those described in the preceding chapters of this book. In terms of vocabulary, the jargon of shoptalk should be avoided in all except the most technical kind of writing. And it should go without saying that slang should never be used in any kind of serious written English, except intentionally. All this does not mean that the written language should be stiff and dull, wholly lacking in colorful or racy expressions. The tendency to be too formal and stiff, whenever a person takes a pen in hand or sits down to his typewriter, is often the worst fault of student writing and of amateur writing in general.

XIV

PROPER FORMS IN PROPER PLACES

No description of modern English grammar, no matter how detailed and accurate, is of much value in a vacuum. For the student, such a description should ultimately lead into the numerous problems of usage which those who speak and write the language must encounter every day of their lives. The earlier chapters of this book provide the terminology and a practical approach for dealing with the 'rules' of such usage—rules which, even after years of hearing about them, remain mysterious to many people because they do not have this background.

As we have said, acceptable usage is relative: its rules depend upon time and place. There is, therefore, no such thing as 'correct' and 'incorrect' English—there is only 'acceptable' and 'unacceptable' usage in a given situation. The grammatical standards presented in the remainder of this book are those which are generally expected in the writing and, in some situations, the speaking of college graduates and of educated people generally. Obviously, this will be a different English from that which a student would use at a 'bull session' or on the football field, or that a businessman would use in the locker room at the golf club.

Broadly speaking, there are two kinds of grammatical mis-usage, which we shall call 'social' mis-usage and 'communication' mis-usage. The second of these is more important than the first. By social mis-usages we mean those which do not seriously impede communication but which educated society has decreed are unacceptable. By communication mis-usages we mean those that mislead the reader or destroy linguistic communication altogether. In general, the social error results from the faulty use of the device of inflection, the communication error mainly from the faulty use of word order. This situation, of course, is to be expected in a language in which grammatical meanings are largely determined, not by inflection, but by the devices of function word and word order, especially of word order. This point is illustrated by 'pidgin English,' which has no inflections at all, but manages to communicate with little difficulty—although to a native English speaker this 'language' sounds dreadful, and its area of communication is limited.

The fact that inflectional errors are usually less serious than other kinds does not mean that this type of mis-usage may be ignored by the student. As a matter of fact, success in college and later life may partially depend on his management of this area of grammar. Although *I sung, it don't,* and *between you and I* may communicate as effectively as *I sang, it doesn't,* and *between you and me,* the use of any of the former constructions in an important letter might have disastrous results. In the rest of this chapter we shall discuss some of the most important problems that involve mainly the device of inflection, explaining from the point of view of structural grammar why 'mistakes' are made and how they may be corrected.

NOUN FORMS

Because the vast majority of nouns in modern English are 'regular'—that is, they are inflected by the addition of *-s, -'s,* and *-s'*—their forms cause little trouble in writing and even less in speech. There are a few, however—especially those of foreign origin—which may present difficulties. Most borrowed words (and there are thousands of them) have long since been 'Anglicized' in both spelling and pronunciation, so that their forms correspond to those of most native English words. But a limited number of these foreign words still retain their foreign endings, and it is these that may cause trouble. For example, the words *alumna, alumnus,* and *datum,* which come from Latin, are still not wholly Anglicized. We still are expected to know that *alumna* is feminine singular, *alumnus* is masculine singular, *alumnae* is feminine plural, and *alumni* is masculine plural. But with *datum* the process of Anglicizing is more complete. What has happened is that in informal English the un-English ending -*um* has been dropped, and the Latin plural form *data* has been substituted for it. Thus most people would normally say and write 'the data is' rather than the strictly formal 'the data are.' Similarly, the Latin *gladiolus,* with its plural *gladioli,* has been almost wholly Anglicized and has become, in speech at least, *gladiola* and *gladiolas.* A second possible source of confusion in noun forms is the fact that a few native English words such as *deer, sheep, cod,* etc., have no plural inflection at all. These are listed in Chapter V. There are also a few that become plural through 'internal' inflection: *man–men, woman–women, foot–feet,* etc. Once the nature of these differences is understood, no difficulties need arise.

A more serious and widespread problem has to do with the use of the apostrophe in the genitive forms of the noun. This is a problem because this mark is a device used only in the written language: in speech, the genitive -*'s* or -*s'* endings sound exactly like the plain plural noun ending -*s,* the verb ending -*s,* and even the -*s* that is sometimes used as an adverb suffix. Since we do not 'hear' the apostrophe when we are composing sentences, it is likely to be left out where it should be used, or inserted in the wrong place, or used in places where there should be no apostrophe at all, especially in the plain plural form. Actually, this kind of mistake is easily avoidable by the use of a simple substitution test. If the genitive form of one of the personal pronouns can be substituted for the noun, then the apostrophe must be used. Thus, for *the boy's new coat,* we can substitute *his new coat;* or for *the school's new song,* we can substitute *its new song.* In both of these examples, therefore, the genitive -*'s* must be used. Similarly, if we can substitute *their* for the noun, the plural genitive form must be used, as in *the Smiths' new home* (*their new home*), or *the European nations' non-aggression pact (their non-aggression pact).* Conversely, if the genitive pronoun cannot be substituted for the noun, the *-s* stands for a plural, not a genitive, idea; and the apostrophe should not be used. If this rule is followed, no one would ever write *I visited the Smith's* instead of the correct, *I visited the Smiths,* nor would anyone have printed on his stationery:

> The John Smith's,
> 422 Joyful Avenue.

One more problem remains in connection with noun forms. This has to do with the form to be used—the base form or genitive form —for the 'subject' of the gerund. Should one write, for example,

> I don't approve of Henry's smoking.
>
> or
>
> I don't approve of Henry smoking?

In sentences like the first one above, the third-form verbal is a noun element (gerund) and the genitive noun is a modifier. What we have said in this sentence, then, is that we disapprove of the activity of smoking on the part of Henry. In the second sentence, the noun is *Henry* and *smoking* is the modifier, and the form of this sentence tells us that the writer disapproves of *Henry* when smoking. In this particular pair of sentences, the distinction is a very fine one, so either the base or genitive form of the noun *Henry* would be acceptable to most people.

There are many instances, however, in which the verbal is clearly a noun (gerund) and could not be interpreted in any other way. First, when a third-form verbal appears in the subject territory, one can always tell from the word order whether this verbal is a gerund or not. In the following sentences the first words are clearly gerunds functioning as subjects:

> Failing the course was a disaster.
> Winning the championship helped our morale.

When gerunds are in this position, their 'subjects' must always be in the genitive case form:

> *John's* failing the course was a disaster.
> The *school's* winning the championship helped our morale.

Second, the verbal is often clearly a gerund when it is in either of the object territories, object of the verb or of the preposition, as in

> I regret *Henry's* leaving so soon.

Here it is obviously the 'leaving' that is regretted, so the verbal is clearly a gerund. In speech and in very informal writing, the base form of the noun is often used before such gerunds:

> I regret *Henry* leaving so soon.

In any kind of serious writing, however, the genitive form should always be employed, especially when the subject of the gerund is a person; for this form allows the writer to make a very real and useful distinction in meaning. The two sentences following show clearly how a difference in the form of the noun before the third-form verbal changes the meaning of the sentence:

> I do not approve of that boy walking across the lawn.
> I do not approve of that boy's walking across the lawn.

If the subject of the gerund is a personal pronoun, we have the problem of deciding whether to use the genitive or the objective form. When the gerund is in the subject position, the genitive form of the pronoun must always be used:

> *His* failing the course was a disaster.
> *Their* winning the championship raised the boys' spirits.

The use of an objective form in this position—*Him failing the course*—is pure non-standard English, and as such is completely unacceptable in written English of any kind. When the gerund is in any object position, the objective form of the pronoun is often used in speech and in informal writing. Thus, we hear:

> I do not approve of *him* leaving in this storm.
> Have you heard about *them* buying a new car?

In serious writing, however, this form is still not considered acceptable. The sentences above should be revised to read:

I do not approve of *his* leaving in this storm.

Have you heard about *their* buying a new car?

VERB FORMS

Problems with the forms of nouns are relatively simple compared to verb-form problems, a fact that should not surprise anyone if he remembers the numerous inflectional forms of the English verb. The main problems in connection with this part of speech are of three kinds. First, the natural tendency to regularize the irregular verbs; second, the tendency to confuse the fourth and fifth forms; and third, the tendency to confuse the first and second forms.

The first two problems rarely trouble college students. Only children, the greatest of regularizers, tend to reduce all verbs to the major pattern of inflection: they say, 'I *rided* my bike,' 'he *bleeded*,' 'we *throwed* the ball,' and 'she *sitted* down.' College students, obviously, do not make such mistakes. They do, however, occasionally say, and more often write, regular fourth forms for some of the three-form verbs: *'casted,' 'bursted,' 'thrusted,' 'wetted,' 'sweated,' 'slitted,' 'shedded,'* and *'spreaded'* have all graced—or disgraced—student papers.

The five-form verbs pose another difficulty. We should, no doubt, count our blessings, for Old English had more than three hundred such verbs, and we have inherited only about a fourth of them. But those that still remain in the language are sources of considerable confusion. The problem with such verbs is not that of regularization, even though there is a slow tendency to regularize them (*chide, cleave,* and *thrive* have already established regular forms). The problem is, rather, that of confusing the fourth and fifth forms —or, in traditional terminology, of confusing the past (or 'preterite') form with the past participle. This confusion results, in large part, from the instability of these forms throughout the Early Modern English period and well into the Modern English period. The *'riz'* (for *rose*) and *'rid'* (for *rode*) still heard at times in non-standard speech and the 'he *slud* into base safely,' frequently heard from a radio baseball commentator, are all remnants of a period in our language when such forms were widely used by educated and uneducated people alike. Of course, today few college students would employ such forms. But another group of verbs tends to be troublesome, because the distinction between the fourth and fifth forms has never been completely established on all levels of usage. Chief among these are the verbs from the third class of Old English strong verbs, of which *sing, sang, sung* is a common example. Throughout the eighteenth century, 'I *sung*' and 'I have *sang*' were common among educated users of the language and no serious attempt was made to fix their usage until the appearance of the grammars of the 1760's. Even after that, the instability of these forms persisted and is still evident today. Common verbs affected by this instability besides *sing* are *begin, drink, ring, shrink, sink, spring, stink,* and *swim.* Even in standard English (of a very informal kind) we sometimes hear 'I *begun*,' 'He *rung* the bell,' 'He *sunk* the putt,' etc.

Inheritances from the other strong-verb classes of Old English may also cause confusion, so that in non-standard English we have such 'incorrect' forms as *I have shook* for *I have shaken* and *I have wrote* for *I have written.* Of all the five-form verbs, a few are particularly troublesome today, especially *become, begin, come, do, drink,* and *see.* As a result, the following are not uncommon even in informal standard English, and especially in speech: 'I *become* frightened last night,' or 'He finally *begun* to see the point.' These forms, of course, are unacceptable in written standard English today. (A list of the 'principal parts' of the five-form verbs will be found on pp. 34-6.)

One of the most familiar and involved problems in modern English inflectional usage is that of subject-verb agreement in number and person. This involves mainly a decision as to whether one should use the first or second form of the verb—that is, the form with no ending or the form with the -*s* ending. The difficulty here is caused largely by the fact that the verb inflection usually repeats an idea already expressed in the form of the subject and really has no meaning for the verb itself (see Chapter VII, p. 77): it merely tells whether the subject is singular or plural, or whether it is the first, second, or third person. Since this inflection is usually no more than a formality, it often gets lost in the rush of spoken words and in hasty or careless writing. Also, under these circumstances the inflection may be used where it should not be used.

Except for the verb *be,* which has different forms for singular and plural in the past tense, the problem of verb agreement exists only in the present tense. Again with the exception of the verb *be,* which has irregular number forms, the general rule for this kind of agreement is to use the *-s* form (second form) if the subject is third person singular and the first form if the subject is any other person or is plural in number. This formula may be summarized in the following examples:

> He, she, it, or the boy *eats* heartily.
> I, we, you, they, or the boys *eat* heartily.

Number agreement alone is a problem when the subject is a noun or any pronoun except a personal pronoun. The personal pronoun subject, as the name implies, calls for agreement in both number and person, and will therefore be considered separately. This first part of the discussion on verb agreement will be concerned only with noun subjects (or pronouns other than personal pronouns), exemplified in the last part of the formula above: *boy eats* and *boys eat.* The quixotic state of affairs in which the *-s* ending on nouns indicates the plural number and the same ending on verbs the singular was recently and wittily lamented by Mr. Ogden Nash in his poem, 'A Brief Guide to Rhyming':

> Oh, what a tangled web the early grammarians spun!
> The singular verb has an 's' and the singular noun has none. . .[1]

Of course Mr. Nash (as he probably knows) is historically inaccurate, for the 'early grammarians' had nothing to do with this 'tangled web.' Indeed, they probably would have liked to untangle it, but 'usage' was too strong for them.

In non-standard English, for some reason, the second form of the verb is widely used with plural subjects—in such expressions as 'All my muscles aches' and 'The faucets leaks.' Users of standard English, however, rarely have trouble with these forms when the sub-

[1] Ogden Nash, *You Can't Get There from Here* (Little, Brown and Co., 1957).

ject is clearly singular or plural in both form and meaning and when it is followed closely by the verb, as it is in both examples above. But more often than not the verb is widely separated from the subject, and the number of the subject itself may be in doubt. Under one or both of these conditions, there may be difficulty in selecting the right form of the verb.

Some errors occur because the writer, not knowing how to analyze the sentence, has not properly identified the subject. This confusion usually happens when the subject and verb are separated by long modifying elements, parts of which are mistaken for the subject, especially when these modification groups contain nouns, as in the following sentence:

> The sound of all those shrill voices in the hallways finally *have* stopped.

Here the writer has used a plural verb almost certainly because he has mistaken either *voices* or *hallways* for the subject of the sentence. *Sound,* of course, is the subject and the verb form should be *has. Voices* or *hallways* was mistaken for the subject probably because both are nearer to the verb. Since the subject often does immediately precede the verb, we feel almost instinctively that any noun in this position is the subject. Obviously, this kind of agreement error is caused not so much by failure to know the 'rules' as by a failure to analyze the whole sentence accurately. Following are sentences of this kind in which proper verb agreement is observed:

> Hours of daily practice in front of a mirror *have* made him a wonderful mimic.
>
> A whole bushel basket of apples, just picked from our early bearing trees, *has* been made into applesauce.

Most errors in number agreement probably occur because of uncertainty about the number of the subject. There are many different problems of this kind. One that may cause trouble arises when the subject is a compound or a series. This sometimes creates difficulties because of the confusing fact that the members of the compound or series may themselves be singular or plural or a mixture of both numbers. The rule is that when nouns joined by the co-ordinating conjunction *and* are the subject of the sentence, whether these nouns are themselves singular or plural, the verb must be plural in form. (The only exception to this rule occurs when the two nouns refer to the same person, such as *my lord and master.*) Thus we would write:

> John's children and his wife *tend* (not *tends*) the furnace.
> John, Charles, and Bill *are* (not *is*) arriving on the noon train.

In these sentences the proximity of the verbs to singular nouns (*wife* and *Bill*) might lead to an error in verb agreement. There is also a tendency to want to use a singular noun when two members of a compound subject are thought of as a single process or as closely related processes, such as *reading and writing* or *sawing and hammering.* In serious writing, however, the plural form of the verb will be expected:

> Reading and writing *are* taught in the first grade.
> His sawing and hammering *are* keeping me awake.

Long compound or serial subjects involving complex verbal elements may present a problem in verb agreement, as in

> Practicing on the piano, painting two pictures a day, and weeding the garden really *take* up all my time.

Even though these occupations may be thought of as a single day's activity, this subject is plural in form and a plural verb will be expected.

When the members of a compound subject are joined by the conjunction *or* or the compound conjunctions *either . . . or* or *neither . . . nor,* the verb is always singular in form unless a plural noun immediately precedes the verb:

> Henry or his brother *is* likely to win.
> Either Mary or her mother *has* the tickets.
> Neither the boys nor their father *was* hurt.
> Neither the boys nor their parents *were* expected to participate.
> Neither John nor his parents *were* expected.

Uncertainty about the number of the subject may also arise when a singular noun is modified by a prepositional phrase beginning with *together with, in addition to, along with,* etc. The traditional rule is that in written English the verb after these phrases should be singular in form:

> The house, together with the lot, *is* valued at $20,000.
>
> The subject, along with its modifiers, *precedes* the predicate.

People often use the plural verb in this situation because they feel that the whole subject (the subject and its modifiers) expresses a plural idea—that it is equivalent to a compound subject. It is only by understanding the form of these sentences, as well as their meanings, that these difficulties can be overcome.

This problem of determining the number of the subject is greatly complicated in modern English by the fact that there are many nouns and pronouns which are singular in form but which, in context, may be either singular or plural in their vocabulary meanings. Nouns of this kind are often called 'collective singulars'—such words as *choir, chorus, collection, committee, company, couple, family, group, jury, majority, minority, pair, party,* and *team.* Each of these is singular in meaning when referring to a group as a whole and plural when referring to the members of that group. The verb, therefore, may be singular or plural, depending upon which of these meanings is intended:

> The chorus *were given* their costumes.
>
> The jury *is* out for dinner.
>
> The team *wins* its sixth victory.
>
> The team *were awarded* their letters.

Similarly, some nouns that are plural in form may also take a singular or plural verb, again depending on their vocabulary meanings in a given context. For example:

> Postal savings *is* an anachronism.
>
> His savings *were* confiscated.
>
> Many years *have passed.*
>
> Fifty years *is* a long time.

But there are many nouns with permanent -*s* endings that, because their vocabulary meanings are singular, are always followed by the singular form of the verb:

> Mathematics *is* a basic science.
>
> Athletics *is* overemphasized at our school.

Not only nouns, but some of the quantitative pronouns, may give trouble because of uncertainty about their number. A glance back at Chapter VII (p. 84) will show that there is one group of these pronouns which allows either singular or plural verbs, depending on their contextual meanings. These are: *all, any, enough, none,* and *some.* For example:

> All of the paste *is* gone.
>
> All of the recruits *are* present.
>
> Some of the cream *is* sour.
>
> Some of the voters *are* not registered.

But the group of pronouns that gives the most trouble is: *another, each, either (neither),* and some of the *one* and *body* words, especially: *one, anyone, everyone, anyone,* and *everybody.* The trouble arises because these words, though singular in form, convey in some contexts a plural meaning. *Each* may suggest the idea of *all; either* and *neither* the idea of *both;* and words ending in *one* and *body* often suggest a general plural idea. This is especially true when the plural idea is reinforced by a prepositional phrase modifying the subject. Thus, one may be tempted to use a plural verb form after such phrases, as in:

> Each of the boys *were* (instead of *was*) given a medal.
>
> Everyone in the block *were* (instead of *was*) investigated.
>
> Neither of the girls *know* (instead of *knows*) how to swim.

Although these forms may seem logical enough, the use of the singular verb form in such instances is generally preferred. The rest of the quantitative pronouns are either clearly singular in form and meaning (*anything, everything, much, nothing, nobody, no one, someone,* and *something*) or clearly plural (*both, few, many,* and *several*) and do not present any problems in agreement.

Inverting the normal subject-verb order may also lead to errors in verb agreement. This is not surprising, for under these circumstances we have to decide on the form of the verb before we come to the subject. There may even be some uncertainty as to just what the subject will be when the verb form is being chosen. In writing, however, there is no excuse for this kind of mistake, for in writing there is always the opportunity to revise. Three kinds of inversion invite this mistake. First, in questions with a compound subject, a singular verb is often mistakenly used. In order to avoid this error, one should remember that a plural verb must always be used after a compound subject, whether it appears in a statement or a question:

> *Do* John and Henry *live* with you?
> *Have* your mother and father *decided* to move here?
> Where *are* John and Henry?

Errors may also occur when subject-verb inversion has been used for rhetorical purposes, especially when the normal subject territory is occupied by an adverbial element. There is a tendency with this kind of inversion to over-use the singular verb form, even when the subject is plural. This error probably results from uncertainty in identifying the subject because of its abnormal position, and it can be avoided only by understanding the form of this type of sentence. One should always write:

> Then *come* (not *comes*) the stories we like best.
> Through our property *flow* (not *flows*) two lovely streams.

A problem in verb agreement may also arise when *there* is in the subject position with the subject itself following the verb. In this kind of sentence, the verb must always agree with the real subject:

> There *is* an icebox in the kitchen.
> There *are* six plates on the table.

There is one more situation in which uncertainty about the number form of the verb may occur. This is in the subject-verb-predicate noun type of sentence. Although both nouns (the subject and complement) refer to the same person or thing, they may have different number forms, as in

Apples are my favorite fruit.

The general rule here, again showing the influence of word order, is that the verb agrees with the noun that precedes the verb, not the following one:

Apples are my favorite fruit.
My favorite fruit is apples.

Another verb-agreement problem involves the relative clause. As with other verbs, those in a relative clause are expected to agree in number with their subjects. When the subject is the relative pronoun itself, however, its form gives no clue to the number. (*Who, which,* and *that* have no number forms.) Therefore, this has to be determined by the number of the antecedent. For example, in the following sentence the verb *break* is plural in form because the antecedent of *who* (*students*) is plural:

Students who *break* rules are usually punished.

Verb agreement in relative clauses is important, since under some circumstances this inflection may be more than a mere convention. It actually may serve as a grammatical signal to tell the reader which word is intended as the antecedent of the relative pronoun. This is particularly important when phrasal modifiers containing nouns come between the pronoun and its antecedent. The sentence following shows how the form of the verb may solve the problem of identifying the antecedent:

The sons of the banker who drive a Cadillac were arrested for speeding.

Here the form of the verb *drive* tells us that the sons drive the Cadillac, not the banker, and a possible ambiguity is eliminated. In relative clauses after *one of those who* (*that, which*), the plural form of the verb is preferred, unless the pronoun refers clearly to *one* instead of the group.

John is one of those men who *love* to argue.

The house is one of those which *show* its age.

Personal pronouns as subjects are in a class by themselves with respect to verb agreement in the present tense, because they involve person as well as number agreement. The rule, as we have noted, is to use the second form of the verb with third-person singular subjects (*he, she,* and *it*) and the first form with the other persons and the plural number (*I, we, you,* and *they*). There is no serious problem here, for college students are rarely tempted to say, 'I eats' or 'She eat.' We do, however, often hear, 'I says' even among speakers of standard English. Obviously, this is very bad usage. A special problem arises with the contraction *doesn't.* Since *don't* is used with all persons except the third person singular, the principle of attraction (or inertia) leads many speakers of non-standard English (and some who otherwise speak standard English) to say *he, she, it,* or *the boy don't.* This usage is frowned upon by careful speakers and is always unacceptable in written standard English.

PRONOUN AGREEMENT

As with the verbs, the selection of certain pronoun forms involves a problem of agreement; for the forms of these words are expected to correspond in number, person, and gender with their antecedents [2] (the words for which they are substitutes). That they should correspond in this way is to be expected, since the pronoun and its antecedent both stand for the same vocabulary idea. This kind of agreement may be seen in the sentence

The boy raised *his* hand.

Here the pronoun *his,* like its antecedent *boy,* is singular number, third person, and masculine gender.

Problems in pronoun agreement usually involve only the selection of the correct number form; and, when the antecedent is

---

[2] The word 'antecedent' is derived from Latin and means 'going before,' but this word does not always precede the pronoun. In the following sentence the antecedent comes after the pronoun: 'When *she* is able, my *mother* helps with the housework.'

clearly either singular or plural, mistakes are not often made. It is when its number is not clearly defined that difficulties sometimes arise. The number of the antecedent may be doubtful under several circumstances. First, it may be doubtful when the antecedent is singular in form, but is modified by certain words that express group ideas and therefore suggest plurality. Two of the most common expressions of this type are *this kind of* and the indicator *the* when it is used to show that the word modified represents all the items in its class, as, for example,

> *The* groundhog (meaning all groundhogs) is a rodent.

When a pronoun is used to refer to these two types of antecedents, the singular form should be used:

> When you use *this kind of word,* you should put *it* (not *them*) in quotation marks.
>
> Now we shall study the habits of *the* groundhog. *This* animal spends (not *these* animals spend) most of the winter in hibernation.

Second, the number of the antecedent may be doubtful when the word referred to is a collective singular noun, such as *team, family, crowd, committee, majority,* etc. This is the same type of word that causes difficulties in verb agreement. Although these nouns are singular in form, singular or plural pronoun forms may be used after them. If we wish to express the 'collectiveness' of the antecedent, we usually use a singular pronoun form:

> The team won as *it* should have.
> The family is proud of *its* heritage.
> The choir was at *its* best last Sunday.

But when the emphasis is on the members of the collection, the plural form of the pronoun is usually allowed:

> The team played in *their* traveling uniforms.
> When the family heard the news, *they* shouted with joy.
> The choir will not wear *their* vestments today.

Most collective singular nouns may be interpreted in these two contrasting ways. A few of them, however, such as *couple* and *pair,* always require a plural pronoun when these words refer to human beings. (We never speak of a couple and *its* child.) The plural pronoun form is used even when the verb form is singular: *The couple loves their children* is standard usage, although the use of the plural verb form would seem more logical.

Third, the number may be in doubt when certain quantitative pronouns serve as antecedents or as modifiers of antecedents. These pronouns are *any, anyone, anybody, each, every, everyone, everybody, either, neither, nobody, no one,* and *none.* Although singular in form, all of these words suggest a plural meaning in some or all contexts. *Everybody* means all people, *either* may mean both, and *each* may mean all. Consequently, there is a widespread tendency to refer to this kind of antecedent with plural pronoun forms:

> *Everybody* wants to have *their* own way.
> When I make *either* salad dressing, *they* get lumpy.
> *Each* student received *their* medals.

Most teachers of English and most style manuals, however, still insist (in writing at least) on the use of the singular pronoun forms except when referring to *none,* which for some reason seems to be exempt from this rule; so one should write

> When I make either salad dressing, *it* gets lumpy.
> Each student received *his* medal.
> Anyone can take *his* own pulse.

Everybody and *everyone* are being used so widely at this time with the plural pronoun that this form cannot be considered 'wrong' except in the most formal writing.

Another reason why pronoun agreement raises so many problems —in addition to the frequently ambiguous number of the antecedent—is a deficiency in the language itself. This is the lack of a common gender personal pronoun in the third person singular: *I, we, you,* or *they* may refer to members of both sexes or to either sex, but this is not true of *he* or *she*. (*It,* of course, is not a common gender pronoun, for it applies only to objects without sex or to collections like *team,* etc.) This fact raises quite a problem if the sex of the antecedent is not indicated or if the meaning includes both sexes, as with the quantitative pronouns listed above, with other indefinite pronouns such as *one, someone, somebody,* and with such indefinite nouns as *a person, the winner, the buyer,* etc. These antecedents are, of course, singular in form and meaning; but, if we use a singular personal pronoun to refer to them, we must choose between two rather unsatisfactory alternatives: first, use the masculine pronoun (even though we know that the antecedent might be feminine), as in

> Somebody has lost *his* notebook,
> The winner may select any prize *he* likes,

or use both the masculine and feminine forms (*he* or *she*). The latter alternative is, of course, impossibly awkward, and the other strikes many people as being too formal, and rather unrealistic in addition. For this reason, the third person plural pronoun (*they, their, them*) is widely used in this situation. Such practice has led some modern grammarians to conclude that *they* has changed its status in the language: that it is no longer merely a third person plural pronoun, but a common gender pronoun for both numbers, and as such may be used quite properly to refer to many singular antecedents when their gender is not clear. Most college students, however, are expected to use the masculine singular form in their themes and term papers, unless the antecedent specifically refers to members of the female sex:

> Nobody will hurt you unless you hurt *him* first.
> The buyer should watch out for *his* own interests.

When the antecedent specifically includes the members of both sexes, as in *each of the boys and girls,* the masculine singular pronoun obviously cannot be used, so the sentence must be rewritten in order to eliminate the word *each.*

FAULTY PRONOUN REFERENCE

In addition to the problem of agreement, there is another problem in connection with pronoun antecedents. This has to do with the correct designation of these words. Often there are several words either in the sentence itself or in the preceding sentence which might qualify as antecedents of a personal or demonstrative pronoun. And we need some grammatical means of showing which word is intended to function in this way. This is called a problem in pronoun 'reference.' In some situations, the gender and number form of the pronoun will make clear which word is intended as the antecedent. This point is illustrated in the sentence

> John and Mary talked about *his* grades and *her* dates.

Here the gender forms indicate that *his* is a substitute for *John* and *her* for *Mary*. In the sentence,

> If the first two words in the phrase are reversed, *it* will mean something quite different,

the singular number form of *it* indicates that *phrase,* not *words,* is intended as the antecedent. If *words* had been intended, the pronoun would have been *they.* Inflections are a convenient device for designating an antecedent, but unfortunately the language does not have enough kinds of formal pronoun distinctions to make this method work under all conditions. Obviously, there are many situations in which the number and sex of the various words a pronoun could refer to are the same. Then we must find another grammatical device to establish the reference.

The other device is, of course, word order. The word-order rule for pronouns and their antecedents is as follows: If we wish to designate a word as the antecedent of a pronoun, the words in the sentence should be arranged so that the antecedent comes as close as possible to the pronoun. The reason for this rule is obvious: If the antecedent is too far away, other words which might qualify as antecedents may intervene and cause ambiguity or completely alter the meaning intended. This kind of confusion occurs in the following sentence, in which the antecedent *western states* is too far away from the pronoun *they:*

> I enjoy the western states with their rugged scenery and dry climate, but they also have disadvantages.

In this next sentence the antecedent *girl* is too far away from the pronoun *her:*

> I would like to help the girl and will talk to old Mrs. Green in the hope of getting her a scholarship.

In fact, the antecedent is so far away that another noun phrase (*old Mrs. Green*) has intervened with the resulting foolish implication that it was this person, not the girl, who was seeking a scholarship.

Ideally, the antecedent should be the first noun (or indefinite pronoun) before the pronoun in question. But, unfortunately, this rule does not solve all problems of this kind, for the patterns of reference in the modern English sentence are so variable that vague and inaccurate references are always a danger, even if this rule is followed literally. One difficulty is caused by the fact that being close to a pronoun does not always mark a noun unequivocally as the antecedent. Sometimes a noun functioning as subject of the sentence has a strong pull on the pronoun, putting this noun in competition, as it were, with another noun that is closer. When this happens, neither word will emerge clearly as the antecedent, and the reference will be ambiguous. The following sentences show this kind of ambiguity:

> When the car ran into the fence, *it* was badly damaged.
> The parents of the girls were ashamed of *their* conduct.
> Because of *his* friendship with the Joneses, Jim asked John to write the letter.

Of course, the vocabulary meanings of the words often clear up ambiguities when other devices fail. In the sentence

> When the prowler struck Mr. Smith, he screamed for help

the entire meaning of the sentence makes it fairly clear that Mr. Smith, not the prowler, screamed for help. However, students should not depend too heavily on this device. Often the writer may think the reference is made clear by the context of meaning, when this meaning is not at all clear to the reader, who may see a second meaning that has not even occurred to the writer. In the sentence above about Jim and John, the ambiguity was undoubtedly not apparent to the writer.

The fact that our language does not have any cut-and-dried rules for pronoun reference is one of its greatest weaknesses and probably the most dangerous source of ambiguities. Directions of all kinds— in cookbooks, on packages and food cartons, dressmaking patterns, and various put-together-at-home articles—abound in these vague references and are the bane of everyone who has to struggle with them. We find such ambiguous sentences as,

> Before you beat the egg into the batter, be sure *it* is at room temperature.

We may also find such 'howlers' as the following:

> If this milk disagrees with the baby, boil it.

There are at least three ways to avoid these ambiguous references. First, the sentences may be arranged so that only one noun precedes the pronoun:

> The car was badly damaged when it ran into the fence.
> Boil the milk if it disagrees with the baby.

Second, a function word may sometimes be used to point the reference more closely:

> The parents of the girls were ashamed of their *own* conduct.

Third, the pronoun may be eliminated entirely by simply repeating the word intended as the antecedent (or by using a synonym for it):

> Before you beat the egg into the batter, be sure the egg is at room temperature.

This course is surely the best one when the antecedent is widely separated from the pronoun. In the following sentence—

> We like to visit the country because of the beauty and quiet,
> but, of course, the country has its disadvantages too—

the use of a pronoun in place of the second *country* would have made the sentence ambiguous.

Another type of faulty pronoun reference results not from there being too many nouns which could be antecedents, but from there being none at all. The following is an example of this kind of sentence:

> This poem is so obscure that I cannot grasp *his* meaning.

Here, there is no word to which the singular masculine pronoun *his* could refer. The writer, no doubt, thought that he had written a correct sentence because the antecedent is 'understood.' But this is a mistaken assumption, for in good writing the antecedents of all pronouns must be clearly expressed. This sentence could be revised either by changing the form of the pronoun to *its* so that this word could refer back to *poem;* or, we could put in an antecedent to which *his* could properly refer, as in

> This poem by T. S. Eliot is so obscure that I cannot grasp *his* meaning.

Reference mistakes of this kind are very common. Other examples are:

> The steeplejack hasn't fallen yet, but he is always afraid of *it.*
> We now have a sound farm policy, but young people are still leaving *them.*
> Henry is studying chemical engineering. *That* is what I want to be too.

The first of these sentences may be corrected simply by substituting the noun *falling* for the pronoun *it.* The mistake in the second sentence is caused partially by the fact that the pronoun refers back to the subordinate (attributive) noun *farm.* In general, pronoun references to any subordinate noun, including those in the genitive case, should be avoided in good written English.

To sum up what has been said about pronoun reference problems: Whenever a pronoun, especially a personal pronoun, is used, we must make sure that the word for which it substitutes (the antecedent) is definitely expressed in the same sentence or in the sentence immediately preceding, and that the antecedent is clearly marked by the inflectional form of the pronoun itself, by a function word, or by the positions of the pronoun and antecedent. When two or more words could qualify as the antecedent by virtue of their forms and meanings, the sentence must be recast so that one of these words is eliminated, or the antecedent must be repeated.

Pronoun Case Forms

As we pointed out in Chapter VII, the case functions of pronouns are exactly like those of the nouns: subject, predicate complement, genitive, the various objects of the verb, the object of a preposition, and the subject of the infinitive. The case forms of the personal, relative, and interrogative pronouns, however, differ from those of the noun in one important respect: There are three of these forms, whereas nouns have only two (the uninflected form and the genitive with -'s); the pronouns, of course, have an extra form to correspond to the various object functions.

This difference between nouns and personal pronouns may be seen in the following pairs of sentences:

Mary loves John.   She loves him.
John loves Mary.   He loves her.

Obviously *Mary* and *John* have the same forms regardless of whether they are subjects or objects, but *she* and *her* and *he* and *him* do not. As we have said before, these are really not 'live' grammatical devices in modern English: They do not actually determine function; they do not tell us whether the word is a subject or an object. As with nouns, it is the word-order device that does this, except under rare circumstances when normal word order is not used (see Chapter X, p. 133). Since *Her did it* communicates just as accurately as *She did it,* this change in form might be regarded more as a grammatical convention than a device. Because the forms of these pronouns are not necessary for communication, they are used rather carelessly by many people.

In standard modern English it is generally accepted that we should use the subject forms of the personal pronoun (*I, we, he, she,* and *they*) in the subject territory, and the object forms (*me, us, him, her,* and *them*) in the object territory. For anyone who has studied structural grammar and understands the positions of the various noun functions, there will never be any uncertainty about these forms—no matter how complex the sentence may be. But people who are not acquainted with this approach to grammar often do have trouble—even highly 'educated' people.

When such 'mistakes' are analyzed, we discover the curious fact that they are often caused by a zeal for overcorrectness, resulting from a fear of using forms which are associated with non-standard English—such crudities as 'Him and her done it,' or such talk as one hears in old gangster films of the 1930's: 'Youse and me will bump him off.' One of the most common mistakes made in reaction to this kind of English is the use of subject forms in object territory. This presumably results from a fear of the object forms, which do seem to pop up in almost every part of the sentence in non-standard English. This use of subject forms in object territory usually occurs in the second member of a compound functioning as the object of a verb or of a preposition. For example,

> Mr. Smith saw Mary and *I* on the porch.
> The police didn't know about Mrs. Jones and *I.*
> They wouldn't allow John and *he* to leave the city.
> Between you and *I,* Smith is going to quit.

This mistake also may occur in appositive and parenthetical expressions following any type of object, as in

> The neighbors have been good to our family, both my husband and *I.*

Let's you and I is a mistake of this kind, for *you and I* are in apposition to the contracted object form *us.*

Since the great majority of people know little about grammar, and have no way of knowing how to use these pronoun forms, they have devised a way of circumventing their dilemma. This involves the use of a kind of personal pronoun that does not have formal case distinctions. This is the reflexive pronoun, the forms of which are: *myself, ourselves, yourselves, himself, herself, itself,* and *themselves.* This strategy on the part of speakers to avoid making the choice between case forms of the personal pronoun was described in Chapter VII (p. 80). As we stated there, such sentences as 'John and myself will pick up the tickets' and 'Unknown to myself John took out more insurance' are widely used in colloquial English. In writing, however, this usage does not have such wide currency. A few reputable authors use these forms regularly and in a few of our better publications, such as the *New York Times Book Review,* it is apparently accepted, but in many others it is editorially banned. College English teachers generally tend to expect the correct form of the personal pronoun unless the meaning is clearly reflexive or 'intensive.' Thus, the sentences above should be written:

John and I (not myself) will pick up the tickets.
Unknown to me (not myself) John took out more insurance.

These problems concerning personal pronoun forms bring us inevitably to the question of whether one should use the expressions, 'It is *me,*' or 'It is *him*' (or *her, us,* and *them*). Unfortunately, there is a wide, but unfounded, belief that the object form is 'wrong' here because in some way it violates a language principle. The truth is that 'It is me' was standard usage for several hundred years before people started to worry about it and to conclude that 'It is I' is more 'logical' and 'polite.' Actually, either form is quite acceptable today, but 'It is *I*' (*we, he, she, they*) is probably preferred by teachers of English generally.

Using the 'proper' case forms of the interrogative and relative pronoun *who* is apparently a matter of considerable interest to many persons who are anxious to make a good impression with their grammar. This is true, in spite of the fact that the *who–whom* distinction is probably the least 'live' of all the inflections in the language. It has no more effect on communication than the color of the tie a man chooses to wear on Sunday. Yet, since so many people want to 'play it safe' with this pronoun, out of fear that their 'mistakes' will brand them as uneducated or gauche, we must make an attempt to describe the practices of the majority of educated people.

Confusion in regard to the distinction between *who* and *whom* is caused primarily by the peculiar word-order patterns of the interrogative sentence, of the relative clause, and of the clause that expresses an indirect question. As we saw in Chapters X and XII (pp. 125 and 177), the object form *whom*—as well as the form *who*—appears at the beginning of the sentence or clause before the verb, not in the object territory after the verb where it would be expected. In other words, *who* and *whom* both occupy the same general area in the clause. This is bound to cause confusion, and a tendency to use the subject form *who* whether the pronoun functions as subject or object, or to use the object form *whom* indiscriminately out of a zeal for 'correctness.'

The 'rules' for the use of this pronoun are not difficult to understand. In the interrogative sentence, the use of *who*, when the pronoun is the first word in the sentence, whether it is subject, object, object of a preposition, or subject of an infinitive, is all but universal:

> Who is coming to the party?
> Who did you ask to the party?
> Who were you speaking to?
> Who have you asked to dance?

Only when this interrogative pronoun follows a preposition is the object form always used:

> To whom were you speaking?

However, when this pronoun is employed in a dependent clause, either as relative or interrogative, we have a different pattern of usage. For in these situations most speakers of standard English do try to distinguish between the use of *who* in the subject function and *whom* in the non-subject functions. Fortunately this is not too difficult to do, since there is a convenient rule of thumb which may be used as a guide. We merely have to remember that if a subject (other than *who*) is expressed in the clause, the *whom* form should be used; if there is no subject, then the pronoun itself must be the subject, and *who* should be used. Because of the set subject-verb word order in dependent clauses, this rule can be formulated in terms of word-order patterns. The subject form WHO should be used when this pronoun, or a single-word or phrasal modifier of it, is FOLLOWED by a verb or a verb phrase. (The only exception to this part of the rule occurs in an unusual kind of sentence in which the relative clause is introduced, not by the relative pronoun, but by a noun subject of that clause: *There is Mrs. Jones, a picture of whom appeared in the paper.*) The object form WHOM should be used when this pronoun, or a single-word or phrasal modifier of it, is FOLLOWED IN ITS OWN CLAUSE by a noun, a noun phrase, or another pronoun. The following sentences illustrate these patterns:

> The housemother wanted to know *who was making all that noise.* (The form is *who* because the pronoun is followed by the verb phrase *was making.*)
>
> Last night we saw John Blank, *whom the whole town is discussing.* (The form is *whom* because it is followed by the noun phrase *the whole town.*)
>
> There is John Blank, *whom I must speak to immediately.* (The form is *whom* because it is followed by the pronoun *I.*)
>
> There is John Blank, *whom everybody wants to represent us.* (*Whom* is used because it is followed by the pronoun *everybody.*)
>
> There are many people *who, calling themselves friends, will stab you in the back.* (*Who* is used because it is followed, after its modifier, by the verb *will stab.*)
>
> The decision about *who should be on the committee* will be made tomorrow. (*Who* is used because it is followed by the verb *should be.*)
>
> The decision about *whom we should dance with* will be made in advance. (*Whom* is used because it is followed by the pronoun *we.*)

There is only one exception to this rule—where a linking verb, such as *be, become, appear,* etc., is used in the clause and the *who* functions as a predicate pronoun, as in the sentence:

> He couldn't decide *who he would be in the masquerade.*

If the rule above were followed literally, *whom* would be called for in this situation because it precedes the pronoun *he.* However, most teachers will insist on the use of *who*—a position they maintain because of the linking function that *be* performs between subject and predicate noun. The truth is that this distinction is rarely observed even in the writing of highly educated people, so under most conditions either *who* or *whom* would be acceptable in this type of clause.

An important part of the rule given above is the phrase 'in its own clause,' and failure to observe this qualification causes the most common 'mistake' made in choosing between the forms of *who* and *whom.* The qualification is necessary because the element that immediately follows this pronoun is often not a part of its own clause, but rather another clause, called a 'parenthetical' one, such as *I think, the people believe,* or *we suspected.* Sentences of this type are very common:

> The prize was won by John Smith, who the whole town thinks will go far.

Here, *who* is followed by *the whole town,* a noun phrase, so if the important qualification 'in its own clause' were ignored, the form *whom* would be indicated. But *whole town* is not in the same clause as *who.* It is the subject of a tertiary clause, *the whole town thinks,* which nests within the relative clause. This phrase, therefore, has no influence over the forms of the words in the secondary relative clause. The element that follows the pronoun in its own clause and thus determines the form of the pronoun is the verb phrase *will go far,* so according to our rule the *who* form should be used. This problem shows once more how important it is to be able to sort out the various structural levels in a sentence.

This rule we have given for the selection of the *who–whom* forms in dependent clauses should eliminate a misconception which often occurs in connection with indirect questions introduced by this pronoun, such as:

> Will you suggest who would be the best candidate?
> It is a question of who should be notified in case of death.

Some people mistakenly believe that the *whom* form is indicated because of the position of the pronouns following the verb *suggest* and the preposition *of*. This would be a correct deduction if these were simple sentences, but these are complex sentences with two clauses, the structures of which must be analyzed as separate units. When the elements of the sentences are sorted out, it will be apparent that *suggest* and *who* (and *of* and *who*) are not a part of the same clause and, therefore, neither one can influence the form of the other. One will never make mistakes with this kind of sentence if he remembers that it is the word or word group FOLLOWING the 'who' pronoun that generally determines its form (see Chapter XII, p. 178).

Selecting Adjective and Adverb Forms

Very often we are faced with the problem of deciding whether a modifier should have an adjective or adverb form. This problem occurs only when there are separate but similar forms for adjectives and adverbs. Obviously, there is no problem when there is only one form for both parts of speech, as with the one-form modifiers, *early, far, better, fast, hard,*[3] *straight, low, little, long, daily, weekly, monthly, yearly, first, second,* and other numerals. These words are used regularly in all adjective and adverb positions. The most common situation in which separate but similar forms occur is when the uninflected adjective is converted into an adverb by the use of the suffix *-ly,* as in *happy–happily, sad–sadly, fortunate–fortunately,* etc. If we think the construction in question calls for an adjective, we use the plain form, if an adverb, we use the *-ly* form.

---

[3] In modern English the adverb *hardly* does not correspond in meaning with the adjective–adverb *hard.* George Eliot writes of a horse's 'hardly earned feed,' but the word is not used in this sense today.

But one should be careful not to assume that all words ending in
-*ly* are adverb forms, because they are not. As we pointed out in
Chapter IX, many adjectives also have this suffix, such as *lively,*
worldly, deadly, lowly, kindly, manly, etc. But distinguishing between -*ly* adjectives and adverbs ending in the same suffix is not a
serious problem. Any native English speaker can easily test words
of this kind by placing them in the attributive position before an
appropriate noun. If the word in question makes sense in this position, it is an adjective. Thus, *a lively dance, a worldly man, a deadly*
weapon are possible, but not *a quickly fox* or *a fortunately person.*
A few of these -*ly* forms may be both adjectives and adverbs. Most
of these have to do with time, such as *daily, weekly, monthly,* and
yearly. The other -*ly* adjectives can be made into adverbial elements
only by putting them into adverbial prepositional phrases, such as
in a worldly manner, in a lively way, etc.

After thus distinguishing the adjective from the adverb forms, the
question arises: Where does one use each of these forms? This question is not as easily answered as one might think, for in many of the
'adverb' positions described in Chapter IX, adverb forms are not
always used. For the sake of convenience, this discussion may be
divided into five parts.

First, there is fortunately one situation in which adverb forms are
always used. This is the movable position. Any two-form modifier
that can be moved about freely within the sentence—that is, not
only from front to end position and vice versa, but from an outside
position to an inside position and vice versa, must have the adverbial form. The following sentences illustrate this kind of adverb:

> *Fortunately,* the rain held off.
> The rain *fortunately* held off.
> The rain held off, *fortunately.*
>
> *Finally,* we reached New York.
> We *finally* reached New York.
> We reached New York *finally.*

Second, there is one situation in which adverb forms are never
used. This is when the modifier is a complement after the linking

verbs, such as *be, become, feel, smell, look, appear, taste, sound, keep, get, prove, turn, turn out,* and *come out* (see p. 99). An important point to remember in connection with this construction is the fact that there are many more verbs which perform the function of linking a predicate adjective with the subject of the sentence than most people imagine. All the verbs used in the following sentences are linking verbs:

> The clothes washed out clean.
>
> She passed out cold.
>
> The shutter broke loose.
>
> The string pulled tight.
>
> Milton ranks high among the poets.
>
> We all remain healthy.
>
> Swift went mad.
>
> I woke up shivering.

Many people get into trouble with modifier forms because they think that the only linking verbs are *be, seem, appear,* and those expressing the operations of the five senses. This leads them to use the adverb form in places where it does not belong, as in

> The pudding came out too *sweetly.*
>
> Milton ranks *highly* in literature.
>
> The string is pulled too *tightly.*

As we saw in Chapter VIII, many verbs in the passive form also may take adjective complements. Some examples are:

> Her hair was cut *short.*
>
> The barn was painted *red.*
>
> The streets were washed *clean.*
>
> His injuries were not considered *serious.*

Some of these verbs may be used both as linking verbs with adjective complements and as non-linking verbs with adverb modifiers—usually with very different meanings. *Turn* and *go,* for example, may be used with adjective complements, as in *turn brown* and *go mad,* or these verbs may be used with adverb modifiers, as in *turn slowly* and *go silently*. Sometimes the *-ly* ending may make an enormous difference in meaning. Clearly the sentence *His injuries were not considered serious* is quite different from *His injuries were not considered seriously*. And *Her hair will be cut short* is quite different from *Her hair will be cut shortly*. Even such typical linking verbs as *smell* and *taste* may be used in a non-linking way with adverb modifiers, but only when the modifier expresses the manner of smelling and tasting, as in

> Since she caught that bad cold, she hasn't been able to taste very *well*.

Since the linking verbs are too numerous to memorize and some may be both linking and non-linking in function, we must fall back on a rule based on meaning: Any modifier in the predicate position that clearly modifies the subject must have an adjective form, and a modifier that expresses the notion of 'manner' must have an adverb form. The most serious usage problem in this construction results from the tendency, as we have said, to over-use the adverb forms, even after the most common linking verbs. Thus we often hear, 'The roses smell *sweetly*,' 'The sun feels *wonderfully* on my back,' or 'That dress looks *well* on her.' Some usages of this type are completely unacceptable, but such expressions as *feels badly* and *looks well* (not meaning healthy), while often prohibited in the classroom, are used by many respectable writers. In fact, they are actually considered more 'correct' by some persons probably because the words *bad* and *good,* for some reason, have developed a bad reputation among users of the language, so they tend to use the forms *badly* and *well* wherever possible.

Third, modifiers following noun complements must have adjective forms when they express the idea of result and clearly modify the preceding noun. Examples of this kind of predicate adjective are: *Hold her close, Hang the picture straight, Spread the paint smooth, Play something nice,* and *Store the eggs separate.* Adverbs may, of course, also appear in this position, as in *Hang the picture carefully, Spread the paint quickly,* etc. Sometimes there is only a slight difference in meaning between the adjective and adverb functions in this position, sometimes a very great one. *Play something nice* is indeed very different from *Play something nicely*. But one has to think a few moments before seeing that *Store the eggs separate* expresses a meaning subtly different from *Store the eggs separately*.

Fourth, there is a group of verbs after which either an adjective or an adverb may be used without any real difference in meaning, as in *John stood rigid (rigidly), He dug deep (deeply), She speaks loud (loudly), It comes easy (easily), She acted peculiar (peculiarly), He played fair (fairly)*. It is hard to describe the meaning of this kind of predicate modifier. It is not so clearly a modifier of the subject as are the modifiers which follow the traditional linking verbs; and the emphasis is not so much on the manner of the action (as it would be if only an adverb could be used), but on the result of the action. Actually this kind of modifier partakes of the meaning of both these constructions. And, since either form is acceptable, no problem of usage is involved. Almost any modifier except *good* and *bad* may be used in this dual function. *Good* and *bad* are universally banned as predicate modifiers except after the conventional linking verbs *be, become, appear, feel, taste, look,* and *sound,* and many people do not like these adjectives even after certain of these verbs.

Fifth, another position in which both adjective and adverb forms are used involves tertiary modifiers. Two types of tertiaries may have the adjective form. The first of these is the modifier of certain verbal adjectives. As might be expected, when linking verbs are made into verbals and the adjective complements of these verbs are turned into attributive modifiers of the verbals, the adjective form is always retained, as in *an awful looking dress,* a *foul tasting medicine,* and *a beautiful sounding instrument.* Such attempts at 'refinement' as *foully tasting medicine* should be strictly avoided. Before other verbals, of course, the adverb form is used: *a highly regarded person, a widely read man,* etc.

Certain other tertiary modifiers that express the idea of 'degree' may also use the adjective form: *bright blue cloth, dull blue cloth, deep red color, bitter cold day, great big dog, white hot iron,* and *high-up officials.* The number of degree modifiers that can be used in this form is strictly limited. We can say *a bitter cold day,* but we do not say *a fair cold day* or *a miserable cold day,* unless we want these phrases to mean something quite different from *a fairly cold day* and *a miserably cold day.* There is no set rule regarding the form of degree modifiers, but at least six adjectives are usually banned in this position in written standard English. These are *mighty, real, right, terrible, dreadful,* and *awful,* as in *a mighty fine steak, a real good breakfast,* or *a right handsome woman.*

Most of the problems discussed in this chapter have involved quite literally the 'forms' of words—that is to say, we were largely concerned with the ways in which certain inflections are used. The inflection, of all the grammatical devices, as we have pointed out before, is the least important device for communicating grammatical meaning, especially in those situations where 'mistakes' are made in selecting the acceptable forms (see Chapter II, p. 17). This means that even if all these forms were properly chosen (no *he don't's,* no *whom's* for *who's,* etc.) one's writing still could be wholly lacking in many of the other qualities which characterize good sentences. In fact, if the proper forms are not in their proper places and not accompanied by the proper function words to convey the meaning intended, the sentences could be utter nonsense. Some of these problems involving the construction of the sentence as a whole, especially the ordering of the words, phrases, and clauses in all their structural complexities, will be the principal subject of the chapter that follows.

XV

CONSTRUCTIONS AND COMMAS

The misplacing of the parts of sentences is one of the most per-
sistent of all problems in the use of English. This kind of error
results, of course, from the fact, repeated so often in this book, that
the position of a word, phrase, or clause gives a strong signal concerning its grammatical meaning. That is, its position indicates
whether a given word is intended, for example, as a subject, verb,
or object, or whether it is intended as a modifier or a word modified. And, in more complex sentences, the position will signal which
of the various structural groups the word belongs in. Unlike the
so-called 'social' errors involving inflection, these word-order errors
may result in serious weaknesses in communication; nor do we have
'divided' usage in this area: if a word is misplaced, it is wrong. It
is because of this connection between word order and grammatical
meaning that so much emphasis has been placed upon the positions
occupied by words belonging to the various grammatical classes.

I

It is perhaps paradoxical that words which depend most heavily
on fixed positions to express their grammatical meaning are rarely
misplaced by a native English speaker. Yet the reason is clear
enough, for if such elements were put in the wrong position, the

meaning intended would not be communicated at all. This is why we do not often make mistakes with the subject-verb-complement pattern. For example, we would never say, 'The policeman shot the prowler,' if we knew that the policeman was lying dead on the living room floor and the prowler was fleeing down the back alley; for this 'mistake' in word order completely reverses the meaning intended. It is only when other grammatical devices are also present to direct the reader and the word order is consequently less fixed (but nonetheless important) that mistakes in word order are likely to be made.

Most grammatical word-order errors occur in connection with the placing of the many kinds of modifying elements. These range all the way from the single-word adjective, adverb, or attributive noun to prepositional phrases, infinitive phrases, participial phrases (including third, fourth, and fifth forms), conjunction-headed phrases, and the several kinds of dependent clauses. The traditional rule is that modifiers of specific words should be placed as near as possible to these words, either before or after them. This rule often works very well, but there are a number of weaknesses that limit its usefulness. These weaknesses should therefore be thoroughly understood.

In the first place, the usefulness of this rule is limited by the fact that so many modifying elements modify not a specific word but an entire statement. These are of course the 'movable' modifiers. Obviously, such modifiers cannot come 'as near as possible to the word modified,' and students often have trouble when they try to find such a place for them. The second weakness in this rule involves the words 'as near as possible'; for, when we compose very complex sentences, 'as near as possible' varies greatly, depending on the type of modifier and the specific context. This problem is caused, of course, by overcrowding. If there are three modifiers that are supposed to go in the same place, 'as near as possible' is obviously of no help. And the problem of finding 'parking space' for them becomes acute as the sentence grows longer and the traffic of modifiers increases. Therefore, it is often necessary to work out a kind of priority system for the different types of modifiers that normally belong in the appositive position, with the single-word modifier taking the spot closest to the word modified—then the phrase and finally the clause. A third weakness in this rule arises from the fact that sometimes it is not right at all to place a group modifier as near as possible to the word modified. For example, in the sentence

She sat at the window brushing her golden hair

the modifying phrase *brushing her golden hair* is as far as possible from the word it modifies, but this is idiomatically the best position for it. These observations lead to the conclusion that placing modifiers is a very complex problem—one that cannot be solved by the use of any one simple rule-of-thumb. However, this 'near as possible' rule should be understood and remembered, but also its limitations should be clearly recognized.

II

The single-word adjective modifier is not often misrelated; this is true for the same reason that we do not misplace the members of the subject-verb-complement pattern; for here again the set word order is usually the only device used to signal the meaning, so if the correct word order is not observed, complete failure in communication results. It was pointed out in Chapter VIII that drastic changes in meaning occur when we reverse the word order in such structures as *dog house, bird song, box lunch,* and *barn red.* There is just one situation in which the placing of a single-word adjective has to be closely watched. This is when two nouns come together and the first is a modifier of the second, as in *boys' sweaters* and *boat anchorage.* In *boys' sweaters* and other such genitive-noun combinations, one should remember that a word intended as a modifier of the second noun should never be put before the first one; for, in this position, the word will inevitably be interpreted by the reader as the modifier of the closer noun—often with the most ludicrous results. The copy writer who wrote the advertisement:

Imperfect boys' orlon sweaters $3.95

apparently did not know this rule, or had forgotten it. This problem is merely a matter of misplacing a modifier and may be corrected by placing the word in the proper position before the word modified: *Boys' imperfect orlon sweaters.*

As for *boat anchorage* and other attributive noun-noun structures, an adjective placed before the attributive noun will be interpreted by the reader as a modifier either of the first noun or of the combination of both (see Chapter IX, p. 118), depending on the vocabulary meanings of the respective nouns. In *steam boat anchorage,* obviously *steam* modifies *boat,* but in *shallow boat anchorage, shallow* modifies the entire phrase *boat anchorage.* If the vocabulary meanings do not make the direction of modification clear, ambiguity may result, as in *small boat anchorage.* Or, it may cause unintentional humor as in *heavy equipment manufacturer.*

Unfortunately, we cannot clear up this kind of difficulty simply by moving the adjective. But there are two other ways to solve it. The first is to use a hyphen between *small* and *boat* if we want the adjective to modify *boat* and between *boat* and *anchorage,* if we want it to modify the combination of the two nouns. Or we may substitute a prepositional phrase for the first noun, thus eliminating the problem of the two nouns coming together: *anchorage for small boats; small anchorage for boats,* or *manufacturer of heavy equipment.*

But problems with single-word adjectives do not occur frequently. It is when devices other than word order are used and the word order is more elastic that writers become most careless about relating modifiers to the correct word. This happens sometimes with single-word adverbs, which not only frequently have another device—the *-ly* permanent form—but are also often not in a fixed position. Because adverbs are movable in some contexts, there is a common tendency among writers to be rather careless when placing those that should be fixed.

The following groups of sentences show how a change in the position of the adverb subtly alters the meaning:

> This book is *more* for advanced students.
> This book is for *more* advanced students.

Truly, I love you.
I love you *truly.*

How many men *roughly* play football?
How many men play football *roughly?*

He spoke of seeing me *also* in New York.
He spoke of seeing me in New York *also.*
He *also* spoke of seeing me in New York.
Also, he spoke of seeing me in New York.

In the last group of sentences *also* appears in many different positions, but it is not a movable modifier, for each position conveys a subtly different meaning. A close look at this last group will show, in addition, that two of the positions of *also* make the sentences ambiguous. In the first sentence, the meaning is ambiguous because the word could modify either *me* or *in New York.* If it is intended as a modifier of *me,* the sentence could be improved by finding some other word or phrase which could be interpreted unmistakably as a modifier of that word, like *as well as you.* In the third sentence, it is ambiguous, for it could modify either *he* or the entire predicate *spoke of seeing.* . . In the spoken language, a change of pitch after *also* would indicate that it was intended as a modifier of *he.* If it is to be intended as a modifier of the entire predicate, it would have been better to place it after *spoke,* where it could not be attracted as a modifier to any other word.

Many of the difficulties encountered in placing adverbs occur because a distinction is not made between the movable and the fixed positions and the different kind of meaning each conveys. It must be remembered that if what we intend as a movable adverb, modifying the entire predicate, is put in a fixed position before or after a specific word which could attract it as a modifier, a fixed-position meaning will be conveyed. In other words, the reader will interpret it as narrowly restricting the meaning of a single word. In any of those sentences above illustrating the position of the adverb *also,* the writer may have intended *also* as a movable modifier loosely restricting the general meaning of the sentence ('he spoke, in addition to other topics of conversation, of seeing me in New York').

But only when this word appears before *he* and after *spoke* is this meaning clearly expressed. In every other position *also* is placed next to a word which can attract it as a fixed modifier, thus narrowly restricting the meaning of that word and that word alone (*me* also, *in New York* also, *he* also).

III

But more important than misplacing the single-word modifier is misplacing the various kinds of group modifiers. Whether it is a simple two-word prepositional phrase or a ten-word dependent clause, a group modifier is always in danger of slipping into a place where it is related to the wrong word, with a resulting failure in communication. There are several reasons for this tendency to misplace group modifiers. In the first place, devices other than word order are always present. For example, a function word is always used with a prepositional phrase and usually with a dependent clause, and inflection is always used with participial modifiers. The presence of these other devices allows for more elasticity in the word order—demoting its importance somewhat—so that careless writers have a tendency to ignore it altogether or at least to forget that in our language, no matter how many other devices are present, word order still remains the most important for determining grammatical meaning.

Another reason why group modifiers, especially adjective group modifiers, are so often misplaced is that all adjective modifiers of this type normally fall in the same position following the noun. Sometimes two or three phrases, both verbal and prepositional, and several clauses may compete for position in this place. Handling this problem requires considerable knowledge of and skill in the art of sentence construction. We have to know, for example, what type of modifier should be awarded the choice place close to the word modified and which element may be safely moved to a distance, and under what circumstances this may be done. We must also know how to reduce the number of modifiers by recasting the sentence completely, if recourse to this strategy is the only way to solve the problem.

Probably the most frequently misplaced of the group modifiers is the prepositional phrase. In Chapter IX the positions of both types of prepositional phrases (adjective and adverb) were described in general terms. The adjective phrase most commonly follows the noun modified, as in *the picture on the dresser* or *an era of good feeling*. Sometimes, however, such a phrase may not directly follow the noun: it is possible for a single-word adjective or another prepositional phrase to intervene. And occasionally an adjective prepositional phrase may come before, instead of after, the noun modified, as in:

> *With a hundred-foot shore frontage,* the lot is very desirable.
> *As an old customer,* I demand good service.

The adverb prepositional phrase usually comes in one of three places. It may come immediately after the word modified, usually an adjective, as in:

> He is delirious *with happiness.*
> Happy *over succeeding,* John treated the whole crowd.

Or the phrase may come at the beginning or the end of the sentence or clause, with the end position being more idiomatic, as in:

> The highwayman held up the stage *with a gun.*

It is a general rule of composition that prepositional phrases should come as near as possible to the words they modify. But this rule is not always easy to follow, since often there are other elements that compete for this same place. Contrary to the rule given in many composition books, it is not always 'incorrect' to allow certain kinds of elements to come between a prepositional phrase and the word it modifies. These elements are: single-word modifiers, other prepositional phrases, and, at the end of the sentence, the various kinds of complements.

When any of these elements intervene, the prepositional phrase is 'misplaced' only if one of the components of the intervening structure could be mistaken for the word to be modified. Unfortunately, this danger always exists, since all structures of modification are extremely 'cohesive,' that is, if two elements are close together in a sentence, the reader tends to interpret them as belonging together grammatically. This is called the principle of 'attraction.' Whether this attraction takes place when elements intervene depends on several factors. One is the vocabulary meanings of both the word intervening and the preposition itself: certainly such a combination as *books by* will be taken as belonging together grammatically; so one cannot say, 'a review of two books by John Doe,' if he means not that the books but the review is by John Doe. Here the prepositional phrase has been misplaced because its position following *books* gives the word group a meaning that the writer did not intend.

Another factor is the position of the phrase in relation to the sentence as a whole—whether it comes inside the sentence, at the beginning of the sentence, or at the end. When the phrase is in an INSIDE POSITION, trouble may occur if another prepositional phrase intervenes; for the object of the intervening phrase is usually interpreted by the reader as the word modified by the other prepositional phrase. For example, in the sentence

The man next to the post in the blue uniform is Alfred

the reader immediately will start thinking about 'posts in blue uniforms,' which is hardly what the writer of this sentence intended! This problem is caused mainly by the fact that the two prepositional phrases are co-ordinate or parallel in structure, but unlike other compound structures, are rarely separated by co-ordinating conjunctions. (We would never say, 'The man next to the post *and* in the blue uniform . . .') If such a conjunction were used in this position, the whole problem would of course disappear, for the conjunction would prevent the second phrase from directly following a component of the first one.

When two of these co-ordinate prepositional phrases come together inside the sentence, humor or ambiguity almost always results, for the attraction is so strong in this position that the object of the first preposition, regardless of its meaning, will be interpreted as the word modified by the second prepositional phrase.

Phrases that are misrelated in this way often cause the broadest kind of humor, as in:

> The farmer in the jeep with the red nose sells potatoes.
> The man with the black hair from Peru is our local consul.

In these sentences, the writer undoubtedly 'heard' a pitch pattern, which indicated to him that the second phrases were not intended to modify the objects of the first. But, alas, these devices, as we have said before, are not a part of the written language, and the reader cannot 'hear' what the writer is thinking. It is thus rarely safe to use two co-ordinate prepositional phrases together in the inside sentence position. The best solution to this problem is to turn one of the phrases into some kind of attributive modifier: *the red-nosed farmer in the jeep; the Peruvian with the black hair.* This change leaves the remaining phrase as the sole occupant of the appositive territory, thus eliminating any possibility of a misrelated modifier.

When the prepositional phrase precedes the word modified, as it occasionally does in such a sentence as this:

> As an investor, I am not being favored by the government,

the first noun or pronoun following the phrase will be taken as the word modified. When the phrase appears in this position, the writer must be careful again not to allow another noun to intervene. If this rule is disregarded, he may write an ambiguous sentence such as

> As an investor, the government is not treating me right.

The prepositional phrase causes trouble particularly when it is in an END OF THE SENTENCE POSITION, following a noun complement, another prepositional phrase, or another single-word modifier. A prepositional phrase in this position normally functions either as a modifier of the noun or adjective immediately preceding it, or of the verb. A problem arises when such a phrase intended as a modifier of the verb is attracted by the preceding word, or when the phrase could be interpreted as modifying either word, thus causing an ambiguous sentence. Unlike phrases in the inside position, end phrases are not always attracted strongly by the preceding word.

This is caused by the rival attraction of the verb. Therefore, the vocabulary meaning of the preceding word becomes more important in deciding whether the phrase may be used in this position without creating ambiguity or unintentional humor. In order to avoid making mistakes in placing phrases in the end position, the following rule should be carefully studied and memorized: If the word preceding the phrase is a noun or an adjective, the meaning of which allows it to attract the phrase as a modifier, this phrase will be interpreted as a modifier of that word, as in:

> The author read the first act *of Pygmalion.*
> The farmers built a bridge *across the creek.*

Under all other conditions, the phrase will be interpreted as a modifier of the verb (or the entire predicate). The following sentences illustrate this part of the rule:

> People work hard *in our factory.* (preceded by adverb: modifies *work hard*)
> The room looks better *at night.* (preceded by an adjective which does not attract the phrase)
> John strolled across the street *in his bathing suit.* (preceded by a noun which does not attract the phrase)

If this rule is not understood, the writer is always in danger of writing ambiguous or ludicrous sentences. If, for example, we should change *John strolled across the street in his bathing suit* to *John caught a prowler in his bathing suit,* we have unconsciously created humorous ambiguity, because of our failure to see that the vocabulary meaning of *prowler,* unlike that of *street,* allows *prowler* to attract *in his bathing suit.* The sentence would be even more foolish if the gender of the subject and the pronoun were changed:

> Barbara caught a prowler *in her bathing suit.*

In the last sentence above, the problem cannot be solved by moving the phrase to another position, for this is the normal place for it and any other would be unidiomatic. Here the only solution is to change the prepositional phrase into a dependent clause, which allows a repetition of the subject:

>Barbara caught a prowler when she was wearing nothing but her bathing suit.

This may seem roundabout and rather wordy, but very often errors in sentence structure are caused by the tendency on the part of inexperienced writers to compress too many ideas into too few words.

It is not always easy to decide whether the word preceding an end-position prepositional phrase has the kind of vocabulary meaning which attracts the phrase away from the verb. In this kind of situation, of course, the sentence is ambiguous: we cannot tell whether the phrase modifies the word preceding it or the verb. The following sentence exemplifies this problem:

>Robert Blair wrote a poem on a tombstone.

Did he write a poem on the subject of a tombstone? (phrase modifies *poem*) Did he write a poem while sitting on a tombstone? Or did he use the tombstone instead of the back of an envelope? (phrase modifies the verb) When prepositional phrases are placed in the end position, they should be carefully checked for such possible ambiguities.

Another general problem in connection with the placing of prepositional phrases has to do with the intrusion of different types of verb elements between the prepositional phrase and the word it modifies. A phrase containing a verbal element is banned in this position, because any member of such a phrase may attract the prepositional phrase as a modifier and create a ridiculous meaning. Sometimes the object of the verbal will do this, as in *the man wearing a panama hat with a beard,* or the verbal element itself: in a student publication, there appeared the sentence

>This is a novel about a girl known as Manty *during the Civil War.*

The position of the phrase *during the Civil War* allows it to be attracted by the verbal element *known,* thus implying that the girl was 'known as Manty' only during the Civil War. This kind of blunder could have been avoided by using an attributive modifier instead of a prepositional phrase:

This is a *Civil War* novel about a girl known as Manty.

In the sentence

> The men will discuss their plan to create a United Nations police
> force *at the headquarters of the Woman's Club*

the unintentional humor is caused by the fact that the verbal element *to create* has been allowed to come between *discuss* and *at the headquarters.* All of these mistakes are clearly examples of misplacing a prepositional phrase, since they violate the general rule that no type of verb element should come between a prepositional phrase and the word the phrase is intended to modify.

This general rule applies also to intervening dependent clauses, because, of course, all such clauses contain a verb element. In the sentence

> A person who likes candy *with diabetes* is unfortunate

the position of *with diabetes* conveys the ludicrous meaning that the candy has the disease! This mistake can be corrected easily by moving the phrase to its proper position—before the clause:

> A person *with diabetes* who likes candy is unfortunate.

In sentences like this, where both the relative clause and the prepositional phrase modify the same noun, care must be taken to select the proper form of the relative pronoun, for often the gender distinction which this pronoun provides (*who,* masculine and feminine; *that* and *which,* neuter) is the only means the writer has of indicating whether the clause is intended to modify the object of the preposition or the noun preceding the preposition. In the sentence above, the use of *who* (instead of *that*) indicates clearly that it modifies *person* and not *diabetes.*

End-shifted prepositional phrases—those that modify the subject but are shifted to the end of the sentence—also violate this rule that no verbal element should come between the phrase and the word it modifies. Here, of course, the main verb intervenes. Sometimes the meaning of the sentence is not affected when the phrase is in this position, but often ambiguity results. In the sentence

John caught the cold instead of Jim

the meaning is perfectly clear; but this slightly different sentence

The cat caught the bird instead of Jim

is ambiguous. Sometimes a radical change in meaning takes place when a prepositional phrase is end-shifted. Certainly, the sentence

The nurse is very pleasant *on duty*

has a very different meaning from

The nurse *on duty* is very pleasant.

Because of these pitfalls in connection with the end-shifted prepositional phrase, the student should be advised not to place this kind of group modifier in the end position unless it is intended to modify either the verb or the word immediately preceding the phrase.

IV

The next general problem in placing group modifiers has to do with all types of adjective phrases other than the prepositional phrase. These are of three types:

1. The non-verbal adjective that has been expanded with other modifiers, particularly with one or more prepositional or infinitive phrases:

   Happy over his success, John will probably work harder now.
   The morning after the tennis game, I woke up *stiff as a board.*
   Anxious to succeed, John studied every night.

2. Verbal adjectives expanded by any kind of modifier or complement:

   I saw Barbara at the window *brushing her hair.*
   Having decided to build a house, the Joneses started to look for a lot.
   A truck *loaded with junk* drew up to the house.

3. Any conjunction-headed adjective (see Chapter XII, p. 171):

   When happy, all people do better work.
   The carpenter broke his arm *while shingling the roof.*

The general problem of placing this type of group modifier is much simpler than any of those connected with the prepositional phrase. But the principle of attraction is also a problem here. We saw in Chapter XI some examples of what ludicrous effects may occur when a verbal phrase is put in a position where some word other than the one intended by the writer attracts it as a modifier. We had corpses swimming in Lake Michigan and sunsets walking down the avenue.

Difficulties occur most often when this kind of phrase appears either at the beginning or end of the sentence or clause. When the phrase comes first, the rule is simple and clear-cut: in a declarative sentence, the phrase must always be followed by the noun modified, or by some other modifier of that noun, as in the three examples above: *Happy over his success* modifies *John, having decided to build a house* modifies *the Joneses,* and *when happy* modifies *all people.* If this rule is not followed, one is always in danger of writing such nonsensical sentences as the following:

> *Forced into idleness by the strike,* the babies of the miners had nothing to eat.
> *Walking down the street,* the poor little houses looked beautiful to me.
> *While shingling the roof,* the hammer fell on the carpenter's toes.

In an interrogative sentence, phrases in this front position must be followed by an auxiliary verb and then the word modified, as in

> *Having looked at all the dresses in the store,* can you make up your mind now?
> *After doing the dishes,* will you wipe off the shelves?

In questions such as these, ambiguity is almost certain to result if this rule is not followed to the letter. In the sentence

> *Having studied for two hours,* do you think the class is ready to recite?

the writer probably meant *class* to be the word modified, but one simply cannot be sure, since it is not in the correct position to convey this meaning.

When any one of these types of adjective phrases appears in the end position of a well-constructed sentence, the word it modifies will appear in one of two places. First, it may precede the modifier—either immediately or with another modifier coming between—as in the following:

> We were fascinated by the sight of the FIREMEN *climbing the high ladder.*
>
> Iron the CLOTHES *when still damp.*
>
> Chaucer's Prioress cried over a MOUSE *caught in a trap.*
>
> We saw a WOMAN at the window *shouting for help.*

Here a problem exists only when another group modifier containing a noun, such as a prepositional phrase, intervenes. The last sentence above is an example of this kind of structure. This is the normal word order for these phrases; but, as with two prepositional phrases in tandem, there is always the danger that the noun in the first phrase will attract the whole second phrase as a modifier—often with humorous results, as in

> It's the man next to the post reading a newspaper.

If the vocabulary meanings of both nouns preceding the second phrase allow either noun to be modified, an ambiguous sentence will result:

> It's the man next to the woman reading a newspaper.

Since there is this possibility of ambiguity, the writer must always be conscious of it and place his phrases in this area with extreme care.

Second, the word modified by any end-position adjective phrase may also be the subject of the clause or sentence:

> JACK AND JILL came down the hill *carrying a pail of water.*
>
> This MATERIAL should not be ironed *when damp.*
>
> MARY returned home *delighted with her purchase.*

When there are two nouns preceding the phrase, one in the subject position and one just before the phrase and when the vocabulary meanings of both nouns are such that either one could attract the adjective phrase as modifier, the nearer noun has the stronger attracting power. Thus in the sentence

> John heard MARY *playing the piano,*

we would interpret MARY as the word modified.

Because of the superior attracting power of the nearer word, the problem of the misrelated modifier crops up whenever the end-position phrase is intended to modify the subject; for here we encounter again the possibility that another noun may sneak in between and attract the modifier away from the subject. Under most circumstances, an intervening noun does not cause any trouble. The following sentences are quite all right:

> Barbara sat in the window *brushing her hair.*
> The huckster was parked at the curb, *shouting his wares.*
> He stalked out of the room, *mad as a hatter.*

In fact, the end position for these phrases is idiomatically the best one. But there are two situations in which an intervening noun may attract the phrase away from the subject and cause ambiguity or foolishness.

In the first of these, the noun intervening is the object of a verb—most often a verb expressing the ideas of seeing, hearing, feeling, tasting, smelling, and touching. Using an end-shifted phrase, especially a third-form verbal phrase, after this kind of verb causes the humor in the following sentences:

> He watched the sunset *driving along Route 1.*
> He saw a corpse *swimming in Lake Michigan.*
> He heard the fire siren *standing on the front porch.*
> He milked the cow *sitting on a stool.*

This type of error may be corrected in one of three ways. First, the phrase may be moved to the front position, either before or after the subject:

> *Driving along Route 1,* he watched the sunset.

Second, a conjunction may be used with the phrase:

> He watched the sunset *while driving along Route 1.*

It is possible to use these conjunction-headed phrases in the end-shifted position because they are more strongly attracted to the subject than any other type of verbal phrase. Third, the phrase may be expanded into a subordinate clause.

The second situation in which the preceding noun may attract an end-shifted phrase away from the subject occurs when the vocabulary meaning of the nearer noun clearly allows it, as well as the subject, to be the word modified. The following sentences show how this attraction may take place:

> Anybody might be arrested by the police *going 70 miles an hour.*
> Proust wrote about the Guermantes family *lying in bed.*

The police as well as *anybody* can, from the point of view of meaning, go 70 miles an hour. Therefore, *police,* because of its position, has attracted the phrase away from *anybody,* the word intended to be modified. A sentence with an end-shifted adjective phrase and an intervening noun of this kind may be even more foolish when a pronoun reference shows clearly that the phrase is intended to modify the subject:

> Proust wrote about the Guermantes family lying in *his* bed.

The errors in these sentences can be corrected by moving the phrases to the front position or by using conjunctions to head them:

> Anybody might be arrested by the police *when* going 70 miles an hour.
> Proust wrote about the Guermantes family *while* lying in bed.

In general, all end-shifted adjective phrases of this type should be watched very carefully for possible ambiguities.

Although the verbal adjective phrase headed with a conjunction, such as *while going* or *when driving,* tends to be more strongly attracted to the subject than to the noun immediately preceding it and therefore can be used freely in the end position, the reverse is true of the non-verbal adjective headed by a conjunction, such as *when happy, while damp,* and *although hot.* For this reason, phrases of this type should never follow any nouns except the ones they are intended to modify. If this rule is not followed, there is always the danger of writing such foolish sentences as:

> He was kind to his old mother even when drunk.
> Don't drink cold water when hot.

v

The next word-order problem involves the position of the dependent adjective clause. Like all other adjective modifiers, this kind of clause, ideally, should follow as closely as possible after the noun or pronoun it modifies. But, of all the adjective group modifiers, the clause is the least 'cohesively' attached to the headword; when there are three types of adjective modifiers competing for the appositive position, the full clause has to take third place, as in

> The people upstairs (single-word modifier) in the front apartment (phrasal modifier), who make so much noise (clausal modifier), have gone away.

When the clause follows a phrasal modifier, as it does in the sentence above, problems may arise; for under these conditions another noun will usually come between the clause and the word it modifies. The vocabulary meanings of the words usually prevent ambiguity: in the sentence above, for example, the meaning of *apartment* would not allow *who make so much noise* as a modifier. If, however, *in the front apartment* were changed to *with the three children*, the sentence becomes ambiguous. Sometimes, when the meanings of the individual words do not clarify the direction of modification, the result may be unintentionally humorous, as in the sentence

> A man with a ten-year-old son who married a widow with five children has bought the house next door.

With a clausal modifier, there are, fortunately, two inflectional devices which may help clarify the direction of modification and prevent confusion. One of these, as we pointed out earlier in this chapter (p. 247), is the gender form of the relative pronoun. It is an interesting fact that when this pronoun is omitted, the clause must follow directly after the noun modified, as in

> This is the book you borrowed last year.

A fixed word-order device thus replaces the missing inflectional one. Failure to observe this rule has caused the writer of the following sentence considerable trouble:

> After the exam was over, I had a grade in an interesting course *I could be proud of.*

Obviously, it was the grade that he was proud of, but his mishandling of the word order has made it appear that it was the course he was proud of. Second, the number form of the verb in the dependent clause may also establish the direction of modification. Thus in the sentence

> The bushes on the fence, which are too high, obstruct the view,

the plural form *are* indicates that the word modified by the clause is *bushes,* not *fence.* In spite of these inflectional aids to clarity, the student should always be on guard against the possibility of ambiguity.

Some writers attempt to solve this problem by setting off the intervening phrase with commas or dashes if they do not intend the adjective clause to modify the closer noun. In the sentence

> I picked up some pencils, from my uncle's study, that smelled of cedar,

the commas are presumably used to tell the reader that the clause *that smelled of cedar* modifies *pencils,* not *study.* Although it is quite proper to use commas in this kind of sentence, it is a rather weak way to solve the problem of the misrelated modifier, and should not be generally used by any except experienced writers.

Not all adjective clauses appear in the positions we have just been describing. Clauses that modify the subject may sometimes be end-shifted:

> A man is foolish who does not heed such danger signals.

This word order is the result of the normal tendency on the part of anyone who has a sense of style to want to 'weight' the sentence at the end with a 'heavy' modification structure. Although stylistically good, this position is grammatically dangerous because of the great distance between the clause and the word it modifies.

THE DANGLING ELEMENTS

One outstanding fact about the modern English sentence is that it is loaded with verb elements of all kinds. These range all the way from the permanent noun forms derived from verbs, such as *arrival, performance, operation,* and *movement,* through the various types of verbals, to the completed clause with its full subject-predicate form. In good writing all of these elements must be fitted like mosaics into the pattern of the sentence. When the sentence is a long one and many verbal ideas are crowded into it, the task of fitting the pieces together requires considerable skill. Inexperienced or careless writers often tend to put in extra pieces that have no place in the pattern. These mistakes occur most frequently with verbal elements, probably because writers who do not fully understand the structure of English tend to think that the verbal has an independent status similar to that of the sentence itself.

Some structural mistakes of this kind will be marked by the teacher as 'loosely constructed sentences.' The following is an example of a very bad sentence of this type:

> After we finished dinner we sat on the porch, watching the sunset, and playing cards later, going to bed at ten o'clock.

The last two verbal phrases (*playing cards* and *going to bed*) are simply tacked on at the end of the sentence; they have no place in its internal structure. They cannot be considered as co-ordinate with the first verbal (*watching the sunset*)—the only possible function that their position would allow—for they could not be substituted for it, as normal co-ordinate elements may be substituted for each other. We cannot properly write, 'We sat on the porch, playing cards later, going to bed at ten o'clock.' A sentence like this can be corrected by breaking it up into smaller completed sentences or clausal units:

> We sat on the porch watching the sunset. Later we played cards, and went to bed at ten o'clock.

During the revision of a theme, all long sentences containing a large number of verbal forms should be carefully examined for such detached word groups.

Another type of mistake caused by the failure to fit verbal elements properly into the structure of the sentence is called the 'dangling modifier.' This is a verbal form which is intended as a modifier, but the writer has not provided any proper word for it to modify. It is usually apparent that some such word is 'understood,' but in good writing it will not be merely understood, but clearly expressed. The following sentences illustrate third- and fourth-form verbals that 'dangle':

> Driving along the highway, the sunset glowed in the west.
> Crowded off the road by the truck, the accident was bound to happen.

Errors of this kind can be corrected in two ways: first, by supplying the missing word—a strategy which usually involves some recasting of the sentence:

> Driving along the highway, we saw the sunset glowing in the west.
> Crowded off the highway by the truck, we were bound to have an accident.

Second, the sentences may be corrected simply by changing the verbal phrase into a completed clause:

> As we drove along the highway, the sunset glowed in the west.
>
> When we were crowded off the road by the truck, the accident was bound to happen.

Infinitive phrases may also dangle, as in

> To get the most out of his life, parties went on all the time at the big mansion on the hill.

This kind of adverbial phrase modifies the whole subject-predicate unit, so the sentence must be revised to supply a new subject-predicate which this particular phrase could appropriately modify:

> To get the most out of life, he had parties going on all the time at the big mansion.

Prepositional phrases containing third-form verbal nouns (gerunds) as objects of the preposition may also dangle when the sentence is not properly constructed. The following sentences illustrate this kind of fault:

> By shifting the gears carefully, the car will not stall.
> Before publishing the book, three years went by.

These sentences too may be revised either by supplying the missing headword or by expanding the prepositional phrase into a clause:

> By shifting the gears carefully, you can keep the car from stalling.
> Before publishing the book, he let three years go by.
> If you shift the gears carefully, the car will not stall.
> Before he published the book, three years went by.

Conjunction-headed adjective phrases, especially conjunction-headed verbals, are often left dangling in the sentence. A few examples of this kind of error were given in Chapter XII (p. 172). Other examples are:

> Cold water is dangerous when overheated.
> My wife never does the washing when damp.
> If kept long enough in battle, breakdown is bound to take place.

In order to correct these sentences, the phrase should be expanded into a clause:

> Cold water is dangerous when one is overheated.
> My wife never washes when it is damp.
> If men are kept long enough in battle, breakdown is bound to take place.

It is likely that the majority of 'dangler' errors are made because the writer is trying to avoid the use of such impersonal pronouns or nouns as *one, you, it,* or *a person.* As we pointed out in Chapter VII, p. 84, we have no real impersonal pronoun, such as French and German have. And many writers of English do not feel at home with any of these words we must use as substitutes. *One* seems too stiff, *a person* seems awkward, and *you* too informal. But we have to make the best of this situation, and the use of any of these words is preferable to any kind of dangling element.

Another common structural error involving verbal forms is typified in the following sentences:

> *By shopping* early before the crowds are in the stores will leave you more time to enjoy Christmas.
>
> *In separating* a dependent clause from an independent clause sometimes requires a comma.

Although the prepositional phrases with verbal objects (italicized above) do not exactly 'dangle,' their use in these 'sentences' is grammatically unorthodox, to say the least. In fact, these are not English sentences at all, for they have no subjects! Blunders like these result either from sheer ignorance of English grammar (ignorance of the fact that prepositional phrases such as *By shopping* and *In separating* cannot be used as subjects) or from extreme carelessness, involving the intention to put in a subject later in the sentence, but never getting around to it. Sentences of this kind, which begin as if they were going to follow one pattern, then change their course in the middle, and end as a hodgepodge, are called 'shifted constructions.'

VIOLATIONS OF PARALLEL STRUCTURE

The use of verbal elements raises the problem not only of fitting them all into the sentence patterns in their proper places, but also of selecting their proper forms. One of the most frequent errors involving the selection of verbal forms is called a 'violation of parallelism.' This simply means that when two or more verbal expressions are structurally co-ordinate (parallel), we should not use different verbal forms in expressing them. The following sentences illustrate this kind of error:

She could not decide whether *to buy a new rug* or *should she make the old one do.* (Here two dissimilar verbal forms, an infinitive and a complete clause, have been used in a co-ordinate structure.)

To go out to play after dark when the lights were on, and *having our hair cut* by a real barber were two things that we children wanted most when we were five years old. (Here an infinitive and a third-form verbal have been used.)

This problem can be solved by *reinforcement* and *moving our left flank* a hundred yards to the south. (Here a simple noun form and a third-form verbal have been used.)

The ocean spray rose gracefully, but *looking like clouds of smoke.* (Here a complete sentence and a third-form verbal have been used.)

In each of these sentences we know that the verbal elements were intended to be parallel because of the use of a co-ordinating conjunction. But the sentences are badly constructed because the writer has not made the verbal elements parallel in form. Whenever we use any of the co-ordinating conjunctions, *and, or,* and *but,* and any substitute for these conjunctions, such as *as well as,* to connect any verbal elements, we should watch carefully to make sure that the forms of both or all of the verbals are the same.

The following sentences illustrate the use of correct forms in parallel structures:

This problem can be solved by *reinforcement* and the *movement* of our left flank a hundred yards to the south. (two simple noun forms)

She couldn't decide whether *to buy* a new rug or *to make* the old one do. (two infinitives)

'*Getting* and *spending* we lay waste our powers.' (two third-form verbals used as adjectives)

Going out to play after dark . . . and *having* our hair cut by a real barber were two things we children wanted most. . . (two gerunds)

Frightened by the rising water, but *determined* to reach camp before dark, we decided to cross the brook. (two fourth-form verbals)

The ocean spray rose gracefully, but *looked like clouds of smoke.* (two complete predicates)

PUNCTUATION AS GRAMMAR

It is often not sufficiently realized that all of the major marks of punctuation may communicate grammatical meanings. When they do, they function as a kind of grammatical device, so their importance in the writing of good sentences is very great. It is also highly significant that most of these punctuation marks in the written language take the place of certain other grammatical devices used in the spoken language. The question mark, for example, signals a question even when the inverted interrogative word order is not used:

Charles is flying to Paris?

In the spoken language this same signal is made by a rising intonation of the voice. Here the question mark is absolutely essential because there is no other means of indicating that a question is being asked. On the other hand, if we use the interrogative word order (which would be more likely), the question mark is still used, but it is not so essential because another grammatical device, the inverted word order, also signals a question:

Is Charles flying to Paris?

(This matter of the interrogative word order is thoroughly discussed in Chapter X, pp. 122-6.)

Because punctuation marks function as a kind of grammatical device, they often create grammatical problems. We shall consider some of these in the remainder of this section. The most important punctuation marks that are used grammatically are: the period, the question mark, the exclamation point, the semicolon, the colon, the dash, the comma, the paired commas, and the hyphen.[1] There are other marks, of course, but they are less frequently used and are not primarily grammatical in function. The first three of these punctuation marks (the period, the question mark, and the exclamation point) usually separate complete sentences. The others separate the various structural groups within the sentence.

The period is often called the strongest mark of punctuation.

[1] The apostrophe is fully dealt with in Chapters V and XIV, pp. 54-5 and 204-5.

This is true because it is always used to separate the largest and most complete grammatical structure—the sentence. But the question mark and the exclamation point are also used to separate special kinds of sentences. They are used, however, far less frequently than the period. If the writer knows when he has a complete sentence, his use of the period will cause no difficulty. But if he does not, then, of course, serious problems will arise; for he will be in danger of punctuating as a sentence what is not a sentence. This brings up the problem of the 'sentence fragment,' a difficult and complicated matter.

An experienced writer might put down the following:

He had the money to buy a car. Even an expensive one.

Not only does this fragment, 'Even an expensive one,' carry on the meaning of the preceding sentence and could be readily incorporated in it, but, more importantly, the reason for this punctuation is the emphasis it gives to the idea in the fragment. In other words, the use of this sentence fragment is a matter of style and rhetorical effect rather than of grammar. If, however, the same writer had written:

He had the money to buy a car. Having worked hard for years.

there would be no justification for the fragment (a participle phrase) in terms of style and rhetorical effect. In fact, no kinds of verbal phrases are ever punctuated with a period. But, unfortunately, this is the kind of sentence fragment that inexperienced writers tend to use, especially if they are weak or uncertain about their grammar. The conclusion is that, unless he knows he is punctuating a sentence fragment as if it were a sentence and has a good reason for doing so, the beginning writer should not use this tricky kind of 'sentence' (see pp. 153-5 for further discussion of the sentence fragment).

The use of the question mark does not, as a rule, give rise to any serious problems. In writing, it should always be used when a question is being asked. In speech, of course, the question mark cannot be used, so in its place we employ a rising intonation of the voice.

But in both writing and speech the inverted word order may signal a question. The important thing is that the question mark is absolutely essential if the written question is not in this inverted word order.

The use of the exclamation point also does not create any serious difficulties. All we need to know when using it is that the sentence must express some intense emotion. As with the question, the exclamatory remark in speech is always made with a special vocal pitch pattern, usually by giving a normally unstressed word or group of words unusual emphasis. Since we cannot do this in writing, we substitute for it by using the exclamation point. This whole matter is thoroughly discussed in Chapter X. Both the exclamation point and (less often) the question mark may, of course, be used to set off units within the sentence.

When we come to the semicolon, we move from the punctuation marks which separate complete sentences to those which set off the various word groups within the sentence—clauses, phrases, etc. The strongest of these punctuation marks is the semicolon. It is always used grammatically to separate independent clauses within the sentence—never to separate phrases or dependent clauses. The semicolon is thus related to the period in that both are used to mark independent clauses, but of the two the period is the stronger, for it signals the end of a sentence as the semicolon does not. Another difference between these two marks of punctuation is that the semicolon signals a closer relationship between the clauses it separates than does the period. In the following sentence the relationship between the two clauses is extremely close:

It had been a stormy political campaign; the issues were crucial.

In fact, the semicolon almost takes the place of a conjunction— in this instance the idea of 'for' or 'because.' In general, the semicolon often functions in this way.

A few examples of how not to use the semicolon will further help to indicate its proper use. No one, we assume, would be likely to place a semicolon after a prepositional phrase, as in

Throughout the long warm summer; we just loafed;

but there are many beginners in writing who would thus punctuate the following participle phrase:

Finding no one in the high-school gymnasium; he returned home.

And there are many more such beginners who would be likely to use a semicolon after a dependent clause:

Since they were from the same home town; they soon became friends.

All of these uses of the semicolon with phrases and dependent clauses are, by definition, errors: they are serious errors because they mark the makers of them as uneducated. This particular punctuation error is the kind that, in another context, we called a 'social' error. But not all punctuation errors are social: many of them seriously impede or destroy the meaning intended and are therefore 'communication' errors.

The colon is a more specialized mark of punctuation than the semicolon and is, for this reason, less often used. In terms of grammatical meaning, the colon tells the reader to anticipate what is to follow: it points ahead to the thought of the remainder of the sentence. And what follows is usually a restatement, explanation, or expansion of what has preceded, as, for example, in the following sentence:

This intellectual quality must encompass the whole poem: it must fuse the poem into a tight logical structure.

The most common use of the colon is to introduce a series of items which follow some statement about them:

The Old English pronoun has three numbers: singular, dual, and plural.

Often in this connection certain specific words or phrases that convey the idea of looking forward will be used—words like *such as, namely, thus,* and *as follows.* There are also, of course, other conventional and mechanical uses of the colon, such as: after the salutation in formal letters and between hours and minutes when they are expressed in figures.

Just as the colon directs the reader's attention forward, the dash may direct it backward to what has preceded:

> A peaceful old house in the country—that was what he wanted.

The dash may also be used to signal an abrupt change in thought, as in the following sentence:

> In most matters he was impractical and romantic—but when it came to money . . .

In terms of emphasis and the sentence units it separates, the dash is roughly equivalent to the comma, although it is a slightly stronger mark of punctuation and draws somewhat more attention to the unit that follows it.

Of all marks of punctuation, the comma is by far the most often used, the most complex, and the most 'tricky' to manage. It is also the most important in terms of grammatical meaning, for its main function is to set off and clarify the great variety of structures, and structures within structures, that make up the modern English sentence. As we know, these range from the single word to the most complex dependent clause. Furthermore, the comma often takes the place of certain other grammatical devices used in the spoken language—such as a pause and a change in the pitch of the voice.

The single comma is used in only two situations. The first and more important use is to separate two or more independent clauses linked by co-ordinating conjunctions (*and, or, but, nor*). There is one exception to this general rule: if the clauses are relatively short, no comma is needed:

> They walked down to the shore carrying their brightly colored bathing suits, but the water was too cold for more than a quick dip.
> They walked to the shore but the water was too cold for swimming.

The second use of the single comma (there are only two of them) is to separate words in a series:

> There were baskets of apples, peaches, pears, and grapes.

The sentence above is conservatively punctuated, for popular usage today has eliminated the comma before *and*. In terms of logic, however (for whatever that is worth), the elimination of the last comma reduces the number of baskets from four to three, the third one containing both pears and grapes.

Paired commas are used in several ways, one of which is to set off or enclose single-word conjunctive adverbs and other short word groups that have similar adverbial functions. These are usually interpolations that momentarily cause a break in the main thought. The most common conjunctive adverbs are: *accordingly, also, anyhow, anyway, besides, consequently, furthermore, hence, however, indeed, likewise, moreover, namely, nevertheless, similarly, still, then,* and *therefore.* The most common word groups with a similar function include such expressions as: *after all, as a matter of fact, I conclude, in addition, of course, that is to say,* etc. An example of each:

> His views on the national debt were, however, given close attention.
>
> His views on the national debt were, after all, his own opinions.

Of course, when any of these words or word groups appears at the beginning or the end of a sentence, only one of the two commas is used. This is true because at the beginning of the sentence another punctuation mark (the capital letter) takes the place of the first comma and at the end of the sentence the period takes the place of the second.

Similarly, the longer adverbial structures (prepositional phrases and adverbial clauses) are set off by commas if they appear at the beginning of the sentence or inside it, and they are set off by commas at the end of the sentence if they are unusually long—otherwise not. For example:

> Instead of going to work, he took in a movie.
>
>   but
>
> He took in a movie instead of going to work.
>
> Because the stakes were high, he decided to risk everything.
>
> He decided to risk everything because the stakes were high.

He decided, since they were in agreement, not to press the
matter.

He decided not to press the matter, since they were in agreement
about everything else.

Commas are less often used when the adverbial element is at the
end of the sentence because in that position a function word (here
the preposition or the adverbial conjunction) itself signals the beginning of the clause. In general, as the examples above suggest,
it is the movable adverbial structures that require comma punctuation, especially if they appear at the beginning or in the middle of
the sentence.

The punctuation of adjective group modifiers, although more
complex, is not really difficult. As we noted earlier in this chapter
(p. 248), there are three kinds of such group modifiers: (1) the non-
verbal adjective expanded by other modifiers, (2) the verbal adjective expanded by any kind of modifier or complement, and (3) the
conjunction-headed adjective phrase. All of these modifiers should
be set off by a comma or commas if they appear at the beginning
or in the middle of the sentence. For example:

Happy to be going, John eagerly packed his suitcase.
John, happy to be going, eagerly packed his suitcase.

Having decided to go, Charles ordered the car.
Charles, having decided to go, ordered the car.

While fixing the car, Henry bruised his hand.
Henry, while fixing the car, bruised his hand.

When the adjective group modifier comes at the end of the sentence,
however, several possibilities exist. If the phrase immediately follows the word it modifies, no punctuation is needed:

I like to see John happy over his success.
The police arrested a man driving ninety miles an hour.
Iron the clothes when damp.

If the phrase modifies the subject and is conjunction-headed, again
no punctuation is needed:

Henry bruised his hand while fixing the car.

But adjective phrases that are not conjunction-headed should be set off unless they are very short:

> John eagerly packed his suitcase, happy to be going home again.
> Charles ordered the car, having decided to go immediately.
>
> but
>
> She sat in the window combing her hair.

Probably the reason for this distinction between the conjunction-headed phrase and the others in the matter of punctuation is that the conjunction provides the grammatical device needed in this position and thus makes the comma unnecessary.

The use of commas to set off subordinate adjective clauses raises the problem of 'restrictive' and 'non-restrictive' sentence elements, a problem that is not always easy to solve. In general, a restrictive modifier 'restricts'—that is, it defines, limits, or identifies—the word it refers to. If such a modifier is omitted the meaning of the sentence either becomes nonsense or its meaning is radically changed. Restrictive modifiers are not punctuated at all:

> It was a new woman *who left the beauty parlor an hour later.*
> The dog *that won first prize* is a cocker spaniel.

On the other hand, the non-restrictive modifier does not limit in the same kind of way; instead, it merely adds information that is not essential to the basic meaning of the sentence. Such non-restrictive modifiers are set off by paired commas:

> The house, *which we reached after an hour's drive,* was beautifully located.
> Charles, *who is now a salesman,* is a graduate of Yale.

The difference between restrictive and non-restrictive elements is, of course, a matter of degree, so there are some sentences in which a modifier could be either one or the other, depending on the writer's intention. The following sentence could be punctuated either way:

> The winding path *which seemed to lead nowhere* began at the edge of town.

The so-called 'nouns in direct address' are always set off by paired commas; for example:

> But, mother, I need that dress badly.
> Would you mind, John, if I took the car?

Similarly, words in apposition are usually set off by commas:

> Our banker, Mr. George, is a man of distinction.

One important point should be made regarding the use of paired commas: if commas are needed, there should always be two when the structure to be punctuated is within the sentence. Because we usually sense more of a pause at the end of the internal structure, there is a widespread tendency to use only one comma there and to overlook the necessity for setting off the structure at its beginning—in other words, to write:

> He decided that whatever happened, he would return to college;

instead of:

> He decided that, whatever happened, he would return to college.

If there is any doubt about whether a comma is called for in a given situation, the question should be asked: Would the meaning of the sentence be absolutely clear if the mark of punctuation were omitted? There is one place where the use of a comma is absolutely essential to clarify the meaning. This is where a word or word group comes between two structures and its form and vocabulary meaning allow it to be a part of either structure. Such elements are said to 'squint' in two directions at once. Thus, in the sentence

> In the picture we sold *the author* is a little boy,

the position of the word *author* makes it wholly ambiguous because it could function either as the object of the verb *sold* or as the subject of *is*. Unless such a sentence is recast, a comma must be used to clarify the meaning:

> In the picture we sold, the author is a little boy.
> In the picture we sold the author, is a little boy.

Actually the second sentence above is a very poor one and should be recast to read:

In the picture we sold the author, there is a little boy.

Here greater clarity is gained by the use of another grammatical device, the function word *there*. Similarly in the sentence

After I had listened to the telephone *for a while* I sat down at my desk

a comma should be used either before or after the phrase *for a while* in order to make clear which clause it belongs in. The power of punctuation as a grammatical device can be seen most dramatically in the following sentence, which contains a squinting clause:

After all *we have said* the house must be sold.

If a comma is placed between *all* and *we,* the clause *we have said* looks ahead to the word group at the end of the sentence; on the other hand, if the comma is placed between *said* and *the,* the clause looks back to and modifies *all.* And what a change in meaning takes place when the comma is moved! Here again, a function word could have been used to clarify the meaning further:

After all, we have said that the house must be sold.
After all that we have said, the house must be sold.

There are other similar situations where, although out-and-out ambiguity is not involved, the comma is needed as a guide to the reader to tell him at first reading what structure a doubtful word belongs in. There are many types of sentences in which a word might be interpreted at first reading as part of a structural group in which it does not belong, unless a comma is used. We saw in Chapter VIII (pp. 95-6) how the last noun element in one structural group may 'attract' the first noun in another to form what seems to the reader at first glance to be a modifier-noun combination. In the sentence

On the fire hoses were pouring hundreds of gallons of water

fire, the object of the preposition, and *hoses,* the subject of the sentence, happen to appear together and therefore might seem to be such a combination—*fire hoses.* Unless the sentence is reconstructed, a comma should be used after *fire* to help the reader. Similarly, in the following sentences commas should be used for the same reason:

> From the street, noises were reverberating around the room.
> To many, Americans seem to lack culture.

Very often, also, the first noun in one structure may be taken as an object of a verb or verbal in another, if a comma is not used to show where the break between the structures occurs. Here are several sentences of this type:

> In writing, words are recognized by the spacing.
> In cooking, spices should be added at the last moment.
> After we had picked up, the house looked beautiful.

When a comma is not used in these positions, the sentence may be so confusing that it will require several readings or, if the sentence is long, even a complete analysis before the meaning becomes clear.

There is one place where the comma should rarely, if ever, be used—that is, between independent clauses without a co-ordinating conjunction, as in the sentence:

> The field-house was packed with students, some were even sitting on the rafters.

This is called the 'comma fault' or 'comma error.' Only four kinds of connectives should be used between independent structures. They are the period, the semicolon, the colon, and the co-ordinating conjunction with or without the comma. Thus the sentence above should be punctuated in one of the following ways:

> The field-house was packed with students. Some were even sitting on the rafters.
> The field-house was packed with students; some were even sitting on the rafters.
> The field-house was packed with students, and some were even sitting on the rafters.

Experienced writers do sometimes punctuate short, closely related independent clauses with a comma, but the inexperienced writer should not do so.

The use of the hyphen has changed considerably in recent years. For example, it is now being used much less frequently to set off a prefix from the main part of the word. In fact, such forms as *to-day, to-night,* and *to-morrow,* which we often find in older books, have completely disappeared; and other words which only a few years ago were regularly hyphenated are now usually run together. Some of these are *unclear, misspell,* and *overexposure.* As a grammatical device, however, the hyphen is being used more often today, probably because writers are becoming increasingly sensitive to its importance in taking the place of missing speech devices and thus helping to clarify meanings. In general, the purpose of the hyphen as a grammatical device is to signal that two words have become a compound: that is, they are to be considered as functioning as a unit and are to be run together in speech as if they were a single word. In this capacity, the hyphen is used in two specific ways. First, it is used when such verb combinations as *blow up, hold over, knock out* (see Chapters IV and VI, p. 49 and p. 70) are shifted to the noun or adjective function:

We had a *blow-up* over the problem.
This usage is a *hold-over* from earlier periods of the language.
The *knock-out* blow came in the third round.

Second, the hyphen is often used between a word and its modifier to show that the two function as a single unit—either as a noun or an adjective. Examples of such compounds used as nouns are *half-mast, self-interest, fellow-townsman,* etc. It is almost impossible to give rules for the hyphenating of compound nouns. Some are hyphenated, some are run together, and some are always separated. The best advice, then, is to consult the dictionary. When compounds function as adjectives, however, hyphenation of the two words is becoming the rule rather than the exception. In this book, for example, *word order* is always hyphenated when it is used as an adjective, as in *word-order device.* Other examples are *two-tone fabric, this-year's model, kitten-soft sweater, after-dinner speech, old-fashioned furniture, near-fatal accident,* and *all-purpose tool.* There are two situations in which this type of modifier should always be hyphenated. First, when it is composed of a verbal adjective modified by another adjective, as in *a high-priced car, a slow-moving train, brilliant-hued plaster casts, tight-fitting shorts,* and *fast-growing fame;* second, when ambiguity would result if the hyphen were not used. For example, in the phrase *a light blue coat,* we cannot be sure whether the color of the cloth is light blue or whether the coat is both blue in color and light in weight. That is, we cannot be sure whether *light* is a tertiary or a secondary modifier. But if we write *light-blue,* there is no question about the intended meaning; *light* modifies *blue* (not *coat*) and is a tertiary modifier. Similarly, the phrase *a small boat anchorage* is ambiguous, but either *a small-boat anchorage* or *a small boat-anchorage* is not.

The discussion of punctuation as a minor grammatical device should serve as a reminder that throughout this book the emphasis has been on the operation of all the grammatical devices—both major and minor—in the communication of grammatical meanings. The major devices, of course, operate through the eight parts of speech and as substitutes for some of the devices of the spoken language that are missing from the written; the minor device of punctuation operates only in the latter capacity. In a very real sense, then, this is a grammar of 'structure.' Although from time to time we have had to consider the vocabulary meanings of words in sentences, this has been done only where otherwise the grammatical meaning was confusing or ambiguous: and the necessity for so doing points to the limitations of modern English grammar. The importance of seeing and understanding these limitations is fully as great as seeing and understanding the positive operations of the grammar itself. Finally, with all of its limitations, this grammar is indeed a fascinating product of the human mind; and in the hands of a skillful user, it can become the basis of an ever-increasing clarity, subtlety, and variety in human communication.

AN OUTLINE OF THE LANGUAGE SYMBOLS OF WRITTEN ENGLISH

VOCABULARY SYMBOLS

Aardvark, aardwolf, Aaron, ab-, aba, abaca, aback, abacus, Abaddon, abaft, abalone, abandon, abash, abate, abatis, abattoir, etc., etc., etc. (meanings may be found in a dictionary)

GRAMMATICAL SYMBOLS

The Major Grammatical Devices

I. Word-order Patterns
  A. Full-sentence Patterns
    1. In the declarative sentence:
       a. Subject–verb–complement: *Honey catches flies.*
          Cheaters are fools.
          The city is noisy.
       b. Subject–verb–complement–complement:
          The captain gave the men a lecture.
          The group elected Henry chairman.
       c. Subject–verb: *Time flies.*
    2. In the interrogative sentence:
       a. (Interrogative adverb)–auxiliary verb–subject–complement–(complement): *(When) did you elect John (president)?*
       b. Interrogative pronoun–verb–complement–(complement): *Who elected John (president)?*
       c. Interrogative pronoun–auxiliary verb–subject–main verb–(complement)–(preposition):

Whom did you see?

Whom did you give the money to?

3. In the imperative sentence:
    a. Verb–complement–(complement):
       Bring the men (coffee).
    b. Verb–(modifier): *Stop. Look. Listen.*
       Come quickly.
4. In the exclamatory sentence:
    a. Exclamatory word–subject–verb–complement–(complement): *How you cause (us) trouble!*
    b. Exclamatory word–complement–subject–verb–(complement): *What a lecture John gave (his son)!*
       How pretty Joan looks!

B. Phrase Patterns
    1. Indicator–(adverb)–adjective–noun: *A (very) hot day.* . .
    2. Auxiliary verb(s)–verb: . . . *is sleeping.* . .
       . . . *must have been done.* . .
    3. Preposition–(modifier)–object:
       . . . *into the (deep) woods.* . .
    4. Modifier [usually verbal] or gerund [verbal noun]–complement–(complement): . . . *worth a dollar.* . .
       . . . *giving (John) his lesson.* . .

C. Dependent Clause Patterns
    1. Type-one connective–subject–verb–complement–(complement): *Since we gave (them) our pledge.* . .
    2. Relative pronoun–verb–complement–(complement):
       . . . *who causes (people) trouble.* . .
    3. Relative pronoun–subject–verb–(complement)–(preposition): . . . *whom we chose (president).* . .
       . . . *whom we gave the book to.* . .
    4. Complement–preposition–relative pronoun–subject–verb–(complement): . . . *a copy of which I sent (you).* . .
    5. Verb of mental action–subject–verb–(complement)–(complement): . . . *think you will tell (me) (the story).* . .
       See p. 181.

6. Word modified–subject–verb–(complement)–(preposi-tion): . . . *the man I wrote (the letter) (to)*. . . See p. 183.

II. Inflections

  A. Verb Inflections

    1. Regular inflections: *s, -ing, -ed (-t)*: *helps, helping, helped*

    2. Irregular inflections:

      a. *-en* (or *-n*) suffix of many five-form verbs: *given, drawn*

      b. Internal inflection: *sing, sang, sung*

      c. Radical inflection: *go, went; be, am, are, is, was, were*

  B. Noun Inflections

    1. Regular inflections: *-s, -'s, -s'*: *boys, boy's, boys'*

    2. Irregular inflections:

      a. Internal inflection: *man, men*

      b. Irregular suffixes: *child, children; ox, oxen; alumnus, alumni; datum, data*

  C. Pronoun Inflections

    1. Irregular inflections of personal and of relative and inter-rogative pronouns: *I, my, mine, me,* etc.; *who, whose, whom*

    2. *-'s* of some quantitative pronouns: *somebody's; everyone's*

    3. Internal inflections of demonstrative pronouns: *this, these; that, those*

  D. Adjective and Adverb Inflections

    1. Regular inflections: *-er, -est: bigger, biggest; lovelier, loveliest*

    2. Irregular inflections: *much, more, most; bad, worse, worst; good, better, best;* etc.

III. Function Words

  A. Auxiliary verbs: *be, do, have, will, can, used to,* etc. See p. 37 for complete list.

  B. Noun indicators: *the, a, an, my, our, your, his, its, their, some*

  C. Adjective-adverb function words: *more, most, less, least, as (so) . . . as, than*

    D. Prepositions: *at, by, for, from, in, of, on, to, with,* etc. See
       p. 69 for complete list.
    E. Co-ordinating conjunctions: *and, but, or, nor*
    F. Subordinating conjunctions: *after, although, as, because,* etc.
      See p. 169 for complete list.
    G. Relative pronouns: *who, which, that*

Minor Grammatical Devices
  I. Permanent Forms: *en-, -ize, -ity, -ment, -al, -y, -ish, -ly.* See pp.
     30, 51, 89, 107-8 for complete lists.
 II. Punctuation
    A. Period and semicolon: signal the beginning of a new struc-
      ture not 'nested' within any preceding structure
    B. Colon: may signal the beginning of a new structure or an
      appositive structure
    C. Comma
      1. Sets off transitional words or phrases and non-restrictive
        nested structures
      2. Separates members of a series of grammatically parallel
        words, phrases, or clauses
    D. Hyphen: indicates levels of modification

REVIEW QUESTIONS AND EXERCISES

CHAPTER I

Review Questions

I. Every language has two types of symbols. What are they called? In what important respects do they differ?

II. How does one go about finding the meanings represented by each type of symbol?

III. In what respect are the grammatical symbols like the 'signs' of mathematics?

IV. What is meant when we say that grammar is an 'economical' way of expressing meanings?

V. What determines whether a certain meaning is classified as a vocabulary meaning or a grammatical meaning?

VI. Explain why some sentences are ambiguous when written and clear when spoken? In general, how can ambiguities of this kind be corrected?

Exercises

I. Linguists use the word 'morpheme' to describe the smallest unit of meaning in a language. Some words, like *ask, great,* or *real,* are made up of only one morpheme, but others are composed of several; for example, the word *revitalized* is composed of four of these: *re-, -vital, -ize,* and *-d.* Some morphemes are vocabulary symbols and others are grammatical symbols. In the following list of morphemes, select those which are grammatical symbols and explain why you think so. Remember that some may be complete words and yet also be grammatical symbols.

hat	of	en	ize	pitch
ing	bug	s	ed	here
ly	see	er	top	est
ment	for	ate	be	y

II. The meanings of the sentences below are not clear in writing. What speech devices could be used to clarify the meanings? Can you recast the sentences so that they become clear in writing?

> Have you ever seen a horse fly?
> She went to see her two year old twins.

III. The principle of 'analogy' is used in this chapter to explain grammar by comparing it with mathematics. The following topics suggest other possible analogies. Select one (or devise one of your own) and work out the similarities and differences between the two things. Write a paper of about 500 words on this subject.

1. Registration at our school is like a sudden thunderstorm.
2. Writing a theme is like building a house.
3. Proper conversation is a matter of good sense and respect for others, just as proper dress is.
4. Daily studying is just like keeping in training for football or another sport.

IV. In this chapter we have frequently used the word 'symbol,' which is a way of representing things or ideas. Write a short paper explaining, in detail, what two or three of the following words or word groups mean to you as symbols.

1. the flag
2. a horse and buggy
3. a Cadillac
4. a white collar
5. a kiss
6. a shrug of the shoulders
7. a wink
8. shaking hands
9. clapping hands
10. bowing the head

CHAPTER II

Review Questions

I. Name the three principal grammatical devices in English and give an example of each.

II. Why must modern English depend so much on word order as a grammatical device?

III. In what important way do function words differ from inflections?

IV. Illustrate the statement that more than one grammatical device may be used at the same time in connection with a word.

V. Why are we able to understand some sentences even though they have 'mistakes' in inflectional forms?

Exercises

I. Using the following vertical lists of words, construct sentences. How many different sentences can you make from each list? You should be able to make at least three. Point out a few of the grammatical devices you have used.

1	2	3	4
room	burn	face	baby
old	record	Helen	mother
use	fire	clock	bottle
John	boy	stop	wash
show	angry	old	little

II. In the following sets of sentences, what grammatical devices have been used to alter the meanings of the sentences?

1. I go to bed every night at eleven o'clock.
   I shall go to bed every night at eleven o'clock.

2. In South America people eat alligators.
   In South America alligators eat people.

3. He picked up the book stand.
   He picked up the book on the stand.

4. The children enjoyed playing in the boat house.
   The children enjoyed playing in the house boat.

5. The Indians make beautiful blankets.
   The Indians made beautiful blankets.

6. John was helped in the shipping room.
   John helped in the shipping room.

7. Swimming down the river, Jim suddenly saw his father.
   Jim suddenly saw his father swimming down the river.

8. Jim's father finds him good buys at the store.
   Jim's father buys him good finds at the store.

9. Following the parade down the street, the crowd noticed a large flock of pigeons.
   The crowd noticed a large flock of pigeons following the parade down the street.

10. Mary's mother dresses her burns for her.
    Mary's mother burns her dresses for her.

11. The store finally sent my ties as I ordered.
    The store finally sent me ties as I ordered.

12. Both Bill and Bob feel much better.
    Both Bill and Bob felt much better.

13, Although we hadn't expected him to co-operate, the famous actor took part.
    Although we hadn't expected him to co-operate, the famous actor took the part.

14. He told me to get the shelf.
    He told me to get on the shelf.

15. He considered the matter serious.
    He considered the matter seriously.

16. The large windows of the house appealed to the man on the corner.

The large windows of the house on the corner appealed to the man.

The large windows on the corner of the house appealed to the man.

17. Only I was interested in the dark corners of the closet.
I was only interested in the dark corners of the closet.
I was interested in only the dark corners of the closet.
I was interested in the dark corners of the only closet.
I only was interested in the dark corners of the closet.

III. Establish a relationship between the following pairs of words, first by inflection, then by the use of function words. Example:

Joan   portrait   Inflection: Joan's portrait
                     Function word: a portrait of Joan (or)
                                    a portrait by Joan (or)
                                    a portrait for Joan

1. month   salary
2. night   rest
3. girl   father
4. Columbus   discovery
5. I   pen
6. centerfielder   hit

CHAPTER III

Review Questions

I. How would you describe the meaning of 'parts of speech' as presented in this chapter? How does this differ from other descriptions of them, with which you may be familiar?

II. In the sentences on page 23 using the word *round,* the word *circular* might be substituted for *round* in the second sentence. In what sense is *round* more widely 'distributed' in the language than *circular?*

III. Find synonyms for the *rounds* in the other sentences.

IV. By what method, other than the use of the three major grammatical devices, may a word be changed from one part of speech to another? Give a few examples.

V. How does the 'permanent' form of a word differ from an 'inflected' form?

VI. What is meant by 'functional shift'? Illustrate fully.

VII. Name the eight parts of speech: which ones express 'vocabulary' meanings? Which ones are primarily function words?

Exercises

I. What tells us that the three words in each group below are probably different parts of speech? Be as specific as you can, and work with the grammatical devices.

1. colors	called	brighter
2. judgment	criticize	hardest
3. dirtiest	dirtied	dirtiness
4. creation	creative	created
5. critics	criticize	critical
6. national	nationalize	nationalization

II. In the following sets of sentences, what general method might be used to show that the italicized word is a different part of speech in each of the sentences?

1. The *tax* was too high.
   They *tax* the people who work.
   The bonds were *tax* exempt.

2. I never knew a *squarer* fellow.
   John finally *squared* a circle.
   Peculiar people are sometimes called *squares.*

3. John finally arrived at the *top.*
   Henry had *topped* my highest bid.
   The *topmost* man was little Jimmy.

4. The army *trains* men.
   The army mans *trains.*

III. What unusual examples of 'functional shift' have you heard on radio or television during the past week?

IV. In an essay of about 300 words, apply the 'principle of distribution' to something in your own experience. For instance, what kind of students go out for debate, or football, or dramatics? Or what kind of animals do you expect to see at a circus, in a pet shop, or on a farm? Or what sort of clouds go with certain weather conditions? Or what kinds of crops are to be expected with certain climates, terrains, or soils? Or what sort of merchandise do you expect to find in a haberdashery, or a grocery store, or a tobacco shop?

CHAPTER IV

Review Questions

I. What are the four basic inflectional forms of the verb?

II. Distinguish between regular and irregular verbs, and describe three different kinds of irregularity in the fourth form.

III. List the auxiliary verbs used with the first form, with the third form, and with the fourth form.

IV. What is a defective verb? A modal auxiliary?

V. Explain what is meant by tense, aspect, mode, and voice.

Exercises

I. Give five examples, other than those in the text, of verbs beginning with *be-, en-, em-,* and *re-.* Consult your dictionary if you need help. How many English verbs begin with *with-?* Give five examples, other than those in the text, of verbs ending in *-ate, -en, -ify,* and *-ize.* Check in your dictionary to make sure that they may be verbs.

II. In English a thousand years ago (called Old English or Anglo-Saxon) there were at least 300 five-form verbs. About half of these have since become regular four-form verbs (and about a hundred have dropped out of use). There is obviously a slow tendency in our language for irregular verbs to become regular. Devise 'regular' forms for the irregular verbs listed on p. 33.

III. Using an irregular four-form verb (like *teach, find, build, swing,* or *sell*) write out all the possible variations of this verb which are made with (a) the first form, (b) the third form, (c) the fourth form.

IV. Discuss the difference in the ideas of tense implied in these sets of verbs:

1	2	3	4	5
had drunk	was being read	were to bring	bought	put
was drinking	is to be read	does bring	were to buy	puts
is to drink	will be read	is about to bring	is buying	will put

V. Discuss the difference in the ideas of aspect implied in these sets of verbs:

won	had been about to start	was being hung
is about to win	has been starting	will hang
had won	started	was about to be hung
is winning	will have started	had been hung

VI. Rewrite the following sentences, changing only the verb form, to show, instead of the certainty that the verb expresses, first probability, then doubt, then command, then clear denial of the process the verb expresses.

1. Henry is seeing a good movie tonight.
2. You are to make the closing address.
3. We are having a wonderful time. (For command use 'Let us')
4. John made an egregious blunder.

VII. Keeping the same tense, aspect, and mode, change each of the following passive verb forms into active voice:

was treated	is being taught
was about to be stopped	will be drunk
had been done	was to have been helped
will be being developed	is baked
has been cooked	will have been completed
had to be relieved	is going to be dropped
got lost	did get deceived

VIII. In the following sentences, determine whether the italicized word is an auxiliary verb or the whole verb:

1. John *will* quit his job soon.
2. Grandfather *must* have potatoes with every meal.
3. Aunt Ida *cans* peelings and pits with her fruit.

4. Making a model plane *is* work.
5. We *have* copy materials for our new project.
6. You must *have* taken the wrong route.
7. The student *has,* on the other hand, made poor marks.
8. The lost picture *is* like the one in our living room.
9. Your daughter certainly *has* taking ways.
10. The suspect *was* being followed by the detective.

IX. In the following word groups, tell whether the italicized word is part of the verb. Using what you have learned about verb forms and variations, give your reasons for your answer.

1. is *like*	11. will each *dollar*
2. has been *cooking*	12. may *bring*
3. have *gone*	13. is to have *sung*
4. are about to *fly*	14. can *peelings*
5. get *feelings*	15. kept *doing*
6. was *liked*	16. will be the *take*
7. has been having *lessons*	17. does *washing*
8. has to be *taught*	18. has been *everything*
9. has got *help*	19. could usually *bring*
10. had been being *happy*	20. is *swing* and sway

X. Pick out the complete verbs in the following sentences.

1. The secret of his winning was inside information.
2. Perhaps your wealthy uncle will will you his money.
3. Mary has been getting help.
4. By then the orchestra will have been playing ten minutes.
5. They might have set us by four tricks.
6. Catherine was going to have a wonderful time.
7. He did know a different way out of the cave.
8. The situation facing him was to be met with courage.
9. The crying child was being ridiculed by his friends.
10. The can cover on Mother's fruit had been leaking.
11. The must covering the fruit had been dangerous at first.
12. The will of the father had overcome that of the son.
13. Immediately noticeable were feelings of intense distrust.
14. The student had to get help on this paper.
15. At nine o'clock Mother had bed ready for us all.

XI. In the following sentences, no words have inflectional forms that distinguish them as verbs. Pick out the words which you think may be verbs and test your guess by changing the word into some distinguishing verb form. There is only one verb in each sentence.

1. We all eat milk and crackers at bedtime.
2. And in the morning my brother takes long walks around town.
3. John read the sports news first.
4. On a foggy night, the lights from the business district color the sky a deep rose.
5. Such people often air their likes and dislikes.

Chapter V

Review Questions

I. Can you always tell whether a word is a noun simply by identifying its permanent form? Give your reasons.

II. If a word ends in -*s*, how can you tell whether it is a verb or a noun?

III. Explain what is meant by number, case, and gender in nouns.

IV. What two devices are used to express the genitive case? Be specific and give examples of each.

V. Name six words that may function as indicators of nouns.

VI. What is the 'indicator test'? Explain how it is used.

VII. Distinguish between grammatical and 'natural' gender.

Exercises

I. How many words can you think of that end in -*ness, -ity, -ment, -acy,* and -*hood?*

II. Write ten sentences (two for each ending) in which words containing the following suffixes are used as nouns: -*al, -ing, -er, -ant,* and -*th.*

III. Which of the italicized words function as nouns in the following sentences?

1. The *superiority* of his brother turned Joe into a *flighty* child.
2. Fathers often *pressure* their children too much.
3. I broke my *filling* as a result of *cracking* walnuts.
4. They cannot *unionize labor* in this area.
5. Our real problem is *spoilage*.

IV. Write all the possible inflectional forms of the following nouns:

1. boy	7. alumnus
2. child	8. alumna
3. woman	9. crisis
4. thief	10. handkerchief
5. pony	11. fly
6. thinking	12. doing

V. Some English nouns, derived from other languages, Latin and Greek especially, retain non-English plural forms in modern English. Look up the plural forms of these words in your dictionary:

1. crisis	8. datum
2. phenomenon	9. automaton
3. stoma	10. stigma
4. seraph	11. cherub
5. alumnus	12. index
6. alumna	13. opus
7. appendix	14. cactus

VI. In which of the following italicized words does the apostrophe function to indicate the genitive inflection of a noun and in which does it indicate the omission of a letter?

> *It's* conceded that *amateurs'* performances *aren't* as consistently good as *professionals';* yet *isn't* it possible that our *club's pro's* scores are consistently lower than some of our *amateurs'?*

VII. In the following sentences, point out the nouns and verbs:

1. Our milkman's helper has been dropping bottles lately.
2. Help with his homework rarely benefits the student.
3. The benefits of the policy didn't help the man's wife.
4. Dropping of courses is discouraged by all officials.
5. Drinks were just being served.

　　6. Can loafers pass this course?

　　7. By that time John's wife will have knitted the sweater.

　　8. John's house could have been 'burgled' while his wife was talking on the telephone.

　　9. Sweat does not always indicate over-exertion.

　　10. Hazing and heckling, present on our campus, have ruined fraternities' reputations.

VIII. Determine whether the italicized words in the sentences listed below are nouns. Give your reasons, based on the presence of an inflection or function word, or the possible presence of an inflection or function word:

　　1. We all have our *likes* and *dislikes,* and the man who denies that *fact* simply refuses to face *facts*.

　　2. This *trifling* is *arousing* the *anger* of all of our *neighbors*.

　　3. Under the *table lies* the *answer* to your *troubles*.

　　4. *Circumstances cause* these *results,* which often *result* in *trouble*.

　　5. *Girls'* excitement often *results* from such silly things as the *screeching* of brakes and the *blowing* of horns.

　　6. *Greens* and *yellows* predominate in *paintings* of Van Gogh.

　　7. *Thieves break* in every year, and *catching* them *waxes* more difficult as *time* goes by.

　　8. The referee will *time* us.

　　9. She hurt the *children's feelings*.

CHAPTER VI

Review Questions

I. By what device is a noun subject expressed in modern English? a noun object? a predicate complement?

II. Describe two ways of distinguishing between an object and a predicate complement.

III. Describe two ways of distinguishing between the two kinds of double objects—the indirect-direct object combination and the direct object-objective complement combination.

IV. What is meant by the term 'noun in apposition'?

V. In what sense is the preposition a function word? In what sense is it a 'dual purpose' word?

VI. By what device does modern English designate a noun as an object of a preposition in simple declarative sentences?

VII. With what other grammatical device may the preposition *of* sometimes be interchanged? Give examples.

VIII. With what other grammatical device may the preposition *to* sometimes be interchanged? Give examples.

IX. How can you tell whether the words *at, by, in, off,* and *up* are functioning in a given sentence as prepositions or parts of the vocabulary meaning of the verb? Illustrate your discussion.

X. Why does the introduction of the prepositional phrase make it necessary to qualify our preliminary rule for word order in the modern English sentence?

Exercises

I. Write five simple sentences containing two uninflected nouns and a verb. Describe each noun fully in grammatical terms.

II. Write ten sentences made up of a subject, verb, and two types of objects. Write five sentences illustrating the use of the predicate complement.

III. There are thirty-four prepositional phrases in the sentences below. How many of them can you find? Put parentheses around each phrase and underline the preposition:

1. Above the river the balloon hung in the air for an hour.
2. After the dance John walked across the room in search of his daughter.
3. That color looks like blue to the colorblind.
4. During the day Henry worked on his invention; at night he tended a furnace near his home till midnight.
5. Everyone in the class but Martha has read *Twenty Years Before the Mast.*
6. The driver was against stopping beside the road.
7. Over the mantel we saw the picture of George with its face towards the wall.

8. *Through the Looking-Glass* is a story concerning the adventures of Alice.
9. According to the witness's testimony before the jury, the defendant drove up the street in his car at a minute after ten.
10. Because of your forgetfulness we are out of provisions.

IV. In the sentences below turn the italicized words into prepositional phrases without changing the basic meanings. The word order may be altered. Be sure to use good idiomatic English:

1. These are just *beginners'* exercises.
2. The *building's* collapse caused two deaths.
3. We showed *the stranger* the way.
4. The *dog's* barking brought the fire to our attention.
5. The *chair's* paint had completely peeled off.
6. We are reading *Milton's* 'Paradise Lost.'
7. The man at the fountain made the *boys'* milkshakes.
8. This farm's yield brought *the owner* a lot of money.
9. We played *John* a long game of chess.
10. He did *the professor* a bad job on the last assignment.

V. Write five sentences in which you illustrate all the positions that the prepositional phrase may occupy in a subject-verb-object-object sentence.

VI. In the following sentences, describe the grammatical characteristics of each noun and show what grammatical device is used to indicate these characteristics. Could any other device have been used?

1. The child carried a gallon of water from the well.
2. The postman handed the woman the mail.
3. In summer the children's interests are concentrated on sports.
4. These problems tax our ingenuity to the utmost.
5. Mrs. Jones called to her husband from the porch.
6. Paul has the physique of a prizefighter.
7. Mary put her hand on the horse's head.
8. Mary put on her dress.
9. Call the plumber. The pipes leak.
10. Put on the tea and put the cake on the table.

VII. Make up four sentences in which:

        1. *Help* is used as a noun.
        2. *Walk* is used as a noun.

What devices have you used?

VIII. By using all three grammatical devices compose a few sentences in which:

        1. *Hit* is used as a noun.
        2. *Man* is used as a verb.
        3. *Water* is used as a noun and a verb.

IX. Write two sentences in which you use *reading* as part of a verb phrase, and two sentences in which it is used as a noun.

X. In the following sentences only the endings, function words, and capital letters are expressed. The vocabulary parts of the words are represented by blanks. Giving all the grammatical information you can about each word (do not fill in the blanks),

    1. analyze the following three-unit sentences:
        a. The —— ——ed ——s.
        b. ——acy is ——ed a ——.
        c. This —— has been ——ing our ——dom.
        d. A —— ——s his ——ment.
        e. ——s ——ize the ——.

    2. analyze the following four-unit sentences:
        a. The ——'s —— will ——ate my ——s.
        b. His —— ——ed the —— a ——.
        c. ——s will be ——ing the ——'s ——.
        d. —— have ——en our —— on the ——.
        e. The —— ——s down the ——.

    3. analyze the following five-unit sentences:
        a. A —— has ——en our ——'s —— a ——.
        b. The ——ion of the —— ——ed ——'s ——ness.
        c. ——'s —— ——s —— for J——.
        d. ——'s —— ——s —— in ——s.
        e. In the ——'s —— the ——s were ——ing their ——.

XI. In which of the sentences below are *up, off, at,* and *down* prepositions? Why?

1. He looked up at the sky.
2. He picked up his room.
3. He put off the work.
4. He jumped off the roof.
5. He put down the rebellion.
6. He walked down the street.
7. The cat climbed up the tree.
8. Even a cat can look at a queen.

Chapter VII

Review Questions

I. In what sense are pronouns not substitutes for nouns?

II. Name the four grammatical ideas that may be expressed by personal pronouns. Describe the following pronouns in terms of these four ideas: *he, she, it.* Which of these ideas is not expressed by each of the following: *I, they, you?*

III. What do we mean when we say that the forms of some verbs 'repeat' the idea of person expressed by the subject?

IV. Discuss the concept of number implicit in the editorial 'we.'

V. Most personal pronouns use two types of devices to express ideas of case. What are these devices? Why is one of them usually not necessary? How does this kind of grammatical redundancy bear on the problem of selecting the 'proper' form of the pronoun?

VI. In what ways do the forms of pronouns differ from those of nouns? Discuss in detail, using illustrations for the different types of pronouns. Are some of these more like nouns than others?

Exercises

I. Of these substitutes for Tom and Bill Jones, which would you consider pronouns, and why?

> the Jones boys
> the Joneses' sons
> the two boys

the two
the boys
the both of them
both of them
two boys
they
these

II. In this chapter various ways of altering the 'natural person' were discussed: Bill Jones calls himself 'Bill Jones' rather than 'I'; the parties to a contract call themselves 'party of the first (and second) part' rather than 'I' and 'you'; the judge calls himself 'the court.' Discuss the concepts of person in the following expressions:

1. The prosecution rests its case.
2. The dean's office will tolerate no more of your delinquency.
3. God save your majesty.
4. Mr. and Mrs. Henry Ward Smith announce . . .
5. I beg the reader to be patient with me.
6. Is the captain of the Blues ready?
7. Let us keep our eyes on our own work.
8. Now your Germans are hard-headed, and your Frenchmen are quick.

III. Comment upon the gender suggested in each of the following quotations:

1. 'The moon doth with delight
   Look round her when the heavens are bare'
2. 'And in my day the sun doth pale his light'
3. 'The cat will mew and dog will have his day'
4. 'Be England what she will,
   With all her faults, she is my country still'
5. 'Earth fills her lap with treasures of her own'
6. 'God moves in a mysterious way
   His wonders to perform'
7. 'The sea that bares her bosom to the moon'
8. '. . . his form had not yet lost
   All her original brightness'

9. 'Hell trembled at the hideous name, and sigh'd
    From all her caves'
10. 'When the gust hath blown his fill'

IV. What case forms of the pronouns would you use in the following sentences? Why?

1. Between you and (I, me), it's a secret.
2. Among (we, us) five girls there sprang up a real friendship.
3. Both (he and she, him and her) forgot their textbooks.
4. Mother gave no allowance to either (he or I, him or me).
5. The boys cut (themselves, theirselves) on the new knives.

V. What form of *who* would you use to fill the following blanks?
Why?

1. —— do you want to see?
2. With —— did Mary come to the dance?
3. —— is the new president of the club?
4. —— did you forget to introduce?
5. —— was given the first prize?
6. —— was the first prize given to?
7. —— gave us the first prize?
8. —— do you think will win the game?
9. —— did you tell to get the checkers out?
10. —— do they believe will finally return the money?
11. —— did Mother give the cookies?
12. —— did Mother give the cookies to?

VI. By using the tests suggested at the end of the chapter, decide
whether you will call each of the italicized words in the following
sentences nouns or pronouns. Defend your decision.

1. The *ones* she gave me are *two* of the best in town.
2. *She* is the *one* who put the *who* in hooray.
3. To *each* we gave the *other's* prize.
4. *Mines* full of dazzling diamonds were now *mine*.
5. Our children sometimes have a whim
   That *he's* a *her* and *she's* a *him;*

But ultimately they will recur
He to a *him,* and *her* to *her.*

6. The *both* of *them* think that the *other* is at fault.

7. *Each* gave *his* most precious possession to the *other.*

VII. Some of the forms of the personal pronoun do not always indicate exactly just what 'persons' they are intended to refer to. For example, the pronoun *you* might refer only to the person addressed, or to this person and any number of other undesignated persons (*you* and your wife, *you* and your children, *you* and some business associate, etc.), or to people in general ('*You* can't judge a book by its cover'), or it might refer in an oblique sort of way to the speaker himself ('*You* can't work at the office all day and then come home and do housework'). This is another one of those weaknesses in our grammatical system which impede communication unless the writer is alert to the problem. Now suppose you are writing a letter and use the pronoun *we* (or *our* or *us*), how many different 'persons' might this pronoun designate? How could you clarify the meaning?

CHAPTER VIII

Review Questions

I. Why is it difficult to 'define' modification?

II. Why does the English language have particular need for modifiers?

III. Under what circumstances may an adjective be inflected? What are these inflections?

IV. Under what conditions are function words used in place of these inflectional forms? What are these function words?

V. Why are the permanent forms not an infallible sign that a word is an adjective? Give five sentences in which words with adjective forms are used as other parts of speech. Example: Mary *prettied* her hair.

VI. What is a verbal adjective? How is it derived?

VII. What is the most common position of the adjective?

VIII. What structural device is most commonly used by the English language to show which noun in the sentence is modified?

IX. What are the five possible positions for the single-word adjective? Illustrate with *five* sentences, showing each position.

X. What is an 'attributive noun'? How does its position in the sentence differ from the positions of other nouns?

Exercises

I. Make up a pair of sentences, the first of which contains an adjective ending in -*ate,* the second of which contains a word ending in -*ate* which is not an adjective. Do the same for -*ous* and -*able.*

II. Make up ten simple sentences containing third- and fourth-form verbal adjectives, such as 'A *rolling* stone gathers no moss.'

III. In the following skeleton sentences, only 'endings' and function words appear; the vocabulary parts of the words are represented by blanks (do not try to fill them in with actual words). Which of these words are adjectives? Why? A sample analysis will show you how this may be done:

In ——y of ——s the ——est ——ments —— the most ——able ——.

First, look for endings which might indicate an adjective form— either a permanent form or an inflection; then look for adjective function words. There are three of these endings and one function word in this sentence. Then (as a final test) examine the position of the words: (1) ——y cannot be an adjective because, when this part of speech follows a preposition, it must be followed by a noun or pronoun; (2) ——est is almost certainly an adjective because it appears in a position between an indicator and a word with a noun form; (3) ——able too must be an adjective since it is preceded by an adjective function word and is followed by an uninflected word, which must be a noun because an indicator precedes the entire phrase. Finally, we should see if any of the other words could be adjectives. In this sentence they could not be, because they do not occupy any of the adjective positions or because they have endings that adjectives could not have.

1. The —ous —s are —ing a — —.
2. The —est — in the —ion —ed —y —s.
3. Our — — —s its —y —.
4. In — —s the —est — —s.
5. —'s — —s —er the —ful — of —ment.
6. —able —s are —ing his —er —.
7. The —s on our — are —ic.
8. —ed the — —ed his —.
9. — is —ing his — —.
10. —ing has —ed him —er.

IV. Name ten verbs after which we might find predicate adjectives. Make up sentences which illustrate the use of adjectives after each of these verbs.

V. Construct sentences in which the following words function (1) as attributive adjectives and (2) as predicate adjectives: *narrow, cool, indefatigable, democratic, falling.*

VI. Select the adjectives in the sentences below. On what evidence did you base your decision?

1. Greater love hath no man.
2. The neighbor children were enthusiastic.
3. A pretty girl is like a melody.
4. On autumn days falling leaves fill the smoky air.
5. Her foolish chatter makes me sick.
6. Mother folded the quilted spread.
7. Into each life some rain must fall.
8. In the city soot is a real menace.
9. This new invention is the greatest thing since the Ford automobile.
10. The old man looked up surprised.
11. The farmer is painting the red barn.
12. I like barn red as a color for a colonial house.

VII. Compose sentences in which the following words are used as adjectives in the attributive position: *book, luxury, animal, tree, United Nations, cook, automobile, house, farm,* and *dance.*

CHAPTER IX

Review Questions

I. Name all the parts of speech that an adverb may modify.

II. List the ten positions in a sentence which an adverb may occupy. Give an example of an adverb in each position. Which of these are exclusive adverb positions? What positions in the sentence cannot be occupied by an adverb?

III. In what important respect does the word order of adverbs differ from that of any other part of speech? Construct a sentence which will illustrate this characteristic. Then construct a sentence containing an adverb which does not have this characteristic?

IV. Describe, in terms of the grammatical devices used, the difference between a prepositional phrase and an attributive noun. Give five examples of adjective prepositional phrases that may be turned into attributive nouns. Do the same thing for adverbial phrases. Use at least one prepositional phrase that contains a plural noun.

V. How can you tell in a given sentence whether such a word as *up* (or *down, before, after, since,* etc.) is a preposition or an adverb?

VI. Write a 250-word paper in which you explain why the 'definition' of the adverb given on p. 116 is not completely satisfactory. Illustrate with examples.

Exercises

I. Which of the following permanent forms might be used as adverbs:

1. forthrightly	5. furiously	8. regally
2. singly	6. friendly	9. swiftly
3. motherly	7. queenly	10. gingerly
4. partially		

II. Construct ten adverbs by using the suffixes listed on pp. 107-8. Do not use the words listed in the text.

III. Why do people often have difficulty deciding whether to use an adjective or adverb form in the following sentences?

1. Come quick (ly).
2. He is real (ly) happy.
3. She looks bad (ly).
4. The venture turned out disastrous (ly).
5. We always dress formal (ly) for dinner.

IV. In the following groups of sentences, which of the italicized words are adverbs? On what 'structural' evidence did you base your decision? Can you give more than one reason?

1. The child is *backward*.
   Our civilization seems to be moving *backwards*.

2. We work *indoors*.
   The job is an *indoor* one.

3. *Unconscious*, he fell on the ground.
   Unconsciously, he assumed her superiority.

4. She liked her food *hot*.
   She pressed the argument *hotly*.

5. Something *definite* must be done.
   Something *definitely* must be done.

6. *Next week* the weather is expected to be better.
   Next week is expected to be better.

7. This old house is called *home*.
   The student was called *home*.

8. It was a *deep*, genuine emotion.
   It was a *deeply* felt emotion.

9. John sat *down* angrily.
   John ran *down* the street.
   John ran him *down* terribly.
   The house was run *down*.

    10. He *righted* many wrongs.

    You cannot make a *right* out of a wrong.

    He worked *right* through the night.

V. Pick out the adverbs in the sentences below. Describe the methods used in reaching your conclusions.

1. They lived happily ever after.
2. The children ran faster than ever after the little dog.
3. The cat came back after we backed the car away from the back porch.
4. He has always taken a daily walk.
5. This mystery has never been too fully explained.
6. The little boy sat down on a rock.
7. He took the news hard.
8. The trumpet came in on the down beat.
9. 'Nobly, nobly, Cape St. Vincent to the north-west died away.'
10. These piecemeal solutions are never very satisfactory.

VI. Compose two sentences in which *corn* is used as a modifier: in the first use it as an adjective modifier, in the second as an adverb.

    Examples: adj. The farmer filled his *corn* crib.

         adv. Her *corn* fed beauty attracted the boys.

Do the same for the words *cream, sand, hand,* and *college.*

VII. In the following sentences the italicized words function as adverbs. Indicate the level of modification expressed by each one.

1. Don't run *so fast.*
2. He performed *satisfactorily.*
3. 'Comes the blind Fury with th' abhorred shears
   And slits the *thin*-spun life.'
4. Her *carefully* worked-out premise collapsed *immediately.*
5. Their baby is a *wonderfully* healthy, *remarkably* handsome child.
6. *School fund* fraud attempts are shocking.
7. The river is *a mile* away.
8. Everyone is excited about the *man*-made satellite.

9. We *almost never* have steak.

10. You must take the matter to the *New York* state highway commission.

CHAPTER X

Review Questions

I. Explain how interrogative, exclamatory, and imperative sentences differ from declarative sentences in terms of the intentions of the speaker or writer. Describe the most common word-order patterns for each of these types of sentences.

II. Why are sentences with predicate adjectives more easily inverted than those with noun complements? Illustrate your answer with examples.

III. Why, from the point of view of its structure, is the subject-verb pattern not the simplest of English patterns?

IV. What are the places of greatest emphasis in any communication? What is the place of least stress?

V. How well does the word order of the normal English sentence square with the places of greatest and least stress? Why do writers of English have to resort so often to underlining or italics in order to gain emphasis?

Exercises

I. Change each of the following declarative sentences to interrogative, exclamatory, and imperative sentences. For example:

> (declarative) John has hit a home run.
> (interrogative) Has John hit a home run?
> (exclamatory) What a home run John has hit!
> (imperative) John, hit a home run.

(Notice that in the imperative sentence the tense must be changed: we have no way of commanding in the past tenses or future tenses.)

> 1. Henry was doing his homework.
> 2. You will forget that nickname.

3. Boys never trust girls.
4. Helen looks happy.

II. Write questions which illustrate each of the following word-order patterns:

1. interrogative pronoun–verb–complement
2. interrogative pronoun–subject–verb–complement
3. exclamatory word–subject–verb–complement
4. verb–subject–complement
5. auxiliary verb–subject–main verb–complement
6. interrogative adverb–auxiliary verb–subject–main verb–complement
7. interrogative pronoun–auxiliary verb–subject–main verb–complement

III. Rearrange the word-order patterns of each of the sentences below in order to stress the italicized word or words. How many different changes can you make?

1. My cousin gave *me* a book.
2. The roses are *gorgeous*.
3. There *remain* five reasons for our leaving.
4. The couple didn't care for the *house* itself.
5. Our landlady never believed *me*, but she always took John's word.
6. My partner was *odd*, but not insane.
7. He praised the people's intentions, but *criticized* their achievements.
8. It will not be easy to win. But we *must win*.

IV. Change each of the following passive constructions to the active voice. What pattern results in each case?

1. Our awards were given to us by the dean.
2. The new system was instituted by our new coach.
3. The story was believed by nobody.
4. Joseph was named honor student by the faculty.
5. Was our team beaten by the Yellowjackets?
6. What a sight was seen by everybody!

7. What a beating we were given by Western State!
8. John's credentials were scrutinized by the committee.
9. Had the accident been witnessed by anybody?
10. Has the claim been settled by the insurance company?

V. Poets are especially aware of the values of word-order inversions to gain stress or greater effectiveness in their sentences. Study the following excerpts from poetry and observe the inversions from normal patterns. Then rewrite the sentences in normal order.

1. 'Towers and battlements it sees
   Bosomed high in tufted trees.'
2. 'What in me is dark
   Illumine. What is low raise and support. . .'
3. 'Him the Almighty Power
   Hurled headlong flaming from the ethereal sky. . .'
4. 'Long is the way
   And dark. . .'
5. 'Their fatal hands
   No second stroke intend.'
6. 'Sweet is the breath of morn. . .'
7. 'On her white breast a sparkling cross she wore.'
8. 'Fair tresses man's imperial race ensnare.'
9. 'The hungry judges soon the sentence sign.'
10. 'The meeting points [of a pair of scissors] the sacred hair
    dissever
    From the fair head, forever, and forever!'
11. 'A man he was to all the country dear.'
12. 'Three sleepless nights I passed. . .'

VI. In the skeleton sentences below, the blank spaces represent vocabulary elements. All inflections, function words, pronoun forms, and marks of punctuation are expressed. Proper nouns are indicated by capital letters. Analyze the sentences completely:

1. That —— we ——ed on the ——.
2. Across the —— was ——ing a —— ——.
3. Has J—— ——en the ——s to his ——?
4. —— the ——s into the ——, J——.

5. There —— two more ——s.
6. Their ——s we ——ed.
7. What a —— J—— can be!
8. —— this —— a ——?
9. Do you —— those ——ish ——s?
10. ——ly must —— some ——.

VII. You probably remember the poem 'Jabberwocky' from *Through the Looking Glass*. It begins

> 'Twas brillig, and the slithy toves
> Did gyre and gimble in the wabe.
> All mimsy were the borogoves,
> And the mome raths outgrabe.

Although these two sentences may seem hard to understand, you should be able to recognize the grammatical forms, even though you do not know the vocabulary meaning of the words. What are the patterns of these sentences? What grammatical devices are used? Is either sentence inverted?

VIII. Make a study of some favorite poem of yours or of the editorials or stories in a newspaper or magazine. What sentence patterns are most often used? How often are there inversions in the word-order patterns? What kinds are they? Are they used to make a type of sentence other than a statement, or to stress some part of the pattern by shifting it from its normal position?

Chapter XI

Review Questions

I. What is meant by (a) 'expansion' and (b) 'duplication'?

II. List the co-ordinating conjunctions. Show how they may be used to compound any element in the simple sentence structure.

III. How does a verbal differ from other forms derived from the verb base (like *betrayal* or *insurance*)?

IV. What is a gerund?

V. In what sense may verbals have the characteristics of two parts of speech at the same time? What verb characteristics do verbals have? What noun characteristics?

VI. What do we mean when we say that word groups may 'nest' in a sentence? Give several examples.

VII. What is the difference between the 'internal' and 'external' patterns in a sentence?

VIII. Explain how a verbal can be an object and have an object at the same time.

IX. What is an 'absolute' construction? Why is it called 'absolute'? Give several examples.

X. In what sense is an infinitive without the *to* a 'stripped down' grammatical structure? By what grammatical device is this kind of infinitive expressed? Why does this infinitive sometimes cause an ambiguity or pun?

Exercises

I. Expand all the nouns in the following sentences by adding one or more co-ordinate (compound) elements:

1. Charles wrote novels out of sheer necessity.
2. Bill looked across the road at the boys playing baseball.
3. Her real love was writing plays for children.
4. The audience waited an hour.
5. The mechanic worked a whole day on the car.

II. In these sentences, expand the modifiers (including phrasal modifiers) in the same way. Use each of the four co-ordinating conjunctions at least once:

1. We have decided on a pink bathroom.
2. The winner of the hundred-yard-dash was tired.
3. He runs a cleaning establishment.
4. The cracked wallpaper in the den gives the room a neglected look.
5. We saw two small boys diving for pennies.

III. Give five examples of third-form verbals functioning as nouns. Make each sentence illustrate a different noun function.

IV. In what two ways could the verbal phrases in the sentences below be interpreted grammatically? Can you recast the sentences to resolve the ambiguity?

1. George liked *thrilling girls.*
2. Our cook prefers *baking potatoes.*
3. *Rubbing alcohol* on the wound will cleanse it.
4. The specialty at Grover Brothers is *washing machines.*
5. *Engineering degrees* for clearly illiterate people should be a source of shame for a university.

V. Each of the sentences below contains a single-word third-form verbal. Expand these verbals by adding a complement. Did you have to make any changes in order to do this? In inflection? In word order? In function words?

1. He had no need for savings.
2. Walking is our favorite recreation.
3. The ice made the driving hazardous.
4. We spent an hour cleaning up.
5. Deliveries are made on the following day.

VI. In which of the sentences below is the verb form a verbal? How does each verbal function in the sentence?

1. Her hobby is finding antiques.
2. The Joneses are finding a new home.
3. The experiment had expected results.
4. The family had expected a large check.

VII. The skeleton sentences below contain third- and fourth-form verbals. Give all the information you can about each verbal. (Is it a noun? an adjective? Does it have a complement? etc.)

1. ——ing the —— ——ed ——.
2. A ——ly ——ing —— is not ——able.
3. —— will —— ——ing a —— in the ——.

4. The —— ——ing the —— ——s will —— a ——.

5. The —— ——ed —— by his —— is a ——.

VIII. Which of the following are complete sentences? Which are not? Why?

1. Laughing, our baby is delightful; crying, she is horrible.

2. Having been up at six o'clock every day this week to tend that balky furnace.

3. Kept in his place all these years by his father's tendency to dominate him.

4. His career having been decided at an early age by his aptitude for mathematics.

5. The shower being a mild one, we went to the picnic anyway.

IX. Compose five sentences illustrating the use of infinitives as nouns in the external sentence structure—one sentence for each of the five functions.

X. Identify the infinitives and infinitive phrases in the following sentences. How does each one function in the external structure?

1. To make mistakes is only human.

2. It is unwise to try to undertake too many things at once.

3. For him to be allowed to play in this game would be foolish.

4. We will be glad to co-operate.

5. You cannot expect the people in the store to refund your money after all this time.

6. To be or not to be, that is the question.

XI. In the following sentences there are several infinitives and infinitive phrases that are not accompanied by the infinitive indicator. Can you find them?

1. The teacher made the boys write the sentence on the board ten times.

2. Did you see the mailman pass by?

3. I have never heard her sing, but her father had her study with a famous teacher.

4. John is out watching the man next door put up his storm windows.

5. Every five minutes we felt the earth tremble.

XII. Analyze the internal structure of the verbal phrases in the following sentences (be sure that you include all of the words in each phrase):

1. Our painting the house red was a horrible mistake.
2. We greatly appreciated his having gone quietly to bed.
3. On hearing the news about Henry's promotion, we all cheered.
4. The devil having been given his due, we agreed to limit the discussion to happier subjects.
5. Following the path marked by the advance patrol, we easily found our way to the village.
6. The area bounded by the town line on the south and by the highway on the north seemed an ideal location for building a super market.
7. It is ridiculous to fill your days with senseless activities.
8. The doctor applauded our determination to stop smoking cigarettes.
9. Given the proper incentives, most students will do good work.
10. For us to give a final answer at this time is impossible.

XIII. How do the phrases above function in the external structure of the sentences?

XIV. In the following sentence several verbals are nested within verbals. Identify each one and explain its function in relation to the others:

We asked the station-master, waiting to signal the train, to give us an idea about the time remaining before its arrival.

Compose a sentence of your own, in which verbals are similarly nested.

CHAPTER XII

Review Questions

I. What is a simple sentence? a compound sentence? a complex sentence?

II. Grammatical dependence is not a matter of logical dependence or of vocabulary meanings. Explain why. What, then, is the meaning of grammatical dependence?

III. Give an example of a noun clause operating in each of the eight noun functions.

IV. Give an example of the adjective clause operating in the appositive and in the end-shifted positions.

V. Distinguish between movable and fixed adverbial clauses, with examples of each. What determines whether they are movable or not?

VI. Explain the difference between connectives of the first type and of the second type.

VII. What is a relative pronoun? a relative clause?

VIII. What is an indirect question? How does it differ from a direct question, in word order and in verb tense?

IX. What connectives may be dropped with adjective clauses? with noun clauses?

X. State the rules for determining adjective clauses, noun clauses, and adverbial clauses in terms of the grammatical devices used.

Exercises

I. In each of the following exercises, combine the two sentences into one, so that the first sentence includes the second as an internal structure. In order to do this some of the sentences must be reworded and in some the word order must be changed. What function word did you use? Can you rearrange the word order of your new complex sentences or not? In terms of their function as parts of speech what kind of clauses have you made?

1. Henry brought us the news. He received it from Mr. Jones.
2. It was great news. The rebate was coming to us at last.
3. There was one big question facing us. What would we do next?
4. The house stands on the corner. Mr. Brown built it.
5. Henry wouldn't speak to me. I stole his best girl.

6. We put alcohol in the gas tank. It keeps the gas lines clear of ice.

7. We were in doubt. Would our team win the championship?

8. Mother tucked us in. We had already gone to sleep.

9. I left school early. Thus I was able to help with the chores.

10. George has published a new novel. He has just sent me a copy of it.

II. What function word or words are missing in the following sentences? Would you use them in writing? In speech? Why?

1. The house John built the man he hated most was a bad one.

2. The best buy there is on the market now is the car we bought.

3. The last time we saw Henry he was the naughtiest boy I ever saw.

4. The girl you like best is the one you have left behind.

5. The only place you are going is to the bed you just left.

III. Make sentences in which you use the following function words to introduce noun clauses, adjectival clauses, and adverbial clauses: *that, when, where*. Make others in which you use the following function words to introduce noun clauses and adverbial clauses: *because, if, whenever, wherever, whether*. Make others in which you use the following function words to introduce noun clauses and adjectival clauses: *which, who,* and *whose*.

IV. By adding modifying words, phrases, and clauses, construct as elaborate sentences as you can from each of these simple sentences:

1. The farmer ploughed the field.

2. There stood the man.

3. The man gave the boy a bat.

Explain in grammatical terms every addition that you have made.
V. Analyze the sentences below in full. First find the dependent clauses, and then explain their function.

1. Whether we won or lost was not of such great importance that we would cheat.

2. If you decide that we are welcome, we will be glad to come to your party.

3. When the team was defeated, the coach who had been at the college for five years took the responsibility he should have taken.

4. Inasmuch as Henry was absent, we cannot believe that he took the book from your desk, and we are not going to question him.

5. The more fully we discover that English is a complex language, the more we understand why we have trouble with it.

6. That she told the story she heard was so unlike her that I couldn't believe she had done it.

7. That he had quit his job and that he had not told anyone were things that hurt his friends and pleased his enemies.

8. The guide told the men they couldn't go into the cave.

VI. In the following sentences, set off the dependent clauses with parentheses, underline the connectives, and describe the function of each connective in its own clause:

1. There are no troubles that cannot be overcome.

2. I tried on the dress that you liked so much.

3. His wife objected to the man whom he had asked to join them.

4. Let's send whatever toys are left to the Children's Home.

5. This meeting, a notice of which was in yesterday's paper, has been postponed again.

6. This is the corner where we had the accident last year.

7. I am not sympathetic with what you have proposed.

8. He is not the kind of person in whom you could place any real confidence.

9. Whatever happens, we must save our ammunition.

10. The actress whose play closed last night was seen this morning in Central Park.

VII. Complex sentences with their many intricately related parts are often difficult to construct. One must be sure that each clause has the requisite number of parts (at least a subject and a verb), and conversely that there are no extra parts that do not fit into the structural pattern of the clause. Furthermore, one must be sure that there is no more than one connective for each dependent clause. In what ways have the writers of the sentences below failed to observe these rules?

1. This is the problem of which I told you about.
2. We should cut down on the time which crime stories are told.
3. There are several names on the list that I don't know who they are.
4. I believe that besides making profits for the sponsors that commercials also provide a service.
5. It seems as if everything the people get interested in and enjoy that the politicians try to find a way to cash in on it.

VIII. Each of these sentences contains several dependent clauses. Describe the way in which they are nested.

1. It embarrasses me that I blush every time I am introduced to a girl I like.
2. We feel that, if all goes as we expect it will, the job can be completed before snow falls.
3. Rome was ready to act the moment it appeared the Carthaginian fleet proved a threat to its security.

IX. The two following sentences are alike except for one letter in the verb forms *sing* and *sang:*

> We heard Marie sing in Paris last month.
> We heard Marie sang in Paris last month.

Yet, this one small inflectional change makes an important structural difference between the two statements. What is this difference? Could another grammatical device be used in either sentence to point up this difference?

X. The kinds of sentences employed by a writer usually reveal a significant aspect of his thinking: we see in the forms of the sentences something of the complexity or lack of it with which the writer regards his subject matter. Writers of instructions on a can of shoe polish write simple sentences because they regard shoe polishing as a simple process. Most of the sentences in this book, on the other hand, are complex because we regard grammar as a complex subject. Great authors, too, vary in this respect. For example, the early novels of Ernest Hemingway report a world in which noth-ing makes much sense—a world in which things happen, one after another, with no logical pattern: men's hopes and plans are shat-tered, the good die young, the brave are killed and the cowards live, the generous are thwarted, the greedy are rewarded—but even this is never really certain. Things just happen. In such a book as *A Farewell to Arms,* you see this view clearly reflected in the sentence patterns. Simple sentence follows simple sentence or simply com-pounded ones ('Charles danced and Alice sang'). The few complex sentences involve time complexes ('After this happened, then that happened'). The number of logically complex sentences in the whole novel is hardly a handful. In contrast, the writing of another modern novelist, Joseph Conrad, is heavily weighted with complex sentences. Conrad's world is one of mystery and meaning. Things happen in it, too; but Conrad is preoccupied with what they mean. Though he is not certain, he continuously gropes to find relationships and mean-ings in the world he portrays, for he cannot believe that his world doesn't make sense. Hence, his writing is full of long, loose, complex sentences, in which the report of a fact or event is followed by com-parisons or suggestions of significance.

Take a theme of your own and make a critical analysis of its sentences. Note for each sentence its length, its structural type (simple, compound, complex), and if it is complex the relation, word-order-wise, between the external and internal clauses. (The length of your sentences may be judged against the 'norm' for sentence length: grade-school writers average between 15 and 20, college freshmen average about 20, and the sentences of graduate students range up to nearly 25 words.) Now note the relative fre-quency of simple, compound, and complex sentences. There should be more complex sentences than either of the other type (but, of course, this depends upon what you are trying to do; there is no hard and fast rule about it). Also, there should be some variation in the word-order patterns. Bearing in mind what the purpose of your theme is, write a criticism of it. Is the sentence length what a reader should expect? Or are you writing childish sentences about an adult subject, or conversely 'high-flown' sentences about a simple matter? In other words, are you reporting accurately your impression of the complexity or simplicity of the subject, or are you obscuring your attitude with the wrong types of sentences?

CHAPTER XIII

Review Questions

I. Give the names and the dates of the four periods in the history of the English language.

II. To what continental European languages is English most closely related?

III. What do we mean when we say that Old English is a 'synthetic' language? What do we mean when we call modern English 'analytic'?

IV. Name a few of the changes that took place in English grammar between the Old and the Middle English periods and between the Middle English and the Modern English periods.

V. Point out the chief differences between the doctrine of usage and that of authoritarianism as linguistic principles.

VI. Modern English grammatical usage may be divided into two broad areas, depending upon the background of the user: what are these two areas and give a few examples of these two kinds of grammar.

VII. Name a few of the influences which determine what is 'right' and what is 'wrong' in English grammar.

VIII. In what ways does serious written English differ from spoken or 'colloquial' English?

IX. Why is non-standard English not 'incorrect'? For whom is it 'correct'? Why?

X. What are the main differences between formal and informal English? Under what conditions is the use of each appropriate?

Exercises

I. The following sets of words have approximately the same meaning. The first set are native English words, the second and third sets are borrowed from French or Latin. Comment on the levels of usage in which they might appear. Are some of them more 'learned' than others?

1	2	3
thrill	excitement	agitation
drink	carouse	imbibe
draw	lure	attract
ask	question	interrogate
fear	horror	trepidation
glad	joyful	elated
slow	retard	decelerate
proud	haughty	supercilious
brethren	people	congregation
fire	flame	conflagration

II. Study these Middle English lines from the Prologue to Chaucer's *Canterbury Tales*. How many words do you fail to recognize? How many can you guess? Are there any inflectional endings no longer used in modern English? Do you recognize any other differences, grammatically, from the English of our day? Explain.

But nathelees, whil I have tyme and space,
Er that I ferther in this tale pace,
Me thynketh it acordaunt to resoun
To telle yow al the condicioun
Of each of hem, so as it semed me,
And whiche they weren, and of what degree,
And eek in what array that they were inne;
And at a knyght than wol I first bigynne.

A Knyght ther was, and that a worthy man,
That fro the tyme that he first bigan
To riden out, he loved chivalrie,
Trouthe and honour, fredom and curtesie.
Ful worthy was he in his lordes werre,
And thereto hadde he riden, no man ferre,
As wel in cristendom as in hethenesse,
And evere honoured for his worthynesse. . .
At mortal batailles hadde he been fiftene,
And foughten for oure feith at Tramyssene
In lystes thries, and ay slayn his foo.

III. Now study these extracts from Early Modern English. What differences do you find in the grammar of these passages from English of our day?

1. Near about this place inhabited certain Indians, who the next day after we came thither came down to us, presenting mill and cakes of bread, which they had made of a kind of corn called maize, in bigness of a pease, the ear whereof is much like to a teasel, but a span in length, having theron a number of grains. Also they brought down to us hens, potatoes, and pines, which we bought for beads, pewter whistles, glasses, knives, and other trifles.

These potatoes be the most delicate roots that may be eaten, and do far exceed our parsnips or carrots. Their pines be of the bigness of two fists, the outside whereof is of the making of a pineapple, but it is soft like the rind of a cucumber, and the inside eateth like an apple, but it is more delicious than any sweet apple sugared.

2. But studies have their infancy, as well as creatures. We see in men, even the strongest compositions had their beginnings from milk and the cradle; and the wisest tarried sometimes about apting their mouths to letters and syllables. In their education, therefore, the care must be the greater had of their beginnings, to know, examine, and weigh their natures; which though they be proner in some children to some disciplines, yet are they naturally prompt to taste all by degrees, and with change.

3. That women are inconstant, I with any man confess, but that inconstancy is a bad quality, I against any man will maintain. For every thing as it is one better than another, so is it fuller of change; the heavens themselves continually turn, the stars move, the moon changeth; fire whirleth, air flieth, water ebbs and flows, the face of the earth altereth her looks, times stays not; the color that is most light will take most dyes. So in men, they that have the most reason are the most alterable in their designs, and the darkest or most ignorant do seldomest change; therefore women changing more than men have also more reason.

IV. In a paper of about 500 words, explain as fully as you can some sort of slang or shoptalk you are familiar with. Perhaps you have worked at something which has a specialized vocabulary (stores, filling stations, farms, business offices, etc.) or are interested in some sport or a kind of popular music which has a special 'lingo.' Explain this vocabulary with good illustrative details, organizing what you have to say under such headings as vocabulary, peculiar word order or other sentence construction features, odd functional shifts, and other grammatical peculiarities.

Chapter XIV

Review Questions

I. What is the difference between 'social' mis-usage and 'communication' mis-usage? Which grammatical devices are primarily involved in each type?

II. What is meant by 'agreement' of subject and verb?

III. In the inflectional system of the English personal pronoun, what weakness in the language makes agreement difficult when the gender of the antecedent could be either masculine or feminine? How can this problem be solved?

IV. Formulate a good workable rule that will help writers avoid faulty pronoun references. What three methods may be used to correct ambiguous references?

V. Suppose someone you know uses subject forms of the personal pronouns when object forms should be used (as in 'George hasn't spoken to Jim and *I* for a week'). How would you explain to him, using your knowledge of structural grammar, a method of avoiding this kind of error? (Do not say that the object form should be used because the word 'functions' as an object!)

VI. In the sentence 'Our neighbors drove John and *myself* to the station,' explain why *myself* is not used as a true reflexive pronoun.

VII. Describe the word-order patterns of all dependent clauses introduced by the pronouns *who, whose,* and *whom.*

VIII. State the word-order rule by which we can determine what form of the pronoun *who* should be used in a given dependent clause.

IX. *Keep* and *turn* belong to a large group of verbs which may be followed by either adjective or adverb forms. How do you decide which form to use? Compose sentences in which each of these words is used, first with an adjective, second with an adverb.

X. Explain why 'the organ sounded *beautifully* this morning' is an example of an attempt to be 'over-correct.'

Exercises

I. Some of the noun forms in the sentences below are not good usage. Correct each mis-usage: there is at least one in every sentence.

1. The Smiths and the Joneses took the Smiths car on the trip, and the Joneses paid for the gasoline and oil.

2. The girls' marks on the tests were higher than the boys, but the boys' general class average was superior to the girls.

3. Margarets staying home from the meeting was a great mistake.

4. Whether the Presidents signature will be put on the bill remains uncertain, but his aides are reported in favor of most of the bill's sections.

5. We were at our wits end when we found we owed three months rent.

6. Spenser is sometimes called a poets poet, but I find him more difficult to understand than most other poets.

7. How much Harold's appointment meant to him I cannot say; but his bosses confidence in him meant a great deal, I am sure.

8. The two childrens' features were entirely different.

9. The Hall's house is on the same side of the street as ours.

10. We stopped off to see the Phelp's, the McNutt's, and the Overton's in Smithfield.

II. What forms of the italicized nouns are preferable in each of the sentences below? Defend your answer.

1. *Herbert* running at the crucial moment gave away our carefully laid plans.

2. I prefer *Lois* singing to *Elizabeth* playing, but neither is of professional quality.

3. I have always had a secret admiration for that *professor* reading in the corner.

4. *Teachers* marking us down for late papers is unfair, for we cannot always do our work on time.

5. I doubt *John* being sincere when he gives that kind of advice to *students* entering college.

6. Apparently this is a case of no one *person* being responsible.

III. In the following sentences choose the verb form which properly agrees with its subject.

1. Neither the circumstances nor the ignorance of the defendant (is, are) sufficient reason for the jury to acquit him.

2. The reason for his leaving without permission and the general sympathy of his classmates (count, counts) in his favor, of course.

3. The supervisor, together with the workmen involved, (face, faces) the actual problems of the job and must solve them.

4. The crew (work, works) hard only when their boss is watching.

5. Mathematics (is, are) difficult, but I think physics (is, are) more so.

6. Each of the men (is, are) responsible, and all of them (is, are) bonded.

7. In the inability of the new workmen to understand our problems (lie, lies) the heart of our difficulties.

8. There (was, were) several good reasons for firing the engineer, but there (was, were) only one given—his inability to write clearly.

9. Engineering drawing, physics, chemistry, algebra, and English (make, makes) a tough schedule.

10. Barbara is one of the few girls who (do, does) well in medical studies.

11. What the manager thinks, in this instance, (doesn't, don't) make much difference.

12. Neither the student manager nor the members of the team (is, are) allowed to break training rules.

13. The reaction of all the students involved and of all the faculty members (was, were) immediate and intense.

14. My old friend and long-time associate (is, are) finally going to retire.

15. "The acoustics in this room (is, are) perfect," the engineer said; but acoustics (is, are) a less exact science than such a statement suggests.

16. Either solution (is, are) coherent; but both of them (is, are) not possible, and hence each (is, are) subject to a careful re-examination.

17. In the reports of the commission (is, are) to be found the answer to our difficulties.

18. It (is, are) exhilarating to skate and ski in the winter, but there (is, are) reasons for studying, too.

19. Five men, three boys, and a mascot (comprise, comprises) our squad.

20. Mr. Richards is the only member of the faculties who (seem, seems) to care about student discipline.

IV. Each of the sentences below contains a faulty pronoun agreement or a faulty or ambiguous pronoun reference; some contain two. Recast the sentences to make all agreements proper and all references clear.

1. Our group is determined to present their case to the Dean.

2. Does everybody know what they must do next?

3. John told Henry that he was expected to make the presentation.

4. That set of dishes is my favorite, and I hate to sell them.

5. Apparently no one used the new boulevard, which came as a surprise to us.

6. The boys told the girls that they were naturally superior to them.

7. Uncle Oscar and Cousin Vaughan both practiced law, and because I admire them I naturally want to be one, too.

8. Every one of the applicants has copied their answer to the last question, I suspect.

9. We decided against swimming when the weather turned cold and stormy, for it seemed dangerous to us.

10. We took every precaution for the success of our trip, because it was necessary.

11. Because of the new office management, the girls don't want to work in it any more.

12. When they returned, the Browns told the Smiths of their bad luck.

13. It turned out to be the son of the prospector who sold us the worthless claim.

14. Any of these recipes are good, if they are used by a good cook.

15. The movie is badly written, and that is a field that should attract good writing.

V. Correct any improper case forms of the pronouns in the following sentences (some are correct and some incorrect).

1. Only three of we students were aware of whom the winner was.

2. The trouble with us liberals is that we hate practical politics; and it is the practical politician who, whatever we think of him, gets things done.

3. All of us—both you winners and us losers—should be more interested in safeguarding the rules of the game than in winning.

4. Everyone except Mary and I was tardy.

5. Leave the burden of proof to James and myself.

6. 'Then I ripped me and searched where hearts did lie.'

7. Who do you think would prefer chocolate cake?

8. We offered the reward to whoever brought the dog back.

9. The man whom they suspect of stealing is very rich and cannot have a motive.

10. We all wondered who they would select to supervise the new office.

11. The man who in the course of time will be selected is the one who we feel we can trust with the proper execution of the duties of office.

12. He is the kind whom everyone hates and who hates everyone and also the kind whom flattery cannot move and who is undaunted by threats.

13. We are all in favor of Richard Roe, whom we hope will be our next representative.

14. Please leave the message with whomever comes to the door.

15. There is Sarah Jones who I have been looking for all day.

VI. Which form of the modifier is preferable in the following sentences and why? Might either form be used? If so, is there a difference in meaning between the two forms?

1. He acted (furious, furiously) at her remarks.

2. Our prospecting for uranium came out (bad, badly).

3. The motor ran (good, well), and we agreed that the mechanic's work seemed (good, well).

4. The next time we met, she cut me (cold, coldly), but later we became good friends and she apologized (sincere, sincerely).

5. In order to get to the ball game on time, the professor cut his lecture (short, shortly); and as a result we did rather (bad, badly) on part of the next examination.

6. Every critic in attendance considered the painting (serious, seriously).

7. We were attacked from all sides, but we held our position (secure, securely).

8. In the past decade, Charles has many times proved himself (satisfactory, satisfactorily).

9. There we all stood (tense, tensely) in anticipation of his next move.

10. Your brand may draw (smoother, more smoothly) but mine tastes (good, well) and is packed (tight, tightly).

11. Hers was the most (beautiful, beautifully) sounding voice I had ever heard.

12. His (dirty, dirtily) blue overalls and his (bare, barely) decent shirt contrasted with his (real, really) fine shoes and a (general, generally) fastidious appearance.

13. The day has turned out (wonderful, wonderfully) after all.

14. The valley lay (peaceful, peacefully) in the summer sun.

15. Everyone is buying (high, highly) priced cars these days.

Chapter XV

Review Questions

I. What is the general 'rule' for placing modifiers? What are the weaknesses in this rule?

II. Why are group modifiers more likely to be misplaced than single-word modifiers?

III. What is meant by the 'principle of attraction,' as described in this chapter?

IV. Under what conditions is a prepositional phrase 'misplaced' (a) when it is inside the sentence and (b) when it is at the end of the sentence?

V. When an adjective group modifier, other than a prepositional phrase, comes at the beginning of the clause or sentence, what is the rule regarding the position of the word modified? In a declarative sentence? In an interrogative sentence?

VI. When an adjective group modifier, other than a prepositional phrase, comes at the end of the sentence or clause, what is the rule regarding the position of the word modified? Under what two circumstances may a phrase that modifies the subject not be end-shifted?

VII. What three methods may be used to correct a misplaced end-position adjective phrase?

VIII. When a prepositional phrase precedes an adjective clause, what two grammatical devices may be used to clarify the direction of modification of the clause?

IX. What is a dangling modifier? Give several examples.

X. In what sense is a mark of punctuation a grammatical device? Show how the comma may be used to express grammatical meaning. Do the same for the semicolon and the hyphen.

Exercises

I. Each of the sentences below contains a misplaced single-word modifier. Revise these sentences to correct the errors.

1. He nearly wrote the whole report without aid.
2. The man was an old car hobbyist.
3. A handsome doctor's colonial house is for sale on Main street.
4. He only had two dollars in his pocket.
5. The fire had almost burned to the attic.
6. It takes a lot of intelligence to become a dumb animal trainer.

II. Explain why the italicized prepositional phrases in the following sentences are misplaced or ambiguous. Apply the explanations given in this chapter. What can be done to improve the sentences?

1. We telephoned our relatives *from California.*
2. Simpson will be remembered after his death *by this poem.*
3. It's that man selling herbs *from the South.*
4. He saw Mrs. Smith counting the money *through the key-hole.*
5. The teacher gave us a lecture on how to behave ourselves in school *about every two weeks.*
6. *In his hesitancy to shoot,* Jacob killed the intruder.
7. The dean called in the student *instead of Professor Craig.*
8. The heroine kissed the poor fellow *at the end of his tether.*

III. Show how the meanings of the following sentences would be altered if the positions of the italicized prepositional phrases were changed.

1. Any man *with children,* who likes to work, will get the job.
2. The employees *in our factory* work hard.
3. This is a story about people during the war *in Poland.*
4. The farmers *across the ravine* have built a new bridge.
5. The girls are very nice *at the office.*

IV. In the following sentences, there are a number of misplaced group modifiers. Find these modifiers and revise the sentences to eliminate the errors.

1. Too tired to play any longer, Mother put us to bed.
2. The entrance to the cave did not impress us, being rather small.
3. When clean, polish the car briskly.
4. The vine on the north side of the house, which has to be torn down this year, is one of my favorites.
5. Fishing in the icy waters of the stream, the largest trout of the year was caught by Bill McHenry.
6. We all noticed the stopped-up storm sewer, riding on top of the bus.
7. Having promised the dress for tomorrow, are you driving around to the dress-maker's before going to work?

8. The train pulled up to the station platform crowded with sight-seers.

V. Each of the following sentences contains a dangling modifier. Revise the sentences to eliminate the errors.

1. Knowing it might rain, alternative plans for graduation were carefully made.
2. Wanting an immediate solution, a disinterested bystander was asked to decide the argument.
3. Walking to the window, the snow gleamed on the front lawn.
4. With his temper under control, the party turned out a successful one.
5. The elevated train roared past his window, but being very tired, his sleep was not broken by the noise.
6. Looking at Salisbury Cathedral, the past seems very real.
7. Specimens should keep almost indefinitely, using alcohol.
8. Flattered by all the praise, his poise and confidence were restored.
9. If bumped into accidentally, no complaint should be made.
10. To be received in good condition, you should wrap carefully and label clearly.

VI. Compose five sentences with prepositional phrases at the end of a clause or sentence. What word does each phrase modify? Have you allowed any word to intervene which might 'attract' the phrase as a modifier? Does the position of the phrase make the sentence ambiguous or nonsensical?

VII. Compose five sentences, each with three types of adjective modifiers—single word, phrasal, and clausal—modifying the same word. First, put them all in the appositive position. Then rearrange them in the sentence if you think that this new arrangement would be an improvement.

VIII. Compose five sentences with verbal adjective phrases at the end of the sentence. Designate which words you intend these phrases to modify. Are your phrases placed correctly?

IX. The following sentences exhibit various kinds of violations of parallel structure. Revise each to express parallel ideas with parallel grammatical forms:

1. Walking takes longer and is less pleasant in bad weather, but it is more healthful than to ride to work.

2. An artist must stress certain features of his characters and ignores others.

3. Our critic has fallen into the error of confusing what is profitable with how difficult something is to comprehend.

4. The plane's duty is to hunt for enemy submarines, for fighting enemy planes, and for locating as well as destroying enemy sea forces.

5. I was getting the best food in the land and no worry about ration points.

6. New York is huge, thrilling, and which I should like to visit again.

7. She is often seen in class badly groomed, wearing house slippers, or has oversized blouses on.

8. Anyone earning a 90 average and who has given evidence of interest in the course was excused from the final examination.

9. Sell it to whomever it fits and wishes to buy it.

10. Sitting crowded together on shaky bleachers, however frightening it may be, is still not so forbidding as to stand throughout the game.

X. In the following sentences there are numerous punctuation errors, varying in degree of seriousness. Correct the errors and be prepared to give your reasons for doing so.

1. Do you suppose that only the men who received second notices will show up for the meeting.

2. The manager said that he would put our organization on a businesslike basis, what he did, however, is quite another matter.

3. There stood the old mansion; nearly hidden in a grove of trees, only its chimneys rising above the protective greenery.

4. We had prepared a more than usually detailed report for the new supervisor had a reputation for precision.

5. His performance by and large, was nothing to become excited about, but the half-gainer was perfectly done.

6. He was an imposing man, with a powerful body, erect carriage, a tan complexion and the head of a god.

7. Mr. Smith the boarder was an obliging man in most respects. Never too busy to help Mrs. Wheeler with her heavy work.

8. Joseph never asked for explanations of the problems. The answers being all he thought he needed.

9. This company seemed apprehensive about our paying for the supplies it sent us; whereas the others often took ninety days to bill us.

10. The play has four outstanding features, a first act, a second act, a third act, and plenty of boredom throughout.

11. Dependability, honesty, patience, and a complete lack of ambition; these are the qualities that will keep a bookkeeper a bookkeeper forever.

12. 'Would you mind Baby if I play golf this morning?' Harold asked his new bride.

13. Rubber, which has been used, can be reworked and used again.

14. While we ate the animals were fed.

15. His decision in spite of all their attempts to change it remained the same.

16. Georges light tan topcoat came from Scotland.

17. He is a self-made man a man after my own heart.

18. Although Henry is not happy here is there any good reason why he should leave.

19. These ornaments are made of gold, silver and copper or platinum.

20. After peeling the fruit should be plunged into hot water.

21. The Jordans sent us a beautiful plant for my birthday, they are certainly very pleasant people.

22. When we remembered it was too late to catch the bus.

23. We decided to stay home, because the weather was so cold, we even had to light a fire.

24. The countries of Europe have recovered remarkably since the war, however there are many scars still remaining.

25. To get up late, have a big breakfast and read all afternoon. That is my idea of a wonderful vacation.

INDEX

Major references are in **boldface** type

Absolute construction, 156-7
Acceptable grammar, **195-201** (*see also* Standards, grammatical)
Active, *see* Voice, active
Adjective, **88-105** and *passim*
  appositive, **101-2**, 105, 233-4, **237-8**, 253
    clause, 167-8, 186, 253
    verbal phrase, 149-51, 155-6
  attributive, **93-8**, 105, 115, 151, 231, 234-5, 244, 246-7
    levels of, 117-18
    verbal, 103, 147, 150, 151, 154
    with gerund, 142
  clause, **174-80**, 186 (*see also* Relative clause)
    positions of, 167-8, 253-5
    punctuation of, 267
    without connective, 182-4, 253-4
  comparison of, *see* Comparison
  confusion with adverb, 111-12, 230-35
  conjunction-headed, **171-2**, 237
    dangling, 172, 257
    positions of, 248, 251-2, 252-3
    punctuation of, 266-7
  end-shifted, **103**, 105
    ambiguity in, 150, 250-53
  front-shifted, **102-3**, 111 (*see also* verbal, positions of, *below*)
  interrogative, 124-6
  of degree, 234-5
  of result, 100, 233-4
  phrasal, 118-19, **147-62**, 171-2 (*see also* Prepositional phrase and verbal, *below*)

Adjective, phrasal (Cont.)
  positions of, 119, 241-53
  punctuation of, 254, 266-7
  predicate, **99-101**, 105, **111-12**, 130, 142, 147, 152, 231-4
  verbal, **103-5**, 118, **147-57**, 158, 159 (*see also* Participles; Verbals)
    confused with finite verb, 153-6, 207-8
    dangling, 256-8
    phrase, 148-53, 158-9, 248-53
    positions of, 147, 149-51, 159, **248-53**
    punctuation of, 261, 266-7, 272
    reduced forms of, 104-5
Adverb, **106-20** and *passim*
  and adjective confused, 111-12, **230-35**
  clause, **168**, **170-71**, 182, 186, 265-6
  conjunctive, 106, 265
  infinitive as, 159
  interrogative, 124
  misplacing of, 237, 239-41
  positions of, 110-14, 129, 231-5
  prepositional phrase as, 119
    positions of, 119, 242
    punctuation of, 265-6
  squinting, 184-5
Adverbial
  conjunction, 168-72
    punctuation of, 265-6
  noun, 118
African language, 9
Agreement
  adjective, 90-91